How to Avoid the Divorce from Hell*

*and Dance Together at Your Daughter's Wedding

How to Avoid the Divorce from Hell*

*and Dance Together at Your Daughter's Wedding

M. Sue Talia

Nexus Publishing Company
Danville, California

How to Avoid the Divorce the Divorce From Hell*
*and Dance Together at Your Daughter's Wedding
Third Edition

Nexus Publishing Company
P.O. Box 2335
Danville, CA 94526-7335

Photograph by The Image Maker

ISBN 10: 0965107566
ISBN 13: 9780965107563
Library of Congress Control Number: 2015920190
Nexus Publishing Company, San Ramon, CA

First printing 2016

Although the author and publisher have made every effort to ensure the accuracy and completeness of the information contained in this book, we assume no responsibility for errors, inaccuracies, omissions, or any inconsistency herein. Any slights of people, places or organizations are unintentional.

The quote of Lucy Van Pelt from "Peanuts" is used with permission of Charles M. Schultz and United Media

Printed in the United States of America

Other Books by the Author

Unbundling Your Divorce:
How to Find a Lawyer to Help You Help Yourself

Everything I Needed to Know I Learned *AFTER* Law School:
Memos to a Young Family Lawyer*

Uncoupling in Three-Quarter Time:
Life-Affirming Divorce Poetry*

*available for download at www.nexusbooks.com

Dedication

To Lee,

*who came home one night and told me about a new client he had seen that day.
She wasn't ready to file for divorce yet, but wanted to know if there was a book
she could read to learn about the process. He told her there wasn't one, but a
good friend of his was writing it. She just didn't know it yet.*
*Thanks for the countless hours spent trying to figure out how to make the divorce
process work better for parents and kids, how to reduce conflict and help people
resolve their differences with dignity.*
*Thanks for the endless discussions about how to protect children, educate
parents, find creative solutions, and create new tools to reduce the pain, trauma,
cost and duration of divorce litigation.*
*Thanks for believing in every word of this book,
and participating in its creation.*
*Thanks for recognizing that this book, and others,
were in me, waiting to be born.*
*Thanks for the inspiration, the encouragement, the participation, and most of
all, thanks for the love.*

Table of Contents

Preface

EVERYONE WHO GETS married assumes and hopes it will be forever. It isn't always, and the fact that things turned out differently than you expected should not have the power to ruin your life. I'm here to help you move on, be whole, and have the most positive relationships you can with your ex, your children, and your extended family. I'm not a therapist – see somebody else for that. I'm a lawyer, a judge, and a pragmatist, not necessarily in that order, and my goal is to help you navigate the experience of divorce in the most constructive and healing way I can.

Although I have been a divorce lawyer and private family law judge for many years, this book is not just about law. Its purpose is to let you know that despite the fact that the divorce process is foreign and frightening, grindingly slow, sometimes intensely painful and almost invariably frustrating, you have a great deal more control over your divorce than you probably realize. You are not solely at the mercy of your spouse, the lawyers and a stranger in a black robe. Just as the choices you have made throughout your life have brought you to the point where you are charting this new course, you have choices to make at the outset of your divorce and at hundreds of forks in the path thereafter. Those decisions will largely determine the degree to which you come out the other end bitter and scarred for life or whole, strong, and ready to tackle the next phase of life's adventure.

Most people don't want war. They just want to move on with dignity intact from a situation which once worked for them (or else they wouldn't have chosen it in the first place) but which isn't working now.

If you choose to engage to the adversarial hilt, consumed with hostility toward your spouse, I guarantee that hostility will be returned in spades. If, instead, you commit to steering through the process as cleanly as possible, the rewards will be manifold.

The title of this book comes from a technique I developed to use with clients who told me they wanted their divorce to be amicable. If they had children, I reminded them that they would remain the parents of those children forever. I told them to consider how they wanted their interaction with their ex to be after the divorce was over. They were to think of a very specific interaction at some time in the future. It could be as simple as civil conduct at graduation or as emotionally charged as being at the hospital for the birth of their first grandchild or dancing at their daughter's wedding. Whenever they were tempted to react in a hostile manner during the divorce, I told them to consider the interaction they had envisioned and ask themselves whether the action they were contemplating now would make it easier or harder to accomplish that goal in the future.

Something is not working in your life or you would not be reading this book. You are either considering making some major changes which you believe will improve the quality of your life, however difficult they may be, or those changes are being forced upon you by your spouse. I am here to tell you that the process can be constructive, cleansing and, oddly enough, positive. It is possible to come out on the other side, look at yourself in the mirror and know in your heart and in your soul that you did the best you could, that you did nothing to unnecessarily contribute to your own or another's pain, and that when you made a mistake, you corrected and learned from it. We can ask nothing more from life.

Divorce, usually, but not always, involves a man and a woman. The impact of gender is unavoidable. In order to avoid the cumbersome he/she, I have chosen to use gender-based pronouns interchangeably. An example referring to how "she" reacts may just as well mean "he." Also, in the era of same sex marriage and other forms of domestic partnerships, the couple may be she and she, or he and he. Same sex marriage and domestic partnerships have been around long enough in some jurisdictions that we are now seeing same sex divorces and custody disputes. The principles which I discuss here apply equally to same sex partners and heterosexual couples.

You may find the same subject woven through several chapters. There is a reason for that. Many readers will use this book as a resource and consult isolated chapters rather than reading from cover to cover, and I want the discussion to be complete. In other instances, the topic is just so important that I want to reinforce it.

This book is the product of nearly forty years as a divorce lawyer and private judge. It is designed for the ninety percent of divorcing couples who are basically sane, reasonable people who want to get through the process as whole and unscarred as possible. Most people facing divorce are scared. The system is public, cumbersome and, considering the emotional content of the subject, oddly impersonal. You must put your faith in strangers you hire to protect your interests and guide you through a dizzying maze of legal concepts, many of which will make no logical sense to you. The very fabric of your life is being transformed, from where you live to how often you see your children to whether you can pay your bills. This book is designed to give you the tools to make good decisions as you wend your way through the process.

It is not designed to give legal advice. That is for the lawyers. Neither is it a substitute for a therapist. Most importantly, it is not intended to replace your own judgment. Each person is responsible for the manner in which he processes this, just as any other life experience.

As with any other life-transforming event, each of us ultimately faces divorce as an individual. We are the sum of our past experiences and imprinting, and the experience will not be the same for any two people. You must thoughtfully consider your options, decide what works for you, and disregard what doesn't.

As you read the following pages, many of you will have no difficulty seeing your spouse in examples I give. Do yourself a favor. Be honest and look again to see if you find yourself as well. No marriage is entirely one-sided, and a little introspection into your own contributions to the situation you find yourself in will go a very long way in helping you stay on the right track.

I know it hurts now. But one of the goals of this book is to give you the tools and perspective to not let the hurt today drive you to make mistakes now that you will be paying for financially and emotionally for years to come. I have made a number of suggestions you can use to make good decisions. You can choose to make the process a healthy, growth-inducing passage or dig a bitter, vengeful pit in which you wallow for the rest of your life. Choose wisely.

PART I

Getting Started: Introduction to Reality Testing

CHAPTER 1

Choices — the Divorce Everyone Wants

OF COURSE YOU want your divorce to be amicable. Only a lunatic would prefer to sit across a courtroom and battle the person with whom she shared a bed for 5, 10 or 20 years. What parent in his right mind would choose to subject his children to the trauma and uncertainty of a bitter custody fight? In my many years as a divorce lawyer, I've found that most new client consultations start out with a variation of "Now, I want this to be amicable." Then all hell breaks loose. So, what goes wrong? Lots of things. People let their fears take charge and act in ways the other party, equally frightened, perceives as a hostile attack. Friends and family take sides and inject their own agendas, further polarizing the situation. A parent who doesn't really want a custody fight starts a defensive one because he's afraid that if he doesn't fight for custody, the kids will think he doesn't love them, or worse, that if he doesn't have custody he'll be a stranger to his own children.

Is it possible to have a successful divorce?

The good news is that yes, it is possible. It isn't easy, and requires maturity, focus, and commitment to the goal, but it is possible.

Every divorce is a compendium of choices, both past and present. If you and your spouse decided that one of you should stay home and raise the children, that is going to have far-reaching impact on custody, as well as child and spousal support rights and obligations. If you are the one who stayed home, that decision will impact your present and future career opportunities. If you lived beyond your means as an intact family, the split into two households will create a serious financial hardship. All these choices are part of the fabric as it exists when you first decide to divorce.

So, what can *you* do to pull it off, to have a successful divorce? You have options which, if exercised wisely, will substantially increase your chances of success.

- Commit to keep lines of communication with your spouse as open as possible.
- To the extent you can, separate your feelings of hurt, guilt or rejection from decisions regarding property, money and especially, the kids.
- Try to remember that even if you can no longer live together, you once loved and respected your spouse enough to marry her in the first place, probably to have children with her. Remember that you are *both* human and are entitled to your dignity.
- Divorce doesn't happen in a vacuum, and, just as it takes two to make a marriage, it takes two to make a divorce. Each of you must accept some responsibility for the chain of events which brought you to this point (including poor judgment on your part in the selection of a mate). You must also accept 100% responsibility for your own conduct through the divorce.

Realize that whatever pain you are feeling, your spouse is probably experiencing comparable, though equally unique and personalized, pain. More important, whatever fear and insecurity grips you, it is much worse for your children. At least *you* have some control over your life; they have none.

Commit to ensuring that your children have two parents. You gave them that in the beginning. It is their birthright. Remember, too, that however angry you may be at the other parent, this is the parent *you* chose for your children.

Accept the reality that the process is not going to change the other party. It won't make your spouse more cooperative, less controlling, more financially responsible, more honest, more mature, or a better parent. If you couldn't change him in 20 years of marriage, you won't be able to do it now, and your lawyer and the judge can't do it either.

Be realistic. Most of this book is devoted to telling you not what you want to hear, but what *is*. The sooner you get clear that the legal system cannot solve all of your problems and relieve you of the consequences of decisions you made years ago, the sooner you'll accept responsibility for making the best decision you can and be more likely to have a successful life after divorce.

CHAPTER 2

Gold Stars and Magic Wands

MANY DIVORCES GET off on the wrong track at the beginning because one party either wants credit for having been an exemplary spouse or parent in the past, or refuses to accept the reality that a divorce is inevitable. This isn't all a bad dream from which you will awake in the morning. Divorce, even under the most auspicious circumstances, is disruptive, traumatic and painful.

If you've been "spouse of the year" for the last 20 years, don't expect a gold star for it. That means nothing to your mate if you've just walked out, whatever the reason. Don't keep looking for validation of all the good you did over the years; it isn't going to be forthcoming, at least not for now. Maybe in the hazy future, perhaps when you're dancing at your daughter's wedding or celebrating your first grandchild's birthday, you'll each be able to acknowledge the other, but don't expect it now. And don't give away the store trying to buy validation from your ex. It doesn't work that way. You'll just end up feeling like a chump.

Similarly, don't check out of the process just because it is painful. It isn't going to go away or get better if you ignore it. You'll have major problems if your attitude toward your divorce is "Wake me when it's over." You probably won't like the decisions which have been made for you during the course of the proceeding. If you elect not to participate, it may be too late to influence the result when you finally decide to pay attention.

Gold Stars and Magic Wands

The greatest assets you can have at the beginning are a realistic attitude, honest self-examination, and a willingness to learn what you need to know in order to make the best possible decisions under the circumstances.

I have in my office a wand, complete with bells, streamers and gold glitter. It was given to me by a client who went through a gut-wrenching two-year divorce after a thirty year marriage. She really, *really* didn't want the divorce, and constantly railed against the unfairness of it all. The suburban fairy tale she thought she had been living abruptly turned into a nightmare when her husband left her for a younger woman who, in her words, "didn't have two brain cells to rub together." She was hurt, angry, rejected and terrified, a most volatile and inauspicious combination. She was now going to have to assume financial responsibilities she thought her husband would handle for the rest of her life and the prospect horrified her. I heard constantly how unfair it was and couldn't get her to look far enough beyond the failure of her expectations to focus on the decisions she needed to make now. I often told her that I wished I had a magic wand which could make it all better, but I didn't. My job, unpleasant as it was, was to tell her the truth, however unpalatable it might be to her, and help her make the best decisions she could under the circumstances. Once she finally got the message, the case settled, and after it was all over, she made me my own "magic wand." I've used it countless times since, always to make the same point. I'm not in the business of telling you what you want to hear. I'm in the business of telling you the truth and helping you deal with the reality of your legal situation in the healthiest and most responsible way I can.

So, if you want to do yourself a favor at the beginning, promise to deal with the process as clearly, cleanly and responsibly as possible. Separate dollars from emotions, kids from property, and don't try to rewrite the past. Of *course* you wish things were different. Accept what is, take responsibility for the decisions you have made, and actively plan for your future. Don't just drift aimlessly through your divorce. Otherwise, you'll come out on the other end profoundly unhappy with where you find yourself and with no clue how you got there.

"But it's not FAIR . . ."

To paraphrase a quote from William Goldman's *The Princess Bride*, "Life isn't fair . . . it doesn't have to be." The concept of fairness is utterly subjective. In a divorce, there are as many definitions of fairness as there are parents and children. The first awful truth about divorce is that you and your spouse will never agree on what is "fair." You will each feel that you are giving more and getting less than the other.

Divorce isn't fair. Don't expect it to be and don't complain because it isn't. Divorce isn't fair because life isn't fair.

The fact is:

A husband who worked 20 years at a job he hates will think it is "unfair" to have to "give" his wife half of his pension while he still has to work at the same lousy job to pay her alimony.

A wife who gave up her career dreams to move from state to state with her husband's job transfers will think it "unfair" that she is now expected to take her rusty education out into the workplace and maximize her earnings.

That's the way it is. They made choices and those choices have consequences.

If you start out chasing "fairness," however you subjectively define it, you are doomed to a long, bitter and expensive divorce. I don't mean by this that the law is arbitrary, capricious and cruel, even if it sometimes seems to be. It just isn't designed to solve all the problems of a failed relationship. It certainly can't meet a litigant's subjective definition of fairness.

One of the most damaging fallacies which we entertain as a society is the belief that there is legal redress for every wrong. That simply isn't the case with the legal system in general, and couldn't be more starkly untrue than in family law.

Forgive me for digressing into a little law.

The legal system which we inherited from our forbears was designed to resolve boundary disputes, criminal guilt and punishment, and who breached the contract to deliver ten sacks of flour. It was not designed to decide where children live, who the better custodial parent is, or how long one party should receive support payments from the other. The church took care of families back then. I can think of no issue less suited to the traditional hour's worth of direct and cross examination in a courtroom than child custody. Yet, the vast majority of custody decisions don't even get one hour of court time.

When the legal system addresses those issues, it tries to establish a general rule, a rule that will be equitable (a better term than the endlessly loaded "fair") in more situations than not. There are always some cases which will not fit the rule. Therefore, by definition, there always will be situations in which, given the specific facts, the rule will operate inequitably. That's the way it is. Cases and fact situations slip through the cracks, and there's little that either lawyers or judges can do about it.

A good example is "pillow talk." Husbands and wives quite literally do not deal with one another at "arm's length," even though the law of contracts usually assumes that they do. They make agreements and promises to each other, sometimes spoken, often just implied or inferred, all on the assumption that they will always be together. They regularly base those agreements on unspoken assumptions which they believe (but don't verify) that their spouse shares. These agreements are rarely reduced to writing, and when the marriage falls apart, each remembers at least some aspects the agreement differently, if they remember it at all.

Suppose a husband owns the house where he and the wife and children live. He intends to stay married forever. He says he'll put her name on it, but somehow, in the press of getting the kids to soccer practice, going to work, and the business of day-to-day living, it doesn't get done. So, what happens when somebody decides that "forever" just ended? The law has to make a rule, which means that if it didn't get handled "legally," that wife may very well lose out. Whenever there is a general rule, there are going to be individual cases where it works a hardship.

So, why make the rule in the first place? Why not simply let a judge decide each individual case on its merits? Assuming for a moment that there was money to fund and staff the thousands of new courtrooms that would be required to handle the volume of cases (and do you really want to pay the taxes necessary to sustain that many courts?), how could anyone plan and make decisions about property during marriage with any degree of predictability? The whole point of having rules is so that people can have some expectation of a predictable result in their dealings with each other.

You may find several instances in your own divorce where you think the rule is inequitable in your case. *Don't* keep bouncing from lawyer to lawyer and judge to judge trying to get someone to tell you what you want to hear. You'll just end up spending lots of money trying to buy something that isn't for sale. Equally importantly, don't dig in your heels on another issue, trying to get more there to "make up" for the fact that you lost on something else you think you should have won. If the law doesn't support your position on the house, don't insist on trying to recoup your "loss" by taking an unreasonable position on alimony or the pension.

Instead, think of "fair" as a four-letter word and lose it from your vocabulary for the duration of your divorce. Instead of looking for what is fair, look for what is practical, what works, what results in maximizing the estate being divided, what minimizes the cost, and what leaves each party with the best chance of starting over with their dignity intact.

"I want to be protected . . ."

A corollary to "but it's not fair" is "I want to be protected."

Everyone wants to be protected from the vicissitudes of life, and there are many areas where the law can accommodate them. However, in thousands of other areas neither the law, your lawyer, nor the judge can protect you. Remember that life involves risk, and there are countless risks from which there is simply no protection. That's life. You are not going to obtain greater protections in divorce than you would have had in an intact marriage.

You may have the best support order in the world. You may have the model ex who not only pays support on time, he pays it early. Not only does he pay it early, he pays for lots of extras for the kids without being asked and voluntarily agrees to increase the payment from time to time to account for adjustments in his income and the cost of living. What happens when he loses his job, a common event these days? Don't beat your breast and gnash your teeth because the legal system failed you. It didn't. He would have lost his job if you had still been together, and you would have shared the financial hardship with him just as much then as now.

Suppose that instead of losing his job, he's hit by a truck? OK, you say, I'll get lots of life insurance. Suppose, instead of being hit by a truck and dying, he gets hit by a truck and survives? No life insurance will pay your mortgage if he is disabled, and very few people can afford sufficient disability insurance to replace 100% of the lost income. That's life, and if that happened while you were still together, you would have suffered the consequences along with your spouse.

The moral of the story is that there are thousands of contingencies for which protection through the divorce courts is minimal at best. The law can't guarantee the vagaries of the economy, the rising cost of a college education, or traffic accidents. Neither the judge, the legal system, nor your lawyer is a guarantor of your future. As with fairness, if you start out with an expectation of protection against every ill wind, you will have a very long, expensive, painful and ultimately bitter divorce and, at the end, you still won't have the protection you wanted.

No Fault

Most states now have some variation of no fault divorce. The definition will vary from state to state. In California, fault only creeps back into divorce tangentially in connection with some (but not most) custody disputes or breaches of fiduciary.

Check with your lawyer to find out what "no fault" means in your state. In the meantime, here are some suggestions for some things that "no fault" probably *does not* mean.

- Since he walked out, I get the house and the kids.
- Since he wants the divorce and I don't, he has to pay for it.
- She left the home, so I can sue her for abandonment.
- I wanted to invest and he spent money frivolously, so I should get what's left.
- The courts aren't going to let her see the kids because she's committed adultery with her boyfriend and is, therefore, an unfit parent.

Most states find "no fault" appealing because they recognize that it is in the interest of families to take "he said/she said" disputes out of the courts, where they never belonged anyway. Again, check with your lawyer. But whether your state is a community property or an equitable distribution state, most courts will try to remove the element of fault as much as possible from the distribution of property and establishment of appropriate support levels.

This means that if what you expect from the legal system is public vindication of yourself and vilification of your spouse, you are going to be disappointed. Instead of getting on the witness stand and telling the world chapter and verse about how you have been wronged, find another outlet for your venting. I suggest you substitute your therapist's office or a lonely mountain top rather than using mutual friends, a local billboard, your spouse's co-workers, his family or, worst of all, your children.

There is a distressing trend in some state legislatures to reintroduce fault into marital dissolution. Some legislators feel that the requirement of fault will deter divorce, and therefore "strengthen the institution of marriage" and aid children. I believe nothing could be farther from the truth. While these attempts are well intentioned, I am convinced that nothing will be more likely to firmly plant children in the middle of their parents' conflict than to tie a financial or other incentive to proof of "fault." Interestingly, these fault-based proposals are opposed by virtually all family lawyers, despite the fact that they would directly benefit financially from increased litigation. That alone should tell you something. If the people who would make money from it oppose changing the law, that's an important clue that the proposed changed in the law really is a bad thing. The Lawyer from Hell is, of course, an exception (See Chapter 13). He would love nothing better than to call out the private investigators and bill thousands of dollars to air somebody else's dirty laundry in public.

CHAPTER 3

Goals, Strategy and Tactics

NOTWITHSTANDING THE PROLIFERATION of goal-setting books and workshops, most people don't have a clue what they want out of life. In that case, how can they possibly know what they want out of their divorce? One of the most constructive things you can do at the outset is to get clear about what you want. If *you* don't know what you want, how is your lawyer going to have any chance of getting it for you?

Recognize, too, that there is a vast difference between knowing what you don't want ("I don't want to be married to this jerk") and what you do want ("If I have to sell the house, I want to stay in the same neighborhood or school district"). Everybody wants the pain to end, but that isn't specific enough to qualify as a goal. Think instead about what you want your life to look and feel like five or ten years in the future.

I often explain to clients that I don't set your goals; you do. There's a very simple reason for this. Years from now, I'll be off doing something else, and you'll still be living with the consequences of the decisions you made in your divorce. If you've failed to set goals for yourself, circumstances will be imposed on you by default and you may be living with repercussions you never would have consciously chosen.

First, you need to be very clear on what you want, and that it is realistic. You may be quite certain you don't want a divorce. Yet, if your spouse has moved in with someone else and filed for divorce, you don't have much choice, do you? Recognize, too, that what is most important to you at the beginning of a separation may be meaningless a few short weeks or months later as your perspective changes.

Goals, Strategy and Tactics

All life goals need to be set, reviewed frequently, and revised as often as circumstances dictate. This is particularly critical at any life-changing juncture such as divorce.

The first thing you should do is to make a list, in no particular order, of everything you would like to see happen in your life. Include both short term and long term goals. Don't try to set priorities yet, and don't worry yet if your goals don't seem realistic. There's plenty of time for that later. Just make sure you have an hour or two of uninterrupted time and allow your mind to free-float, writing down everything you can think of that you would like to see happen. Try to keep focused on what you do want, not on what you don't. A list of things you don't want won't get you anywhere constructive. Don't edit or judge yet. You'll have lots of time later to revise your list.

After you've made your list, prioritize it. Look at it frequently. Revise it from time to time as appropriate. Trust me; your priorities will change with the passage of time. This is particularly important at the beginning of your divorce. What seems most imperative in the days immediately following separation may well become insignificant with the passage of time. For that reason, I suggest you don't make any decisions you don't have to for at least three months after separating. If circumstances demand a decision, that's fine. Make the best decision you can with the facts available to you at the time, but don't go looking for decisions to make. That's why the first goal in divorce is often to stabilize the status quo to the extent you can to allow time for the dust to settle and your perspective to clear. In the days after separation, you may not be able to stand rattling around alone in the house you shared together. Before you run out to put it on the market, wait a while for things to jell. It won't seem so empty in a few weeks or months, and it might be the perfect place to be in the years to come. And always, always, investigate the legal and financial consequences *before* making any irrevocable decision.

When making your list, be specific. It's not good enough to simply say your kids are your highest priority. What does that mean to you? Does it mean possession of the kids, keeping them away from the other

15

spouse? If so, the result may be a turf war which will make Syria look like a Sunday picnic. Does it instead mean that you want your kids to come through the process feeling as loved and secure as possible? That will lead to an entirely different course of conduct. Decide what you want your kids' and your own lives to be like during and after the divorce. What kind of relationship do you want with your kids? With your ex? Given the realities of your financial situation, where would you like to live? Work? When you look back on your divorce in future years, what do you want to be able to say to yourself about how you went through it? That's where the title of this book came from. What actions will make it more likely that you can dance together at your daughter's wedding?

Always keep your goals in mind. It is far too easy to get consumed by minutia in the day-to-day push and pull of divorce. If you remain focused on the long range target, you are less likely to be sidetracked by trivia.

I tell clients that I'll spend as much time with them as they need to evaluate the pros and cons, but I don't make their decisions. My role is to steer them toward what I think is realistic and to make sure that they understand the probable consequences of their choices.

It is important that you understand the difference between goals, strategy and tactics. Clients set goals, the attorney and client set strategy together, and the attorney then develops the tactics to carry out the strategy.

Once goals are set, then it's time to devise a strategy. That's where the client and attorney must be in sync. I'm the one with the knowledge of the process and expertise in the law. Therefore, I'm the one primarily responsible for charting the course, but it must be one with which you are comfortable.

Your attorney should be able to explain her strategy to you, including why one approach is more likely to be successful than another. Ultimately, if you don't like the course your attorney is taking, you may want to change counsel. However, as long as I'm attorney of record in a case, I insist on being primarily in control of the approach to be used.

Goals, Strategy and Tactics

I'm much more effective if I'm doing things in the way that is most comfortable to me. I'm a first rate Sue Talia and a third rate anybody else. If my client wants it done another way, I'll probably be less effective and will most likely suggest that he find someone else who is more in tune with his style.

Strategy needs to be developed at the beginning of the case and periodically revised as circumstances change. This isn't the time to simply let events take their course, or you'll be mired in circumstances and process rather than moving in a positive direction. I was once criticized by another attorney for setting strategy "too early," that is, at the beginning of the case. Say what? When else would you plot out how you expect to accomplish your goals but at the beginning? I suppose that explains why he was not particularly successful in his practice.

Also, note that strategy is not inflexible. On the contrary, it should be periodically reviewed and tweaked as new information comes to light which suggests that another approach may be more appropriate or successful.

Finally, we come to tactics. In divorce, I define this as procedure. I get to decide that. If we're going to postpone a hearing, or disqualify a particular judge, that's my decision. I'm the one who is responsible for steering your case through the system, and I need to be able to use that system as my knowledge and experience dictate and as I see fit.

As your divorce progresses, you will find its course much smoother if you can hold this perspective. And, above all, keep your goals in mind. If you do, you will be much less likely to find yourself standing disconsolate on the courthouse steps wondering how the hell you got there.

CHAPTER 4

Recipe for the Divorce from Hell

IF YOU INSIST on pursuing vindication from the courts, you are going to be disappointed. You will create the "Divorce from Hell." To ensure that happens, just follow this recipe:

- Take a position and staunchly refuse to budge. If your lawyer tells you that even though you may be right on the law, the result simply isn't worth the cost of the fight, insist, "It's not the money, it's the *principle*."
- Demand that all of your family and friends choose sides. Let them know that if they don't stand with you, they're off your list. This will guarantee that your divorce will create the widest possible circle of pain and conflict and generate rifts you'll be regretting for years.
- Insist on litigating every issue. Proclaim that "I'm not doing *anything* until a judge tells me I have to."
- Don't tell your lawyer the whole truth. Then, when you're caught in the lie, tell a little bit more, but still not all of the truth. This process can be drawn out through several stages until your lawyer will either fire you as a client or you will be left with no credibility whatsoever with the judge.
- Engineer an emotional outburst every time there's a four-way settlement meeting or a court appearance. Better yet, remain calm yourself while pushing your spouse's buttons.

Recipe for the Divorce from Hell

- Use each negotiating session as an opportunity to dredge up every instance of marital wrongdoing, real or imagined.
- Define every issue in terms of who "won" and who "lost." I once left the courthouse with a client who got everything she asked for and then wanted me to reassure her that her husband didn't get any of what he wanted. She actually asked me if getting everything on her list of goals "was a win for us." If it isn't enough for you to get what you want, but instead you have to ensure that the other side didn't get what *he* wanted, you're in for Armageddon.
- Tell the kids what a jerk the other parent is, or how he wanted you to abort them when you found out you were pregnant.
- Bad mouth your spouse to the parents of all your kids' friends in the hope that they won't let their kids play with your kids when they are at the other parent's house. Better yet, cut off all contact between your kid and his best friend because the best friend's parents refuse to shun your soon-to-be-ex.
- Cling to unreasonable expectations, even after your attorney says they are not realistic. Then, when the judge rules against you (as your attorney told you all along he would) confront your lawyer accusingly: "We *lost* on *everything!*" Guess what. . .? It isn't a loss unless there was some possibility of a win.

PART II

Resources

CHAPTER 5

Friends, Family and Armchair Quarterbacks

IT IS GOING to be critical at the beginning of your divorce to identify the support systems available to you and use each of them appropriately. Some of your most important resources are:

- Therapist
- Lawyer
- Financial advisor
- Friends
- Family
- *NEVER* the children, even if they are adults

If you are far enough along in the process to be drawn to this book, chances are you've already told at least one trusted friend. You are now about to embark on one of the trickiest of friendship issues. Even the "best" of divorces can be a traumatic experience. You will need to make good use of all of your resources to get through it. You'll need friends who will listen and just let you vent (hopefully with mouths shut). You'll need family to reassure you that you are still loved. Most people have a healthy contingent of both, so what goes wrong?

Well, for starters, many people are ghoulishly fascinated by other people's crises. It can stem from a variety of causes. Some of them shudder and think, quite honestly, "There but for the grace of God go I."

Others love to endlessly dwell on the problems in other people's relationships to divert attention from the problems in their own. And, of course, everyone loves a scandal, especially when they know the participants. If you are confiding in one of these, don't be surprised to find the gory details of your divorce floating through your circle of friends and the local community. And while I'm at it, keep your divorce off social media. *Much* more on that later.

Identify your resources and keep them carefully compartmentalized. Don't turn to your friends for legal advice, or your attorney for therapy. If you do, you'll get yourself in serious trouble.

Everyone has a different privacy threshold. Some people are perfectly comfortable discussing their most intimate business in the grocery store, while the cashier and other customers listen in. Others don't even tell their co-workers when they separate. Whatever your privacy threshold, at least one good, trusted friend is a godsend. A trusted friend who listens sympathetically and gives no advice is a pearl beyond price.

While we're on the subject of friends, don't, repeat *don't* demand that your friends choose sides in your divorce. If you do, don't be surprised that they choose the other side. People don't want to take on someone else's fight as their own, and grownups don't want someone else telling them who their friends can be.

Suppose your friend, although well meaning, can't refrain from telling you how to proceed. Here are a few of the things you are likely to hear:

*"I'd never let anyone treat **me** that way!"*

The implication is that you are being a chump if you don't follow your friend's advice. The problem with this is that no one else is inside your skin. Your friend, however sincere, in truth has absolutely no idea how she would react to your situation until she has had to face it herself. I can't count the times a client has sat in my office, considering whether to stay with a spouse who is having an affair, and confessed that for years she's adamantly told her friends, *"I'd* never take him back!" She is now considering doing just that. You never know what you would do unless it is *your* "him."

> *"My neighbor/cousin/sister in law/ got everything,"* or
> *"My cousin was left with only the clothes on his back, while his wife got the house, the club membership, and everything else."*

Rarely are court decisions or settlements so grossly one-sided. One party may get the bulk of the property, but also all of the debt, which nets out to the same minimal value as the property awarded to the other side. Also, people like to brag/complain about how much/little they got. Stories about the fish that got away are nothing to tales of divorce woe. Frequently, the person repeating the story has no idea what the specific settlement terms were or what tradeoffs may have been made to get there. Its hearsay, and they only know as much as they were told, maybe third or fourth hand at that. Your source probably has few, if any, of the actual facts that led to the resulting trade-offs, and chances are the cousin's spouse feels exactly the same way, and thinks *he* got the short end of the stick.

> *"Your wife spends a fortune on clothes; you'd better cancel the credit cards before she runs them up."*

If there is any hope for retaining relatively good feelings through the course of your divorce, I guarantee that those good feelings will be permanently destroyed if you secretly cancel the credit cards and your wife is embarrassed by having the card rejected by her favorite clerk at the local boutique. Your friend may have been well intentioned. However, your friend is not going to be the one living with the consequences of the resulting distrust and humiliation. You will. This is a perfect example of the type of "defensive" action that is inevitably viewed as hostile by the other party. (See more detailed analysis in Chapter 34, "The Paranoia Factor.") If you're going to follow your friend's advice, at least be sure you're prepared to live with the consequences. You'll have to. Your friend won't.

"You'd better start hiding money so you have a nest egg."

Again, this is very easy advice to give and almost inevitably backfires. It may even be a violation of the automatic restraining orders which went into effect against both of you as soon as the first divorce papers were filed. It's relatively easy to hide small sums of cash and, frankly, quite difficult to hide large ones. It's also illegal, and in some states a serious violation of fiduciary duties. I frequently tell my clients that if someone has been working seriously for years to hide money, we'll never find it all. However, in my experience, *some* almost always turns up. This means that if you have, again for "defensive" purposes, decided to build your little nest egg, the chances are quite good that it is going to be discovered. When it is, trust and cooperation will die, never to be revived, and you will have lost all credibility with the judge.

What if your motivation for creating a nest egg is that you know your spouse is doing it? If your spouse is a pro at hiding money and you've decided to start doing the same to "protect" yourself, you, the amateur, are much more likely to have your stash discovered than the pro. At the risk of sounding moralistic, two wrongs don't make a right, and if you do it, you're no better than your spouse. I once fired a very successful professional client when she insisted I tell her how to hide money from her tradesman husband.

Now, I'm not suggesting that you should leave your finances in the control of your soon-to-be-ex. Quite the contrary. One of the most important steps anyone must take is to assume responsibility for his own financial knowledge and well-being. If you have not been involved in the family finances in the past, there's no excuse for not educating yourself now. However, actively hiding cash, assets or anything else (and I include hiding or withholding pertinent financial or legal documents) is a no-no and is going to hurt you in the long run.

Friends, Family and Armchair Quarterbacks

Suppose some recently divorced friend is crying in his beer to you about being "taken to the cleaners." Consider the possibility that he's deliberately lying. Now, why would he do that, you ask? Perhaps he doesn't want the other side to realize how much money they left on the table. Perhaps his attorney did such a good job that the other party actually thinks *she* came out ahead. I have admonished clients for whom I negotiated particularly good settlements to keep their mouths shut about the fact that the other side overlooked a major weakness in our case. It's just good negotiating to let your opponent think he won, and it's stupid to blow that by bragging on the golf course, at work, around the pool at the country club, or, for God's sake, on social media. That kind of thing *always* gets back through the grapevine.

One final caveat regarding the trusted friend: Your friend probably has a spouse or special someone and, though sworn to secrecy, will tell them your story. Don't be surprised to have your confidences leak out and get back to your soon-to-be ex.

CHAPTER 6

How to Select a Therapist

I RECOMMEND THAT every divorce client consult a therapist. Now, I'm not suggesting six years of psychoanalysis four days a week. However, under the best of circumstances, divorce is an emotionally charged, traumatic experience. Unless nipped in the bud, emotional issues continually bleed through into property, financial, and kid disputes. Even if you are the one who wants the divorce and consider the day you finally had the courage to walk out the best and most liberating of your life, you are still going to hit rough spots. That is simply part of the program. There are going to be times when you second-guess what you have done, why you have done it, and whether there was a better way. I recommend individual counseling at the beginning of every separation and couples counseling for every case in which the parties believe there is even a minute chance of reconciliation. After all, what is the worst thing that can happen? If couples counseling doesn't work and the marriage can't be saved, you find yourself exactly where you were, but with a better understanding of how you got there. And, if divorce is inevitable, your therapist will help you immeasurably in getting through the process. Moreover, a good therapist will help you understand what caused the breakup of the marriage, including your role in it, and help you avoid making the same mistake with a clone of your soon-to-be ex in the future. If you don't understand your part in the dynamic, you are likely to repeat the same pattern in your next relationship, but with a blond instead of a brunette.

So, how do you select a therapist? Among the best referral sources are other professionals: your own attorney, doctor, minister, pediatrician, teachers, etc. They are likely to know who's well regarded in the therapeutic community. Your attorney will also know a little bit about you, your personality and the case and be able to steer you to one or two therapists who are likely to be a good match. Your friends may also be able to give you referrals. Any consumer of therapeutic services should be able to give you useful advice. You may want to talk with two or three therapists before selecting one you will work with.

After the first meeting or two, you will get a sense of whether or not you are connecting with your therapist. It may be that all you need is a couple of sessions to make sure you are on the right track individually and, equally importantly, that you have someone available as a resource when you hit those inevitable rocky spots.

How can you tell if you have a good match with your therapist?

In the first place, a good therapist will give you a very safe place to address your own conflicts and feelings. When you are ready, a good therapist will help you deal with your own role in the marital breakup. At the risk of repeating myself, it always takes two, even if your part is simply that you missed the warning signs and didn't see it coming. Your therapist can help you extract the lessons to be learned from the experience so that you don't repeat them later on, and help you to adopt a constructive and realistic attitude toward the process, your ex and your children. In fact, a good therapist is an invaluable resource in helping you deal with your children and assist them through their own crises.

Find a therapist who's willing to *work* with you. I say this advisedly. Therapy is hard work. If you're not willing to face painful issues, take responsibility, deal with and resolve them, don't waste your money. Avoid what I call a "cheerleader" therapist. This is someone about whom a patient says, "I really feel great for a couple of hours after I leave her office and then I get just as depressed as ever." This is the kind of therapist who (therapeutically speaking) thumps you on the back and says, "You'll be great" and "It's not your fault." In the long run, this doesn't cut it. Therapy is work, not cheerleading, for both of you. A therapist who encourages you to wallow in Victim Lake is doing you a real disservice by depriving you of the opportunity to understand what you contributed to the breakup of the relationship, and what signals you missed in evaluating your choice of spouse so you don't make the same mistakes again. The only lasting benefit of therapy is increased self-knowledge, not an artificial shot of Feel Good.

The other thing a good therapist will do is to keep your legal fees down and help you refrain from poisoning your friendships as a result of using either your lawyer or your friends as outlets for venting.

Many mental health professionals offer sliding fee scales. If you cannot afford a therapist, look into support groups, church or community groups who might offer free or low cost services.

If you can't afford a personal therapist, get into a support group where the cost is shared among several people. It's not the same as individual therapy, but it can be very useful. Most churches and community centers offer divorce support groups, and you can usually find one in your area. A support group can help immensely by demonstrating that you are not alone, thereby alleviating your sense of isolation. It also can provide a range of practical suggestions for coping with specific situations from people who have been there. And don't ever underestimate the importance of having a group of listeners who can sympathetically point out to you the ways in which you are messing up.

Also, don't overlook the possibility that a support group may benefit your children. Many communities and organizations now offer support groups for children of divorce. In Northern California, Kid's Turn does a marvelous job of providing services to kids caught in the divorce of their parents. Check to see if similar organizations or programs exist in your community, especially if your kids are at risk or acting out. Call your community center, church, or social services organization. Such resources may even be available through the schools.

How to Select a Therapist

At the beginning of a divorce, I frequently tell prospective clients that a good therapist is more important than a lawyer. It may be more important to be clear about where you are now and how you got there than to start taking legal action. A good therapist may be the best friend you'll ever hire.

CHAPTER 7

How to Select a Lawyer

ONE OF MY operating assumptions for this book is that you will have competent legal advice. This does not mean litigation is inevitable, but I don't know how anyone can make good decisions about something as important as divorce without understanding their options and the consequences of their choices. For that reason, I am not a fan of online divorce document preparation services. There are just too many nuances, even in a simple looking divorce case, to make irrevocable decisions without buying a couple of hours of a good divorce lawyer's time. I've seen too many documents which came from a document preparation service which leave out important terms, often with disastrous consequences. I understand that people don't have unlimited budgets, and may turn to document preparers as a less expensive alternative. They aren't always. Not only must you consider the expense of correcting what they may do wrong (if it even *can be* corrected), but some of them charge as much or more than lawyers. I've seen agreements which failed to follow the most basic law on the tax deductibility of alimony payments where the paralegal charged twice what a competent attorney would have charged for a correctly drafted document.

Whether you anticipate your lawyer handling all aspects of your case, working "limited scope," acting as a consulting attorney during your divorce mediation, or coaching you to represent yourself, I still believe you have to have a competent divorce attorney (not an attorney who specializes in another field, a paralegal or document preparer) advising you.

One of the most difficult and critical decisions you'll have to make is the selection of that lawyer. You'll need to do a lot of homework in order to make a good choice.

First, ask around. Find out who is reputed to be a good *family* lawyer in your area. When someone's name is mentioned, ask why. Decide if the reasons given are consistent with your goals for your divorce. The fact that her kids are on your kid's soccer team tells you nothing about her skills as a family lawyer. Find out about her background, experience, and reputation in the *legal* community. If the primary recommendation is "She's really nice," and you expect litigation from hell, keep looking. She may be easy to talk to, but get steamrollered in court. While you want to have good communication with your attorney, you're not interviewing for best friend. You want someone who can do the job. Don't go to an attorney who does not specialize in family law except to get a referral to someone who does. In most jurisdictions, family law is extremely specialized. It takes years to learn to do it well. Steer clear of someone who just dabbles in it or takes a custody case now and then when cash flow is down.

One of the best referral sources is other, non-family lawyers. They're familiar enough with the legal system to know who is respected by the insiders. This is always a good place to start.

Ask your friends and neighbors. Find out who represented them, and how they felt about their representation. If they interviewed and rejected other attorneys, find out who and why. Ask them if they wish they had done anything differently. Then decide for yourself. Don't blindly assume you would have made the same decision as your friend.

Ask your therapist, if you already have one. They frequently know who is good. They have the additional advantage of knowing you, and are therefore more likely to refer you to someone who will be a good fit.

Research

It's a good idea to learn something about the lawyers you have been referred to. Ask your referral source what they like about the attorneys they are recommending. Do they have direct knowledge of their work? What did they like about them? Most lawyers have websites now. Remembering that anyone can post anything on the web, see if your prospective lawyer has a website and what it tells you about her. You can also check the State Bar website to see if there is any history of professional discipline.

Don't assume that because your prospective attorney is listed on an attorney referral website that it means anything. These groups are always recruiting people to pay them for a listing, often have no quality control whatsoever, and anyone can list themselves and their "qualifications" even if the latter are entirely fictional.

Here's a caveat. If you Google your prospective attorney and you find a venomous review on a Yelp or a social media website, take it with a grain of salt. If someone says the lawyer is a shark or other negative epithet, take a look at the reasons. It may be a legitimate, "I thought we should have been trying to settle and all he wanted was to go to court." Be especially suspicious if the negative review comes from the party who opposed her in court. People involved in contentious litigation often loathe the opposing counsel, finding it easier to blame the lawyer on the other side for what is not going their way rather than the person they chose as their mate. There may be legitimate reasons. Or, the opposing party may be a card-carrying, certifiable nut job. As lawyers, it isn't our job to ingratiate ourselves with the other party or opposing attorney. That goes with the territory. One of the risks is the ready availability of the web as a forum for venom and the relative inability of the victim of such attacks to meaningfully correct the record. One of the finest family lawyers I know was very successful in a highly contested litigation. The party on the other side was, to put it kindly, nuts. The result was a scathing, personal, and vicious review of the lawyer on Yelp which was the first thing that came up in a Google search of her name. If something like that is out there, it should be looked at, but consider the source. And if you interview the lawyer anyway, don't ask about it. She won't be able to tell you what really happened because that would be a breach of attorney/client privilege with her other client. Use your own judgment and proceed accordingly after considering all of the other factors I've mentioned. It is much more important to get an overall picture of your prospective attorney and how he might be a good member of your team than to reject a good attorney because he pissed off somebody else at some point in the past.

A final word on research: the internet is a place to investigate people you've been referred to, *not* a place to get referrals.

When you've done your research and have amassed a list of names, call around and interview several. I like to talk to prospective clients on the phone before seeing them. I take only a small number of the cases referred to me. If I talk to the client first, it is usually easy to determine if this is a case in which I'm likely to be interested, and if I seem to have good communication with the caller. If not, I make a referral on the spot. I have an extensive referral list and like to suggest two or three attorneys who I think might be a better fit with the client and case. When making a referral, I take care to match the client with the attorney rather than simply reading down the list, and I only refer to attorneys whose work I know personally. By the way, if you are referred on in this way, don't ask, "Is he any good?" If I didn't think he was, he wouldn't be on my list. Before substituting my own referral list, I always ask prospective clients if they were given referrals to any other attorneys. If I can validate people to whom they have been referred from several sources, they will feel more comfortable about the individual. If the people mentioned are not high on my list of competent colleagues, won't say "stay away, he's an ignorant jerk." Instead, I'll say, "Let me suggest a few more names."

This part is critical: Interview at least two, and preferably three, attorneys. Even among the most competent, there are wide variations in style, strategy and personality. How will you know this and make a good choice if you only talk to one and have no one to compare him to? One lawyer may give you much more specialized and thorough information than another. Find one who communicates well with you and is familiar with the legal issues presented by your case.

Don't be overly impressed with the attorneys who offer "free initial consultation." Though practices and the legal culture vary widely, many good lawyers expect to be paid for their initial consultation, and if you limit yourself only to lawyers who offer free consultations, you may be getting exactly what you pay for. Should it be a man or a woman? There are very few good reasons to let gender be the deciding factor. If you think a man will be tougher, or a woman will understand you better, will be "too nice," or will side with your wife, you will be making a mistake. Don't ever allow sexual stereotypes to dictate your decision. When I'm asked for a referral only to a woman lawyer, I usually give a lecture on gender bias. I point out that hormones are a stupid reason to select an attorney. What they really need is the best attorney for their case, court and personality. I was brought up short once by a woman who somewhat timidly responded that the first lawyer whom she had consulted (a well known local Lothario) had suggested taking out his fees in trade. I told her I understood her fears based upon that experience. The proper response, however, is not to assume that all male attorneys will do the same. Instead, she should report the first attorney to the State Bar for professional misconduct and continue her search for the best attorney for her case, regardless of gender.

Prospective clients frequently asked me to take cases in a distant county or an unfamiliar court. This is a mistake. It is important to find an attorney who is familiar with your local court and judges. An out-of-town attorney is going to be at a distinct disadvantage. This isn't because the local guy can get special favors from the judge. He will, however, be much more familiar with the local rules and may even have helped write them. Many areas of family law are highly discretionary, and the local attorney will be more likely to know how a particular judge exercises his discretion on the facts presented by your case. He should know how the judge tends to rule on similar facts and what approach works best with her. He probably knows your opposing counsel, which can be very helpful. For these reasons, I decided years ago never to venture out of my county; I know that I have a huge advantage over out-of-county counsel and I certainly don't intend to find myself in the reverse position on someone else's turf.

How to Select a Lawyer

If, even after considering all this, you insist on Ms. Hot Shot Big City Lawyer who doesn't really know your local court very well, consider this: Do you really want to pay her several hundred dollars per hour to drive from her office to the courthouse and back for each hearing, or to research the local rules that your spouse's attorney knows by heart? Think of the advantage your spouse will have if he knows that each hearing costs you twice as much as it costs him because of the built-in travel expense. Do you suspect that the extra expense might be used as a tactic to drive your fees up and force you to accept an unfavorable settlement offer because you can't afford to continue to fight for a better one? You bet.

Many states have certification processes which help you in locating an experienced family law attorney. This is one of many factors to consider, but is not by any means determinative. I'm a certified family law specialist in California, but know many highly competent professionals who are not certified, not because they couldn't pass the test, but because they didn't bother to take it. I also know certified specialists who are idiots. It's one of several questions to ask, but don't reject the attorney who is knowledgeable, highly respected in the legal community, and with whom you have good rapport just because he's not certified. Experience and familiarity with the local family court are infinitely more important.

What other questions should you ask? I always smile when a prospective client pulls out a laundry list of questions obviously culled from a "how to" book. They'll want to know how long I've been in practice (as though 18 years is better than 15), where I went to law school (unless it's Harvard, they generally won't know the difference between a fine local institution and ABC Law School by Mail), or what my "win/loss" record is (more about this later). These questions are not going to elicit any useful information in the search for a divorce lawyer. Unless the ink is barely dry on the diploma, the name of the law school or the date of admission to the bar is of significantly less relevance than the quality of the lawyer's experience in cases like yours.

What you want to know is how long they've been doing *family* law in this locality. What percentage of their practice consists of cases with estates and factual and legal issues similar to yours? If it's just something they do when receipts are down and they're having a slow month, keep looking. Ask what they know about the local family judges. What are the procedures? If you know who your judge is, does he have any known biases? How much time are you likely to get with the judge? What does the attorney think the chances are of settling your case? If custody is going to be an issue in your case, ask how much custody work he does. Many family lawyers don't like to do custody work and as a result don't do it well. What are the special problems presented by your fact situation? What is their experience with complex business valuation, or commercial real estate holdings, or stock options, or whatever specific assets you and your spouse will have to value and divide? Do they think it will be necessary to retain a forensic accountant, that is, one who testifies in court? Why? On what issues? What do they estimate the cost is likely to be? Who would they recommend, and why? Ditto for custody evaluators.

It is important that your case is neither the largest they have handled nor the smallest in their office. If your case is significantly larger than their other cases, they may not have the expertise, staffing or time to handle it properly. If it is the smallest, they may lose interest in it or it may be lost among the other bigger and more pressing cases. Either way, you are better off if your case is of a type routinely handled by your prospective attorney.

When you get deeper into the facts of your case, your prospective attorney should be able to tell you her likely strategy and why she thinks it would be more successful or cost-effective than another. Ask what she perceives as the weaknesses in your case and listen carefully to her answer. Your attorney should be able to tell you her approach to procedure, and how she likes to run her cases. As professionals, we all have our own styles and should be able to characterize them for the client. I can give a prospective client an excellent rundown on my style, strengths and, yes, weaknesses in about five minutes. If your lawyer doesn't volunteer this information, ask the question. It's a perfectly fair one.

Finally, your attorney should be able to give you a clear understanding of her billing practices and procedures. Almost all family law cases are billed hourly rather than on a flat fee. You need to know how your attorney structures her billing, what she bills for, whether she bills for paralegal time (most do) and what requirements she has for retainers. How is the retainer held, and how often are you billed? What does she expect from you when the retainer is consumed? Is it refundable if not used, or if you change lawyers? Is it "evergreen," that is, does it have to be replenished when exhausted?

If you already know who will be representing your spouse, your attorney will probably be able to give you a better ballpark estimate on total fees (see Chapter 13, "The Lawyer from Hell"). Remember that since fees are billed hourly, it is virtually impossible to do more than give a general estimate the total cost at the beginning of a case. It is going to be up to you to keep tabs on fees as they are incurred. More about this later, too. (See Chapter 41, " Keeping a Rein on Fees and Costs.")

When you are deciding whether you can afford a particular attorney, assume that you are going to be paying your own legal fees, either from the marital estate or personally. I have explained to countless clients that, although we routinely ask that the other side be ordered to pay our fees, they must assume that everyone pays his own. The rationale is that as a matter of policy, most courts don't like to send litigants the message they can litigate at will for free. It tends to lessen the likelihood of protracted and unnecessary litigation if both sides feel they are at risk for the cost. Despite this speech clients still come back later and say, "But I thought *he'd* have to pay for it." Listen, and read my lips. Yes, you will have to pay for it. Assume that to be true and factor it into the selection of your attorney. And don't blithely assume that the hourly rate doesn't matter because the fees will be paid out of the marital estate. Whose estate is it anyway? And if it is reduced by excessive fees, leaving less to divide with your spouse, what makes you think you're not the one who is paying the freight?

Prospective clients frequently don't believe me when I tell them they don't need someone as expensive as I am for a simple case. Divorce fees are hourly. If Attorney Smith charges $350 an hour and Attorney Brown only $250, when should you opt for the more expensive attorney? Do a cost/benefit analysis. If your case involves complex issues which I can handle more efficiently because I have had many similar cases in the past, then you are better off paying the higher rate because I will be more effective. You are not ahead if you hire someone with a lower hourly rate, only to be charged for the time it takes to educate herself in an area of the law which is completely new to her. The initial rate will be lower, but the total bill may be much higher because her education will be on your dime.

By the same token, if the issues are such that no specialized expertise is required, why should you pay the higher hourly rate when there is no savings in time or result? If the issue is simple and your attorney will just be waiting around the courthouse for your case to be called, why not choose the lower hourly rate? I frequently tell prospective clients that they need a competent family law attorney, but that the complexity of their issues is not such that I can handle the case any more efficiently than the next guy. In that instance, there is no benefit to the client (except ego or perhaps scare value) in retaining the Big Gun. It is not a good use of their money or of the attorney's time.

Sometimes, all logic to the contrary, a client insists on retaining a more expensive attorney than he needs. I have frequently been in the position of explaining to a client why he really doesn't need someone as expensive as me for the facts of his case. After I tell him he will be paying far too high a percentage of his net worth for my fees, and there are many other attorneys who are perfectly well qualified to handle the case at a lower hourly rate, he sometimes insists, "But I want the *best*." Whenever I give in and take a case I know doesn't justify my involvement, I end up regretting it. At some point, the client will realize I was telling the truth and start to resent the hourly rate she agreed to pay. So, you ask, why don't I take the case and just charge the lower hourly rate? Most really good family lawyers have many more referrals than they can possibly take. If they turn down one case, it is not as though their caseload won't remain full. Believe me, if your attorney tells you that you can do just as well with someone less expensive, you are being told the truth.

Once you are well into the initial interview, check the quality of your communication. Are you getting straight answers to the questions you are asking? Do they make sense? Do you feel the lawyer is hearing you when you describe your goals and fears? This is a critical issue. The primary cause of a breakdown in the attorney/client relationship is poor communication. It is a truism that the relationship never gets better than it was at the beginning. If you are not communicating effectively then, if either of you is having to repeat and explain things to be sure the other understands what you are trying to say, it isn't a good fit. I'll refer clients out without hesitation at this stage if I don't think the communication is satisfactory. I know from past experience that we can't work effectively as a team if we're not on the same wave length and it will not be a successful professional relationship. I'll also explain to the client precisely why I'm declining the case. Sometimes attorneys take the easy way out. They don't want the client to feel rejected, so instead of telling the truth, they tell a white lie. They quote a fee the client can't afford or say they are suddenly "too busy" to take your case. I've never understood this last one. If they were too busy for your case, why didn't they know that before making the appointment with you and wasting everyone's time?

Instead, they should be telling you the truth, which is that they don't want your case. It is important to be completely honest here. You and the attorney each have a right to decline a professional relationship. Sometimes clients are surprised to learn this, but, after all, it isn't indentured servitude. If I don't think we have good communication, I say so. It isn't personal and it doesn't mean that I don't like you or that you're stupid. I try to keep it from sounding like a rejection. Instead, I explain what I've just said here. In order for our relationship to be effective in achieving your goals, we have to work as a team. That means our communication must be exemplary and we must agree on the goals and strategy to be employed. If either of those factors is absent, it doesn't mean that one of us is bad or wrong. It just means that it won't work and you should keep on looking for the other member of your team.

Remember also that what we do as attorneys is confidential. I can't give you a referral list of satisfied clients or explain just *how* I pulled off a major coup in the Lombardi case last month. If Mr. Lombardi himself told you what a terrific job I did and that's why you're here, that's great. But don't ask, and don't expect me to comment if you do.

And if I refer you to another attorney because I don't think we have good rapport, or for whatever reason, don't ask, "Is she as good as you are?" Of *course* not. If I didn't think my way was better than hers, I'd be doing it *her* way instead of mine.

Six Questions Not to Ask Your Prospective Lawyer

"Are you really tough?"
("No, I routinely surrender at the slightest hint of opposition . . .")

I'm always baffled by the frequency with which I get this question. What do they think I'll say? "Not really, but my assertiveness trainer says I need to practice in adversarial situations so I'll get better at it." If you've done your homework and investigated who has a good reputation in your area, you must assume that there's a reason this attorney is well respected. Don't ask this, but instead, ask the questions I suggested earlier. After all, even if your prospective attorney is the wuss of the Western World, either he thinks he's a tough guy (roar) or he knows he's a pussy-cat but is hardly going to admit it to *you*. Interestingly, the same client who wants to be sure I'm a "barracuda" (a word used only by laymen and never by lawyers) will frequently turn around and tie my hands, not wanting me to do anything that will "make my husband mad."

Corollary: *"I hope you take this as a compliment: I hear you're a real shark."*

I don't and it isn't. If you think being very, very good at what I do is synonymous with being a shark, I don't want you. Sooner or later you'll ask me to do something that I consider unethical (but which any "shark" would do) and we'll have a parting of the ways. I'll be insulted and you will think I "wasn't aggressive enough."

"What is your win/loss record?"

This is a meaningless question in a family law context. Divorce isn't like criminal law where you can quantify convictions per number of trials. How do you even define a win? I might consider it a huge victory to take a terrible case on dreadful facts and turn it into a 50/50.

Suppose there were five issues in my last trial, and I managed to win on the three about which my client felt strongest. Is that a win? What if those other two issues were the ones in which the other party was most invested? Did he think he won, too? Does that mean I didn't?

"What is your track record against Attorney X?"

This question is almost as meaningless as the last. Instead, ask if your attorney has a history against Attorney X. What happened? Did the case(s) settle? Are there residual hard feelings between the two of you because of prior cases you had with her that might affect her handling of your case? Was there a mutual effort to resolve the conflict as quickly and amicably as possible, or was the case pushed to its litigious limits? If so, what would your prospective attorney suggest as a strategy against Attorney X in your case?

How to Avoid the Divorce from Hell

"Can my husband bribe the judge?"

At the risk of sounding naive to those of you who have been watching too many old movies, the days of judges being purchased are about gone. Most judges are underpaid, hard-working and sincere individuals who honestly do their best to dispense justice as even-handedly as possible. For those few who are not, there are judicial watchdog commissions which are becoming ever more vigilant. The fact is, even if the judge were amenable to bribery, the risks are simply too great to take a chance. Besides, your spouse probably couldn't come up with enough cash to make the professional risk worth his while. Though judges are undoubtedly underpaid, only an incredibly stupid one would risk the public and professional humiliation, not to mention the criminal sanctions and jail time which would result.

"You're a woman, so won't you side with my wife?"

Besides being sexist, this is also stupid and insulting. It assumes that your prospective attorney is so unprofessional as to be guided solely by hormones. After a few well-chosen words on my part, the prospective client who asks me this question either sheepishly apologizes or leaves to find a rough, tough, shoot-em-up gunslinger more to his liking.

Corollary: *"I know you'll understand (read: agree with me) because you're a woman."*

When a new client says this to me, I immediately set them straight. This isn't sisterhood; it's business. I find the implication offensive and rarely agree to represent a client who starts out this way. If I decide to work with you, it will be because you have a case that interests me and not because we both have ovaries.

How to Select a Lawyer

"My husband is SO intimidating . . . are you sure you can stand up to him?"

This is a variation on the first comment above and is just as unlikely to elicit any information which will be useful to you in deciding whether you want to retain me as your attorney. *You* might find your spouse extremely intimidating. Chances are I won't. I wasn't married to him and don't have the emotional baggage that you do. He may have intimidated you for 20 years. The fact that he doesn't intimidate someone else is not a criticism of you. It is a recognition of the reality that I have no history or connection with him. Many of my clients are surprised to hear that I don't care what a tough guy he thinks he is. Its business, and he's on *my* turf.

CHAPTER 8

Why You Want Your Spouse to Have a Good Lawyer, Too

THE LAST THING you want when you are starting a divorce is for your spouse to hire a stupid lawyer. More often than not, when my client asks if the lawyer on the other side is any good and I say yes, he winces. That's because he doesn't understand the extreme cost which *he* may have to pay for a stupid opponent. He assumes that if the other attorney isn't very good, that means that we win. There are, in fact, times when this happens. I have, on several occasions, obtained an extremely good settlement simply because the other attorney hadn't a clue what he was giving away. It doesn't happen as often as you would think, however. The stupid attorney is easy to beat at court. But if you really want to settle your case without going to court (and who wouldn't?) the stupid attorney will make it much more difficult to do so. The likely result is that incompetent counsel on the other side of your case will vastly increase the fees, acrimony, and general craziness — all out of proportion to the benefit to you of some issue which he might overlook through ignorance.

Let me explain.

First, we need to define some terms. By "stupid attorney," I mean someone who is incompetent, ignorant, unfamiliar with family law or just plain "doesn't get it." This will distinguish the "stupid attorney" from the "Lawyer from Hell" referred to in Chapter 13. The Lawyer from Hell is someone who very much "gets it." He is generally quite bright, intimately familiar with the ins and outs of the legal system and manipulates it primarily for his own, and sometimes for his client's benefit. The stupid attorney is generally acting from very good motives. He just doesn't know any better and can completely screw up a case as a result.

A stupid attorney will be rigid

On some dim level, he knows that there is a great deal he doesn't know. Therefore, he will cling quite rigidly to whatever he thinks he *does* know. This means that there will be absolutely no creativity in the way his client's case is handled. Because a particular approach worked once for him in another case, he will repeat the same formula, even in the face of irrefutable evidence that it isn't working *now*. If your attorney suggests a novel solution which creatively solves the problem, he will be afraid to agree for fear it is a trick or a trap. Since he doesn't have the ability or the experience to think through all of the permutations of the admittedly creative suggestion, he will stick to the safe, the tried and true. Mind you, he is not doing this out of evil motives. He wants to be sure that his client is protected. He doesn't want to take the risk, and the liability, of making a mistake by recommending something which he doesn't fully understand. And since he knows in his heart of hearts that his opponent is brighter than he is, he will take the safe way out and say no to the novel solution in case he missed something. It is extremely difficult to settle a case with an attorney such as this. The elegant solution to a complex problem is totally impossible.

A stupid attorney will be unrealistic

Because she is stupid, she will be blind to the weaknesses of her own case. This means she won't see the fact that she really can't win on a particular issue because the facts or the law are against her. One of the hallmarks of a good lawyer is to remain objective with respect to her case so that she can spot not only the strengths but the weaknesses. If the weaknesses can't be turned around or compromised in some way, they should be conceded. One of the worst disservices an attorney can do for a client is to continue to fight on a losing issue, even in good, though misguided faith. All this does is increase the legal fees and level of animosity. Some of the worst attorneys I know are in fact very bright individuals. However, they don't see the weaknesses of their case and as a result, they litigate *everything*. You don't want an attorney like this, nor do you want your spouse to have one.

I have literally pleaded with opposing counsel to simply read a particular code section which absolutely demonstrated that his position could not possibly prevail under the law. He was a real estate attorney who decided to branch out into family law because the divorcing couple owned lots and lots of real estate. He assumed that because he knew about real estate law, he knew how to handle real estate in a divorce. Wrong. The only response I got to that letter (which included a copy of the code section I was begging him to read and which said unequivocally that he was dead in the water) was a sarcastic reply demanding to know who appointed me Goddess of Family Law. Before we finally got to trial on the issue he couldn't win, an additional $100,000 in attorneys' fees had been consumed. Now, mind you, after trial my client ultimately came out well ahead. However I can assure you that he would have gladly compromised at the beginning, and in fact offered to do so, because he would have preferred to see his ex-wife have the money rather than pay it to the lawyers. The wife's attorney couldn't see it, insisted on holding out for something he couldn't possibly win, and his client missed out on a very good deal indeed.

A stupid attorney will get emotionally involved in the case

I have said before that one of the most important attributes of a good divorce attorney is objectivity. This enables him to see the weaknesses in your case and prevents him from being blinded to reasonable settlement opportunities and creative solutions. When an attorney becomes emotionally invested in the case and decides to become a "white knight" for his client, he is at risk of becoming a co-dependent. Trust me. This does not help.

We all know that emotions run high in divorces. The client will call his attorney, absolutely outraged at some conduct by the other party and demand that a "strong letter" be sent to the other side. I am not a fan of the "he said/she said" form of correspondence. It serves no purpose other than to momentarily gratify the sender's client and utterly inflame the other party. Some attorneys have turned this into an art form. A bad attorney will literally paper you with these letters (all of which cost money, of course) simply because his client insists on them. The better attorney is the one who refuses to write them unless they serve a useful purpose. I can assure you that the likelihood of settlement decreases significantly once such an exchange is started. Ditto endless accusatory email chains.

A stupid attorney will create unrealistic expectations

Since by definition a stupid attorney does not know the law, either through ignorance or inexperience, the information he gives your spouse may in fact be incorrect. This will create unrealistic expectations. He may lead your spouse to believe that he can't possibly lose an issue which hasn't been won in your state since 1912. How likely do you think it is that your spouse will compromise if his attorney is telling him he can't possibly lose?

Let me give you an example. Let's suppose that you and your spouse have a family business. Let's suppose that he runs it. For purposes of this example, it doesn't matter whether he is a computer consultant, doctor, lawyer, dentist, contractor or consulting engineer. He has a business which depends almost entirely on his personal expertise for its continuing value. In a community property state, that business is likely to be deemed to have some sort of "goodwill," that is, an intangible value for which you, as the nonemployee spouse, are entitled to be compensated.

This has happened to me dozens of times. The owner of the business comes into my office, and when I start talking about valuing the business for the property division, he says:

"It doesn't have any value because I can't sell it," or

"It doesn't have any value because it is worthless without me and I'll just quit."

When I point out the facts of life, he says, "You mean I have to buy her out of the business because it is going to make money in the future, and then I have to *pay her* support from those future earnings?"

Precisely.

Now a good attorney will allow the client to vent and then explain the law. That's his job. It may not feel good and it may not feel fair, but that's the way it is, at least in my state.

If that same person goes to a stupid attorney, the stupid attorney may well tell him that he is right and will agree to make all these ridiculous arguments with a straight face to the judge who knows better. Now, mind you, the Lawyer from Hell may tell the client the same thing, but for different reasons. He knows he can't win but this is a way to make sure that there is a fight which is going to generate lots of fees for him. The stupid attorney doesn't know better, wants to please his client, and will create World War III out of sheer ignorance. You don't want this.

In the fact pattern outlined above, how likely do you think it is that the parties are going to be able to reach agreement on the value of that business? So, what can you do about it?

If you find that your attorney's theory of the case is radically different from the opposing attorney's theory of the case, pay attention. If your attorney is telling you that it is "the law," and the other side is getting the opposite advice, one of them is wrong. Either it isn't "the law," the law is grayer than one of the lawyers believes, or one of them doesn't know the law. This is a good time to get a second opinion and find out which attorney is operating under the proper theory. In all but a few unusual leading edge fact patterns, there is in fact a body of law, and an experienced attorney will be able to give you some general parameters of what to expect. If you are the one who is getting bad advice, this is a good time to change attorneys. At least you have control over that situation.

If you find your spouse is the one getting bad advice, you have a problem. You have *no control* whatsoever. If you tell him that his lawyer is stupid, he will assume the reason you want him to change lawyers is that you are intimidated by the one he has. This will backfire. You may never be able to persuade your spouse to get a second opinion. This is why you want him to start out with a good lawyer. Two good lawyers will know the law as it applies to facts such as yours. They will also know where the gray areas are and can very quickly hone in on those rather than spending lots of time and money fighting over routine issues. Those fights can cost you and your spouse tens of thousands of dollars.

Why not simply let your spouse go off happily misguided in a fog of unrealistic expectations?

First, in virtually every case, reaching an agreement (i.e., settling out of court) is preferable to going to trial. It is cheaper, faster, and preserves more dignity for both of you.

Second, if your spouse's attorney is spending tens of thousands of dollars scheduling depositions and doing all sorts of ridiculous things to try to prove the unprovable, your attorney also has to attend those depositions and review the documents, respond to demands and all of the rest of it. That costs *you* money.

Incidentally, even the greatest civil or criminal litigator can fall into the category of "stupid attorney" as described in this chapter if he doesn't have extensive family law experience and is foolish enough to think he doesn't need it.

Clients sometimes ask me to give them a list of attorneys to give to their spouse at the beginning of the case. I used to refuse to do this on the theory that the spouse was going to assume it was a setup and I was giving them somebody who would roll over and play dead at the first opportunity. However, after a few run-ins with really stupid opposing lawyers, I changed my mind. If asked, I now will give a list of potential opposing attorneys, and they will all be good ones. They will be people who are very knowledgeable in family law, and familiar with our local courts and judges. They will be people I know have a track record of doing a good job for their clients in similar cases and who can find reasonable solutions to difficult problems. The opposing client may or may not select anybody on my referral list, but at least I know that I have done my part to avoid the divorce from hell.

CHAPTER 9

How to Tell if You Are Well Represented

WHENEVER YOU VENTURE into unfamiliar legal waters, one of the hardest things you'll have to do is evaluate whether you are getting good professional advice. This is particularly true in family law. You may not know much about dentistry, but if you have a bad dentist, the filling will fall out or your tooth will start hurting. But how do you know if you have a bad lawyer?

This is particularly difficult in family law because there often is no clear demarcation between win and lose, and no one wins everything. Further, you may *both* feel like you're losing the preliminary skirmishes. Every so often I hear through the grapevine that someone whom I (and the rest of the local family law bar) know to be a flaming idiot is touted by someone as God's gift to family law. I can only assume that the source of the referral is either someone who didn't realize what good representation was, or whose case was such a fluke that even a buffoon couldn't screw it up.

You can't assume that your lawyer screwed up because you "lost" the first hearing (and I remind you that in family law, "lost" is a relative term). I'm a fan of planning for the long haul. If a few concessions need to be made along the way, I don't lose a great deal of sleep if we're still on track for the major goals.

So, what *should* you look for?

First, your attorney should be willing to explain his strategy to you. He should be able to tell you why, in his opinion, one strategy is more likely than another to succeed in your case. He should have some experience with similar situations and the same judge to draw upon. He should have a sense of how this judge is likely to respond to the facts and law of your case. After all, one of the criteria you used in selecting him in the first place was his familiarity with the specific court where your case is pending and with cases similar to yours.

He should be able and willing to look you in the eye and tell you bad news. It's surprising how few people can do this. We would all prefer to be the bearers of only good tidings. That doesn't often fall to our lot as lawyers. One of the hallmarks of bad lawyering is to fail to be honest with the client about the risks of his case. I've sat on many a courthouse bench, listening to the attorney next to me explain the law to his client, only to have him waffle when the client asks the direct question "Does this mean we're going to lose?" instead of just saying yes. A good attorney can and must look you in the eye and answer that question truthfully so you can make realistic decisions about conceding a position you can't win, or trading it for something else you want in a negotiated settlement.

Ask your attorney what the weak areas of your case are and how she intends to address them. People often shy away from bringing up any thought of weakness, but it is one of the most important questions you can ask. Your attorney should be able to explain your options to you, as well as the advantages and disadvantages of the probable result of each. I've separately discussed the issue of setting goals. You, the client, have the right and the responsibility to set your own goals, consistent with the law and your (and your attorney's) ethics. In order to do this, you may need to spend a considerable amount of time with your attorney to be sure you fully understand the options available to you, what is realistic and what is not, the possible consequences, the approximate cost of each and probability of success. This doesn't mean your lawyer can guarantee an outcome. However, he should be able to assist you in pointing out risks and properly evaluating the choices available to you.

If you have any doubts, get a second opinion. I give second opinions all the time, as do most family law attorneys. I'm happy to review a file and tell the client what I think. Sometimes I find that although I might have handled it differently, both strategies are judgment calls. In that instance, I would generally defer to the attorney who has had the case from the beginning and probably knows more about its strengths and weaknesses than I could determine in an hour's consultation. Although I may have approached certain issues differently, I find no particular fault. In those situations, I give the client a list of questions to ask their attorney and send them back to get the answers. I suspect that the problem is not that the attorney is mishandling the case, but rather that he is not communicating effectively with the client. Frequently this is as simple as not taking the time to explain to the client why Course A is better than Course B. I would discuss that with the client and send him back to ask his attorney to explain the reason for the strategy. More often than not there's a reasonable explanation which simply hasn't been communicated effectively to the client.

There is a caveat attendant to this: Have you, as the client, provided a clear and accurate recitation of the facts to your lawyer? Many people don't. You may leave something out, assuming it "isn't important" or, more frequently, out of embarrassment. Before you start complaining about the course the case is taking, make sure you have given your attorney the complete, unvarnished truth, even if you may have done some things you're not proud of. Your lawyer needs to hear it from you before he's blindsided by hearing it from your spouse's lawyer.

When giving a second opinion, I would also not hesitate to tell the client if I think he's being badly represented. This doesn't mean just that I would have done something else; everyone has a different style. However, if I don't think the first attorney is maximizing the strong points of the case or properly evaluating the weaknesses, the client needs to know that.

If your attorney constantly makes excuses to you for bad rulings, take a close look. We've all been in situations where the judge does something unaccountable. They have great discretion in many areas, and they're human. They bring their own baggage of experiences to the bench, and although they try to prevent it from getting in the way, sometimes they blow it; that can happen to anyone. But if it happens every time you go to court, there's something wrong. Either the judge is right, and your attorney isn't telling you that you have a lousy case, you have a good case and your lawyer isn't doing a good job of presenting it, or your attorney doesn't know as much about the judge as he said he did. If the judge has a track record on cases such as yours, your attorney should know about it. And if the judge truly is a loose cannon, why didn't your attorney warn you to try to get the case assigned to a different judge, or advise you to stay out of court and try to settle at the beginning? These are legitimate questions you should be asking.

The second opinion can be invaluable. It may send you back to your first attorney with a new appreciation of what is involved in your representation. It may, on the other hand, result in your changing attorneys. Either way, the cost of the consultation is money well spent, even if all it does is put your mind at rest.

And, if you decide to change, do it sooner rather than later. The longer you wait the more you'll pay lawyer No. 2 to get up to speed and the harder it will be to change strategy. And remember, lawyer No, 2 probably won't be able to undo the adverse rulings lawyer No. 1 already got.

CHAPTER 10

Attorney/Client Relations

("I thought you were on <u>my</u> side . . .")

AT SOME TIME during your divorce, you may start to lose faith in your attorney. Maybe you don't understand why a particular strategy is being pursued. Perhaps you feel you and your attorney are not on the same wave length anymore. In my experience, 90% of the problems that arise in attorney/client relations result from poor communication.

Most attorneys are paid on an hourly basis. This means that time is money and, as a result, all too many attorneys take on more cases than they can comfortably handle. Some phone calls or emails may not get returned as quickly as one would like. I'm not defending it, but simply describing a common situation.

Very few family lawyers make a great deal of money. Family law is notoriously one of the least lucrative areas of legal practice. A very simple fact accounts for this: Our clients usually can't deduct our fees on their income tax returns. Businesses can afford to pay much higher legal fees because, of course, Uncle Sam subsidizes a percentage of the expense by making it tax deductible. Divorce attorneys' fees are generally after tax, after mortgage, after child support, after utilities, and after everything else. This means that they know that after the retainer runs out, they can't assume each bill will be paid on receipt. As a result, many divorce attorneys take on too many cases at once because they know they may be carrying an account receivable for a while. It may take months to be paid for the work they are doing today. They accept more cases because the staff and rent still have to be paid in the interim, while they are waiting for a house to sell or the IRA to be liquidated or for some other source of payment. This is not an excuse for not returning phone calls or answering emails, but it is an explanation of why some divorce attorneys feel compelled to overbook their time for economic reasons.

This does *not* mean that your case should be ignored, that it should not be given full attention, and that your phone calls should not be returned. That is your right as a client and you should insist on it.

There is a corollary here, as well. If you are constantly calling your attorney and screaming at him because of some unrealistic expectation, such as the fact that he can't make your spouse become someone other than the person he's been since the dawn of time (that is, since before you married him), don't be surprised that he is not overly anxious to return the call and get screamed at yet again. You are entitled to be treated with respect, and so is your attorney.

Email

Email has made communication virtually instantaneous. When I started in practice, the rule was that, regardless of whether I was in trial, taking a deposition or whatever, I would return all phone calls in 24 hours. Now people expect instant responses to communications.

Here are some sensible ground rules:

- Set up a separate personal free gmail or hotmail account to use solely for communications between yourself and your attorney and her staff, and don't use it for anything else. Password it, and change the password frequently, especially if your kids have access to your computer or are overly invested in the divorce.
- Ditto a separate email account for communications with your spouse. Don't have emails regarding your divorce going into your general email account.

Attorney/Client Relations

- Never use your office email account to communicate with your lawyer. Your boss owns your work emails and using office email is likely a waiver of your attorney/client privilege. Also, your communications with your lawyer contain some of the most sensitive and intimate details of your life. You don't want them sitting on the office server.

- Don't mix email strings. You may have several email strings going at a given time. Don't just pull up the most recent and respond to that. Make sure the string is coherent and topical. If you've got one email string going on custody issues and another on valuing the business or collecting support, make sure you are using the correct one when you reply. The easiest way to lose an important communication is to bury it in an email string on an unrelated topic

- Don't forget that your lawyer has other cases. He may be in court, sometimes for days at a time. He may be taking out of town depositions. And even if he's sitting in front of his computer working on another case, don't expect him to drop that one to instantly respond to your request. And frankly, you want his studied and considered response, not something he dashes off of the top of his head before returning to writing the brief that is due tomorrow in another case. Instantaneous communication all too often results in ill considered comments and knee jerk responses on both sides. This is the most important relationship in your divorce other than your spouse. Think through what you want to tell or ask your attorney and state it as clearly as possible. Then allow a reasonable time for considered response before demanding action. Don't communicate with your attorney in ways that discourage thoughtful responses.

- Don't share the emails between you and your lawyer with others. Suppose you've been strategizing with your lawyer about an upcoming issue. You decide to share your lawyer's email with your best friend to get her opinion. Or your sister is a lawyer and you want to run it by her before replying. You have just waived the attorney/client privilege attached to that communication. Your best friend or sister can be subpoenaed by your spouse who can obtain a copy of that email, including the entire string of which it is only the latest piece. The attorney/client privilege is one of the most sacrosanct aspects of your relationship with your lawyer. *She* can't waive it, but there are a million ways *you* can waive it inadvertently, and people do it all the time via careless handling of emails and other communications as well as, God forbid, social media postings.

- Finally, don't copy your attorney or her staff on every email between you and your spouse. Most of it is irrelevant, and it is not a good use of money to pay your lawyer or his staff to review all the petty back and forth about where's the homework assignment I put in the backpack or why was he late for school yesterday.

When to change attorneys

If you feel your attorney is not communicating with you, you must insist that she do so. If she doesn't, it may be time to make a change.

Your attorney should be able to explain to you quite succinctly and in layman's terms the following:

- Her strategy for attaining your goal of getting the house (or some other asset) awarded to you.
- Why he thinks Approach A is going to be more likely to be successful with Judge X than Approach B.
- Why, given the dynamics and personalities of your spouse and spouse's attorney, a four-way settlement meeting would (or would not) be likely to be productive, and how to most effectively prepare for it.

- If you insist on keeping all of your pension instead of dividing it in the divorce, the likely result and cost, including expert witness fees.
- Why Ms. Jones is a better custody evaluator for your case than Dr. Smith.
- Why you are likely to lose on your claim that you invested $50,000 worth of your time in the landscaping of his mother's house.

The bottom line in all of the above is that it is your divorce and not your attorney's. Your attorney can only assist you to the extent that she understands and supports your realistic goals.

If you are losing confidence in your attorney, pay particular attention to the reasons *why* she says you're not going to win on a particular issue. As someone who has built a practice and a reputation on the ability to look people in the eye and give them the unvarnished truth (however unwelcome it may be), I am a great fan of the attorney who can give bad news unflinchingly, even if it means the client is going to be disappointed or even angry. I consider that part of my job. If your attorney tells you that your position is (a) legally right, but (b) not cost-effective, you are being told the truth. If she were out to run up your fees, she would like nothing better than to have you spend thousands of dollars to chase a few hundred. When she will tell you instead that even though you are technically right, the cost of winning exceeds the value to be received, you can take it to the bank. The same is true if she says you can't win the issue you want her to fight. And if you insist on pursuing it in spite of your lawyer's advice to let it go in favor of other, more winnable ones, she's going to ask you to put your instructions in writing. Do it. It's only fair. You can't ignore her advice, pursue something she said you'd lose, lose it, and then blame (or worse, sue) her for not winning it for you.

Suppose you're feeling a little uncertain about your attorney's handling of the case. Talk directly to her about your concerns, not her legal assistant, and not her paralegal. The person whose expertise and knowledge you need is your attorney's. You have to have absolutely crystal clear communication if you are going to function effectively as a team.

Make sure that part of your dissatisfaction with your attorney is not because he is refusing to be your shrink. It is fair neither to him nor to you. I frequently tell clients I am a first-rate attorney but that doesn't make me even a third-rate therapist. They can get a first-rate therapist for a much lower hourly rate than mine. Don't expect a lawyer to be a therapist, or vice versa.

Most family lawyers are truly committed to helping their clients survive what is probably the most traumatic legal matter they will ever face. We really do want to make it better. Sometimes that desire seduces us into crossing over the line between attorney and enabler. There may be a very needy client who absolutely has to have daily contact, who is constantly dropping into the office not so much to deliver the paperwork, but to have a "fix," reassurance that someone is there who cares, who is standing up for them, who understands, and who wants to help. Most of us select our staff with an eye to finding individuals with precisely those traits. This does *not* mean that they should be used as therapists.

So, what happens when your attorney looks you in the eye and tells you something you absolutely, positively, in your heart of hearts *do not want to hear*? Well, I frequently get the comment, "But I thought you were on *my* side . . ."

I'm sorry. My job is not to tell you what you want to hear; my job is to tell you the truth. I would much rather be able to tell you that, yes, of course I can get you precisely what you want at a fraction of the cost we originally estimated. You would go away happy, I would feel satisfied that I had gotten a good result, etc. That isn't the reality.

The point is, I *am* on your side. If I weren't, I wouldn't tell you the bad news that you don't want to hear. I would do the opposite. I would shine you on and let you keep paying me to fight for something I cannot possibly win. I don't; instead, I tell you the truth. I don't expect you to say thank you, but it would be nice if you did. You should.

Relationships with Opposing Counsel

Clients often have a very natural fear, which goes like this:

If you are friends with my spouse's counsel, won't you get together over drinks and cut a deal that is not in my best interests? Will you give away my case in order to preserve your friendship?

In all honesty, I have to tell you that there are extremely isolated instances where this occurs. However, in 99.9% of the cases, it is irrelevant.

Most attorneys are acutely aware of these issues. I remember dealing with an attorney with whom I had many cases over the years. I knew her well and yet, whenever we met at court, she insisted on calling me by my last name, as if we were strangers. She explained to me, *sotto voce*, that she didn't want her client to think we were too familiar.

In any family law court, anyone who has been around for a period of time has had cases against most of the other family lawyers. They may have gone to law school together and certainly meet at the continuing education seminars we are all required to attend. The top lawyers will have opposed one another countless times over many, many years. This is true for every level of practice. We may, in fact, have a social relationship with one another.

What I am about to tell you now is the truth: If a case becomes highly adversarial, if it gets out of hand, something is going to have to give. With any good attorney, what is going to give is not the client's interests but the friendship with opposing counsel. I have had too many friendships with respected colleagues suffer as a result of the fact that both of us knew that the clients' interests must come first. There have been moments when I have sworn to the heavens that I will never again take a case against a friend because of the personal price that I (and he) have paid. If my colleague and I aren't willing to pay that price, we simply agree not to take cases against each other anymore. There has never been a case to my knowledge where my client has suffered as a result of my friendship with opposing counsel. On the other hand, there have been countless cases where I believe both clients have benefited from the fact that the attorneys could work together, had an understanding of a reasonable resolution range, and could get to that range early.

There's an interesting note that goes with all of this. A prospective client will sometimes consult with me and want to be sure that I really hate my opposing counsel. They somehow think that if I have personal animosity toward Attorney X, this will help their case. In fact, the reverse is true. The *last* thing you should be paying several hundred dollars an hour for is my personal vendetta against Attorney X because I'm still angry about the last case we had against each other. This is particularly true if it is in your best interests to settle out of court. Enmity of a personal nature between the two attorneys only results in increased legal fees, unnecessary hearings, ugly battles, nasty email chains, and delayed resolution. You want your attorney to be focused on your issues, not his own.

Don't be frightened if your attorney says of his opposing counsel, "Oh, I know Joe, we've had cases for years." Chances are that is going to help you, not hurt you.

The same is true for judges. I have known many judges very well over the years. Not once have I felt that it enabled me to gain an unfair advantage over the other attorney or the other party.

Don't get all excited if your attorney or the opposing attorney is on a first-name basis with the judge. Judges are on a first-name basis with any number of people, some of whom they do not respect. What does matter is that your attorney has developed a reputation for credibility and competence within the court and with a particular judge. The judge will know that if your attorney makes a representation it is because he or she believes it to be true. That counts for a great deal. The reverse is also true. You could be Mother Teresa but if the judge believes your attorney is a liar and a crook, he may not reject your position out of hand, but it may be a much harder sell.

Here is another fact of life: Attorneys don't get to select which side of the case we are on. That is determined by who called us first. Also, we're not perfect and sometimes we hear one side of a story and it sounds quite credible and persuasive — until we hear the other side. I would like to say that I have always represented the guy in the white hat. It isn't so. There were times when I have misread my client and there were times when I have been flat-out lied to. I have tried cases such as these in front of judges who I know respect me. I can tell by the ruling that I didn't get any favors and that justice was served.

So, when you walk into the court for that initial hearing, don't go into a panic because your attorney says to opposing counsel, "Joe, I haven't seen you in a while. How are the kids?" Generally family law is a very small club, we know one another and we are quite professional.

Finally, think about it this way. If you are going into a court where everybody knows everybody, do you *really* want to be the only one with an attorney that no one has ever heard of? Let me rephrase it. Do you want to be the only one with an attorney the *judge* has never heard of? I think not.

CHAPTER 11

The Many Faces of Technology: The Good, the Bad and the Downright Ugly

IN THE TWENTY years since the first edition of this book was published, technology has changed everything, from how we communicate with each other and the world to how we obtain and process information and data or search for a new partner. The impact of technology on divorce has been profound. How you use it will have a direct and immediate impact on your divorce.

Communications with Your Attorney

Email is now the standard form of communication between lawyers and their clients. That means faster response time, faster answers to your questions, and sometimes less time to think about nuances or ramifications before hitting send. You may be sitting at a computer all day, and it is easy to shoot off an email when a thought or question occurs to you. People expect, and generally receive prompt, if not instant replies. Remember, however, that your lawyer has other clients, may be in court, in deposition, meeting with another client, or preparing for trial. Don't get huffy if you haven't heard back within the hour or even the day.

Think about the computer you are sitting in front of. Is it the property of your employer? Aside from the fact that your boss may not want you running your divorce on company time, if the boss owns the computer, he also owns your emails, including those to your lawyer which contain some of the most sensitive and intimate details of your life. There is no attorney/client privilege if you use somebody else's computer to communicate with your lawyer. It's like sending sensitive information to someone at work by fax in the old days, only to have the very private fax sit on the office machine for everyone to read, providing delicious grist for the office gossip mill. Don't do it.

Suppose the computer you are using is at home. Is it passworded? Never leave confidential attorney/client communications where your children can find them. And remember, they are probably more technologically proficient than you are. Just as it is important to keep your paper divorce files out of reach of children's prying eyes, it is doubly true for email.

Here's a good one. I've already warned you about sharing your lawyer's communications with friends or family. DON'T.

Communications With Your Soon-To-Be-Ex

Just as with your lawyer, get a separate email account solely for emailing your spouse. Don't use your general email, and for God's sake don't use your office email account. There can be serious consequences for messing this one up. Email between spouses comes into evidence. You don't get to cherry pick an email string for the one damaging statement your spouse made. The whole string comes in, including your provocative comments and the damaging admissions you may have made on unrelated issues earlier or later in the string.

Which leads me to the most common email mistake people make: never mix email strings. You know how this happens. You have a thought and just pull up the latest email, regardless of content, and hit reply. The quickest way to lose a piece of communication is to bury it in an email string on an unrelated topic. The best result is that it leads to misunderstandings, missed doctor's appointments, and confusion. The worst result is that all of the email string comes into evidence. The judge is not going to be interested in lining up three or four email strings to try to follow a conversation back and forth through them all. He just doesn't have the time. There may be a gem of evidence buried in there, but it will be lost because it is, in fact, buried. And, it bears repeating that the entire string comes into evidence, not just the one entry where he threatened to withhold the kids if you didn't do X. That means that if you said something which provoked the nasty response, the judge will see that, too.

These cautions notwithstanding, there are many ways in which electronic communication is a godsend. Co-parenting of some form is becoming the norm for most divorcing couples. As I've emphasized in other parts of this book, communication between the parents is essential to making it work. Email and text messaging have made it much easier for parents to communicate with each other. If one of the kids is sick and can't go to day care, it is a quick way to work out arrangements for who is going to stay home with him or take him to the doctor. There are also some nifty resources which make coparenting easier. Cofamilies. org is a site which allows secure, free calendaring for parents, children, day care providers, or anyone else who needs to keep up on kids' ever changing schedules. You log in to a calendar for your family, post any changes in scheduling, and everyone who needs to know can find the family schedule on their smart phone or other device. It's a gem. I've listed more in the chapter on "More Resources."

Electronic communication is particularly helpful if telephone conversation is difficult. The obvious benefit of communicating about the children electronically is that it can take the emotional overlay out of the equation. The detriment is that electronic communication lacks the nuance of voice inflection or facial expression. That can make text messages come across as more harsh or demanding than they were intended to be, triggering a similar, or perhaps even escalated reply.

Like emails, text messages also come into evidence. They can be printed off and introduced as Exhibit A. And, no, you don't just get to use the part that you want to use in evidence. The whole string is likely to come in, and while you may have a particularly egregious text from the other party, the judge will also see the text(s) which you sent to which he was responding. Always assume that whatever you put in writing to the other party is potential evidence that a judge might see. Before sending, stop and think how it will be perceived if viewed by a stranger who isn't motivated by the same emotional or other factors that you are in the moment. Keep text strings separate, clear, and businesslike, and assume your spouse's lawyer or even the judge will see them.

Everyone has a smart phone now, and can record anything. There are laws in some states (like California) which prohibit the secret recording of conversations. In others (Colorado comes to mind) anyone can secretly record a conversation on their smart phone and get it into evidence. And even in California people still do it. It's just doesn't get it into evidence. It will still probably be played for the custody evaluator if it paints you in an unflattering light.

A final note on communications between parents: If there really is a problem with one of the kids, use the text message to set up a time to *talk*. It may be difficult, but talking is much more nuanced than the typed word. You owe your children the best you can do for them, and that includes communicating as effectively as possible with their other parent when their best interests are at stake.

Social Media

There are hundreds of ways in which your use of social media can have a direct impact on your divorce, all of them bad. Facebook and Instagram have, in many ways, supplanted other means of direct communication with your friends. You can post pictures and news and it instantly goes out to a large group of people. I hope it goes without saying that you won't post anything which is a privileged communication from your lawyer. When you post something on social media, assume that it will come into evidence. Yes, you can "unfriend" your ex, but I guarantee that somebody you have friended has also friended her.

This takes many forms. It can be as innocuous as posting pictures of you with your new flame, together with a blissful description of how happy you are, which causes your soon-to-be-ex to dig in even more determinedly to guarantee that your kids are never exposed to "that slut." Or, bragging about the expensive trip you just took (when child support is late or you are trying to get alimony reduced). Ditto your LinkedIn profile. Bragging about how successful you are professionally is a great advertising move. But you can't block people from LinkedIn and your ex is probably checking in regularly. I've seen a great deal of useful information come into evidence via LinkedIn, Twitter feeds and the like.

Legal Information and Research

The good part of technology is that the law is readily available on the web. You can access your own case register (or anybody else's for that matter – think about it). The court rules and statutes are out there as well. This means you can do some of your own research, or simply check to see if what you are being told is true. There are lots of user-friendly websites which I've referenced in "More Resources" at Chapter 45. Many courts now have online family law self help centers. Check to see if the court where your case is pending has one. Online help is out there and often it is remarkably good but, as with anything else, you have to use caution.

If you are representing yourself or have engaged a lawyer for limited scope representation, most of your research will likely be done online. You can download and fill out your court forms. You can even do a child support calculation if you have sufficient financial information and the state guideline is posted. As long as you stick to government based web sites and self help centers, you are probably all right, though it is always advisable to consult with a competent attorney as well.

More and more divorce lawyers are opening "virtual" law offices, where they don't meet physically with clients at all. Technology is rapidly eroding the limitation to brick and mortar law offices in favor of other, more flexible delivery systems. That being said, do your research and know who you are dealing with before giving out your credit card information.

The problem of law on the web arises when something posted on an apparently professional website isn't what it appears to be. Internet predation has expanded exponentially in the last decade. Notarios and document preparers posing as lawyers offer document drafting and other services for a fee. Some unlicensed person working out of a back room in Los Angeles or a basement outside Milwaukee poses as a licensed Kansas lawyer who is delighted to draft your Kansas paperwork for a modest (and sometimes not so modest) fee. It is sometimes hard to know the difference between the many reputable lawyers with virtual offices, and charlatans working out of a cubicle someplace. If you decide to go this route, look carefully at the "about" page to get a sense of who you are dealing with. Make sure they are licensed to practice law, and research them just as you would someone you were going to personally interview. And if their website it is just a stock photo of a parent and child, keep looking. Also consider that a cyber lawyer who refuses to talk to you and insists on only electronic communication is likely to miss some of the nuances of your case and will have a hard time getting a sense of who you are.

The fact is that anybody can post anything on the web. Repeat. *Anybody* can post *anything* on the web. Unless you are going to an official legal site or a reputable professional one, you can't rely on the accuracy of the information you are getting. This is particularly true when you are researching your prospective lawyer or judge on Yelp. If companies can hire seventeen year olds to write phony positive reviews of their products, so can lawyers and document preparers. On the other hand, consider what a disgruntled litigant with an ax to grind can do. Good lawyers and good judges have to make hard calls. Emotions run high. Somebody is going to be disappointed that they didn't get what they wanted and blame the lawyer on the other side or the judge. Sometimes they are so disgruntled that they retaliate by deliberately trashing someone's professional reputation. I've seen it happen many times. Never assume that something you read on Yelp is authentic, much less, accurate. Here's a red flag: the longer and more venomous the post, the more likely it is the result of someone who didn't get what they wanted and wants public revenge. The longer and more venomous it is, the more likely it is that the facts have been altered to make the person who posted it look good and make the target look bad. The longer and more venomous it is, the more likely it is that the person who lost did so because he is unreasonable or unbalanced and *should* have lost.

Now to the Truly Ugly

I am constantly amazed by the degree of private information people gleefully post without giving a thought to who might access it and how it may be used. The whole point of social media is to share, right? Well, not only is sharing not always a good idea, in a divorce, it almost never is. That includes posting pictures of yourself apparently drunk and hoisting a glass at a party. You may not even be the one doing the posting. Everyone else at the party has a smart phone and access to social media, too. You have absolutely no control about where things you do in public end up being posted by somebody else. If you're involved in a hot custody battle, the last thing you want is for a video of your party antics going viral or turning up as Exhibit A. I guarantee the judge and the custody evaluator will see it.

And at the risk of giving somebody ideas, it is not unheard of for someone to take a picture of you in one context and photoshop it to look like you're doing something else. Just saying.

Then there is the issue of dating sites. I said at the beginning that technology has changed how we search for a new partner. Assume that everything you have posted on match.com or some other dating site is available to your ex. That means that if you have misrepresented your marital status or custodial arrangement or used photos of your adorable children as bait for new matches, your ex will find out and the judge won't be pleased.

The Many Faces of Technology

The moral of the story is that technology is great when it used thoughtfully and carefully, in a way that things which should remain private do so. The addition of divorce to the equation, however, creates a minefield which can do truly epic damage to the unwary. Be careful and use common sense.

CHAPTER 12

Courts, Judges, and Private Judges

YOU'RE GETTING DIVORCED. That means that if you and your mate are not able to settle your differences, a person in a black robe is going to make decisions which will potentially have consequences for the rest of your lives. Before you delegate this power to a stranger, educate yourself on what that really means. Take a long, hard look at the judge who will be deciding your support rights, where your kid lives and what happens to your worldly goods. After doing so, you may want to reconsider that "outrageous" settlement offer you rejected out of hand last week.

Courts come in all shapes and sizes. Some are majestic and imposing, some downright shabby, some hushed and reverential, others crowded and noisy. Some look just like the set of a court based TV program and others more closely resemble the local Department of Motor Vehicles. All have common characteristics: They are stark, sterile, and public. Secrets you wouldn't share with your dearest friend are freely aired in front of total strangers day in and day out. Litigants are often shocked by the lack of privacy. I tell them most of the people watching are too preoccupied with their own upcoming hearing to pay much attention to your problems. That is true, to a point. It also sucks to have to bare your soul in public. No one in his right mind would do so by choice if there were a reasonable alternative.

Here's another common factor: In this era of reduced government revenue, there is less and less money available to fund the court system. With increasing pressure for more law and order, fewer and fewer of the limited court funds are being diverted to family law courts. Couple that with rising divorce rates and it doesn't take a rocket scientist to figure out there's not enough court time available in family law.

There are many variations between court calendars (sometimes called dockets). A "calendar" refers to how many cases are expected to be heard on a particular day and how much time is allocated to each of them. Most courts have a combination of "short-cause" and "long-cause" court calendars. A short-cause matter is typically limited to 20 minutes and is designed for family law triage: To make quick and dirty decisions about who lives where, what happens to the kids pending a custody evaluation, who gets the use of the car, and how much support gets paid (and by whom) in the interim pending resolution of the rest of your case.

20 minutes for all of that? It would be funny if it weren't true.

Moreover, in a busy court a judge may have as many as 20 to 40 twenty-minute matters on a morning calendar. You heard me. Between 9:00 a.m. and noon, up to 40 cases must be heard and disposed of. They can't spill over into the afternoon because there is another full docket starting at 1:30 which has to be decided before 5:00. It doesn't take a math genius to figure out that it can't be done. And even if each case had the full 20 minutes allotted, what kind of time is that to determine the family income, how the bills are to be apportioned, who is to receive what support and what restraining orders are needed in order to preserve body, mind and the marital estate pending the final resolution? I guarantee you, there is nothing more taxing to judges than to have to make sometimes life changing decisions in what they know is insufficient time, or based on inadequate or incomplete information. But someone has to make a decision if the parties can't work it out themselves, and that someone is the judge.

Suppose you're one of the lucky ones who can afford to wait for a "long-cause" set. Typically, this means one or two hours on the court's calendar. In my county, that will happen three to six months after the initial filing. Assuming that each party has the financial wherewithal to pay the bills during the interim, you may be able to wait that long before the support order goes into effect. Again, think about it: Two hours to decide who lives where, the family income, how much support should be paid, who has custody of the kids, what the visitation schedule should be, etc. Solomon himself couldn't consistently make good decisions under those circumstances.

As a group, family law judges are extremely conscientious and hard working. They sincerely try to do the best they can with the facts before them and are acutely aware of the financial and human cost of a bad decision. There is probably no other area of the law in which the emotional content is so high and the time pressure and volume of cases so great. Family law judges have the highest burnout rate of any judge. Day in and day out, they must make gut-wrenching decisions in cases where there is frequently no clear right and wrong. They have to do the best they can with the information presented to them, often knowing they lack important data. Nevertheless, even on partial information, a decision must be made, and so it is. But let's look a little closer at that one or two hours of court time.

The American legal system is based upon direct and cross-examination, a very stilted form of questions and answers. Thanks to O.J. and Court TV, everyone in the country is familiar with the concept. It may work fine for real estate or contract disputes but, frankly, it's a lousy way to get to the bottom of who's the best custodial parent. It is slow and cumbersome. If you only have an hour, your attorney is probably going to be forced to do one of two things: Either he'll have to consume far too much of that hour's time objecting to questions on technical grounds, or he's going to simply have to let the objections go (because even though the questions may be technically improper, that is the quickest way to get evidence before the judge) and trust the judge's expertise and knowledge to know the difference between hearsay and credible evidence. And *this* is the system that is going to decide your future and that of your kids . . . ?

Courts, Judges, and Private Judges

I say this not to frighten you, but to educate you to the reality. Courts are a place of *last* resort. Someone who has to ask the court to decide these things has failed: Failed to settle, failed to stay in control of their case, failed to accept a reasonable resolution. Of course, some people find themselves in court because the other side is a jerk and has refused all reasonable attempts at resolution. The point is that if you find yourself in court, make sure that you weren't the one who forced it there.

Let's look at it in very practical terms. You've been served a Summons to show up at court at a particular time on a particular day. You walk into the building on a "short-cause" day. This means that 20 or more cases may be pending for that morning. At least two sides will show up on each case, either "pro se" (that is, representing themselves without attorneys) or with attorneys. Between two and four people will be in court for each of these matters that morning. All of them will be milling around the cold marble (or, in some courthouses, scruffy linoleum) hallways awaiting their turn. The competent attorneys are trying to settle their cases, or at least settle some of the issues and thereby make the best use of their time before the judge by reducing the number of subjects which have to be covered. As you sit there on your hard bench, the following questions may be running through your mind:

"Will I be able to pay my house payment next month?"
"What if I don't get to see the kids?"
"What if I'm kicked out of the house; where will I go? How will I pay for it?"
"Will I be able to live on what's left over after the support order is made?"

This is the truth. This is what really happens. So, what can you do about it?

Anyone contemplating divorce should take a morning and go sit in your local family court. It's open to the public and is well worth the cost of half a day's pay to watch the judge who will be deciding *your* fate.

How to Avoid the Divorce from Hell

How do you feel about that judge? Was she hurried or short-tempered? Despite the press of cases, did she seem to be listening and hearing what people were saying to her? Was he trying to be fair to both sides? What was his attitude toward the attorneys and the litigants? Did she seem to favor men over women, or vice-versa?

Then watch the attorneys. Who did you think did a good job? Recognize that as with so much else in family law, "good job" is a relative term. It isn't the attorney who was able to reduce the opposing client to tears in the shortest possible time. More constructively, it is the attorney who was able to get the most relevant information before the judge in the time allotted. If he asks the same question more than once, lose 5 points. Remember, the biggest fault of the system is that there isn't enough time to get sufficient information into the hands of the person who's going to have to make the decision. Recognize, too, that with the press of these calendars, the judge has likely not read the files in advance; it would be simply impossible to do so. That means he probably doesn't know all the evidence your lawyer drafted so carefully for the court papers.

Therefore, the better attorney is the one who can educate the judge about the relevant facts in the shortest time so that the best possible decisions can be made under these totally absurd conditions.

That's the attorney whose card I would ask for.

Another advantage of hanging around the courthouse is to talk to the litigants. If someone has been ordered to "show cause" at 8:30, his case may not even be called until 11:15 or even later. This means that he faithfully showed up at 8:30 because, of course, the one time he didn't get there on time was the day his was the first case called. In the interim, he is sitting in the hall, anxiously awaiting his turn. Perhaps his attorney is there with him, but most likely, the attorney is either talking to opposing counsel trying to settle the case or handling one of a couple of other cases she has going that morning. The experienced litigant will probably pull out a mobile device to while away the time, but most people will be tense and fearful, not knowing what to expect.

Courts, Judges, and Private Judges

They are a wealth of information. Strike up a conversation with someone who looks like they might be in your position. Find out how they feel about their own attorney and the opposing attorney. Ask if they've been through the system before and how many hearings they've had and what happened (if they're willing to tell you). I don't mean you should invade people's privacy. However, the fact is that many litigants are only too glad to talk about the process with strangers they meet at the courthouse. Utilize this as a resource.

If, after doing all of the above, you still don't feel that settling a case is by far the preferable alternative, either you haven't been paying attention or you should review Chapter 4, "Recipe for the Divorce from Hell," and lose 10 karma points.

There's another reason why you should consider turning your case over to a judge as a last resort: Due to the high burnout rate of family judges, there is a great deal of turnover in divorce court. That means that new judges are constantly rotating into the assignment. Many of them have no experience whatsoever in family law. They've been doing criminal law, business litigation, or personal injury. These are very different animals and they are on very foreign turf. No matter how smart they are, there will be a distinct learning curve. I think it takes a minimum of two years to become competent in family law. You wouldn't hire a criminal lawyer who just dabbles occasionally in family law to represent you. The same is true with a judge who has just been assigned to a family law court for the first time. Do you really want them to learn the ropes on *your* case?

A final word on judges: I have said before that the vast majority of them are sincere and work very hard to deliver justice under distressing circumstances. But with the best intent in the world, even on a long-cause case, the best and most competent family law judge doesn't know who really lives inside your skin or that of your spouse, much less your children. With any luck, the judge will never see your children because children don't belong in the courtroom. If you come into court litigating five issues, the judge has no way of knowing that if you could only win on three of them, it would be numbers two, four and five, and you would gladly concede numbers one and three if you could win the others. Why doesn't the judge know that? Because if you told the judge, that's precisely what would happen and you'd never have a chance to win the other two. If you are going to do that, you might as well have conceded them at the beginning.

Even if the judge has read your file, in fact, *studied* your file before your case was called, that file is not going to tell him that since the separation, Jake hasn't been able to sleep with the light out, or that Matthew gets stomach aches at any disruption in his schedule, or that if there isn't enough money for ballet lessons, Emma will fall apart because dancing is the only thing that is giving her any stability and self-esteem at the moment.

If I'm the judge having to make decisions about your kids, I hate not knowing those things because I never have complete information; there just *never* is enough time.

If your case goes to trial, your trial will be, at best, nothing more than a single snapshot of your marriage. Think of your family photo album. How many of those snapshots reflect an accurate image of your family patterns? Would you really want your and your children's futures decided by those photos?

So, let's go back to the beginning. Is this the system you want to decide where your kids go to school, who gets to stay in the house, and what bills get paid and by whom? Think about it.

Private Judges

One recent development in response to crowded court calendars is the increasing use of private judges (sometimes called "judges pro tem" or even "rent-a-judges"). Judge "pro tem" simply means someone is appointed a judge "for a time." In such a case, the trial or some part of it is assigned to a judge who is hired by the parties. A private judge may be a retired judge who works part time on a case by case basis. Increasingly, experienced attorneys are limiting their practices to private judging. In fact, in 1997 after twenty years of complex family law litigation, I limited my own practice to private family law judging.

Private judges are not allowed in all states, but where they are permitted, they are bound by all of the same ethical rules as publicly appointed ones. They must apply the same law, use the same rules of evidence, and be fair and impartial in their rulings. They are not allowed to use the public court facilities, and usually operate out of their own offices and conference rooms.

Your attorney may recommend hiring a private judge for your case. There are many good reasons for doing so. Perhaps he does not believe that the judge to whom your case is assigned has sufficient expertise in family law, or with the issues presented by your case. It may be that in your jurisdiction, it will take many months or even years to obtain a trial date long enough to accommodate your case and the delay does not justify the financial and emotional hardship. There may be one key issue which has to be decided before the rest of the case can be settled, and the most efficient way to proceed is to split that issue off, try it before a private judge, and then explore settlement of the remaining issues after you get the private judge's ruling. For example, if you can't settle the case until you find out whether the prenuptial agreement is enforceable, this is a prime issue to send to a private judge.

On a highly technical issue I always prefer a private judge who is a highly experienced family lawyer to a retired judge (however brilliant) with limited family law experience.

In any event, careful research is required before selecting an individual.

The first thing you need to know is that both attorneys will have to agree on the private judge. For obvious reasons of neutrality, it is simply impossible for one side to unilaterally interview or hire the judge for their case. Also, some private judges won't take cases where the parties are representing themselves without lawyers.

Second, there is a wide variation in the capabilities of the judges who may be selected.

Most retired judges who work as private judges have served for many years on the public bench and are simply supplementing their retirement income by doing private judging on a part time basis. They may be highly qualified in divorce law. On the other hand, they may be total novices when it comes to your particular issue, having spent 20 years handling criminal or business cases. Find out the difference before agreeing to use one for your case.

One of the beauties of private judging is that you have a choice. Public court calendars are usually random assignments, and you have nothing to say in the selection of the judge who will hear your case. Not so with private judges. There are, of course, some pitfalls with retired judges. If I wasn't impressed with a judge I appeared before in the public court, I can assure you I wouldn't agree to appoint him on a private assignment. Also, it is important to be assured that your private judge has kept up with changes in the law since retiring. I would want to know that the private judge I am agreeing to is not only experienced in family law matters, but is also up to date on the current law, since the law can change very quickly. Interestingly, many retired public judges who do private judging do not bother to attend the continuing education courses that lawyers are required to take in order to remain current. As I write this, I have just returned from a two day intensive update program on changes to family law which occurred in the last year. Not a single sitting or retired judge from my county was among the 350 or so lawyers in attendance. I wouldn't agree to appoint any private judge who I didn't see at continuing education programs, either as an attendee or presenter. I would also want to know about any known biases or idiosyncrasies. If the suggested judge is unfamiliar to me or from a different county, I would do some research before agreeing that this is the person who will hear my client's case.

When a private attorney rather than a retired public judge is the private judge, the procedure is a little different. You should still do the research regarding the specific expertise of the proposed judge. One question you should ask is whether the private judge still has a litigation practice, in addition to doing private judging. This is an important question to ask. Attorneys have no control over who is representing the other side in a litigation case. You don't want the private judge in your case to be opposing your attorney on another case. That creates a potential conflict of interest which could impact the dynamics of your case. You should select a private judge who only does private judging, or perhaps a combination of mediation and judging, since both are neutral functions and neither would represent individual clients in other cases. For more information on private judging, including FAQs, visit my website at www. privatefamilylawjudge.com.

Ask your attorney about the expertise of the proposed private judge. How well does it match the issues presented by your case? Does he have a social relationship with your opposing counsel? Find out as much as you can about your private judge. If your state certifies legal specialists, is the proposed private judge certified? Once certified as a specialist, attorneys are required to take continuing education courses to keep their certification. As a result, they are likely to be current on recent changes in the law. Look for information about certified family law specialists on your state bar website. And, of course, never call the judge yourself. Just like the judges at the courthouse, she can't talk to you without the other side present. That is called an "ex parte" communication, and is a breach of judicial ethics.

If you elect to proceed through private judging, there are some decisions which you will have to make. One of these is the formality of the proceedings. Specifically, you will need to determine whether you want to preserve your right to appeal the decision if you disagree with it.

If your case is heard at the courthouse, there may be a court reporter available. This means that either party will have a record on appeal if they wish to challenge the judge's decision.

If, on the other hand, you retain a private judge, either of the retired version or an attorney who has limited his practice to working as a private judge, you must decide whether to have a court reporter present. Doing so will increase the expense of your hearing. On the other hand, if you do not have a written record and the private judge makes a mistake, it is almost impossible to successfully pursue an appeal. Again, this is a cost/benefit analysis which you should discuss with your attorney.

There is one other use for private judges which is becoming increasingly popular. Some of these individuals have developed such expertise and credibility that they are retained as private settlement judges. Settlement conferences often expose the weaknesses of your case. Frequently, attorneys don't want to tip their hand on a sensitive issue by having a settlement conference before the judge who will actually decide the case. In those cases, it is useful to have a settlement conference before a different private judge. This is a wonderful way to test the strength of your case without going to court and getting destroyed. Again, it takes a special individual and both sides have to agree, but I have settled some very difficult and complex cases this way, and the clients didn't have to pay their lawyers for expensive trial preparation time.

If you take your case to a private judge, you can expect to pay the judge by the hour. You will be required to advance a deposit on fees, which will be held in trust until the time is spent and the fees earned. This may be advanced by one or the other of you, or from joint funds. You will be paying for the time you use, including time for the judge to prepare a written decision, if that is required. You don't get to wait until you see the judge's decision and decide you don't want to pay because you don't like the ruling. Talk to your attorney about whether private judging is available in your jurisdiction and, if so, whether it would be a good solution in your case.

CHAPTER 13

What Happens When Your Spouse Hires the Lawyer from Hell?

YOU'VE JUST STARTED your divorce. You've checked out the local bar association, interviewed several attorneys, and selected the one who seems to most closely match your goals of achieving a reasonable, quick and relatively healthy and inexpensive settlement of all your divorce issues. Your spouse then hires the Lawyer from Hell.

What do you do?

When the party on the other side of my case retains a Lawyer from Hell (and we lawyers all know who they are), I know several things. I know the fees are going to be at least triple what they should have been. I know that what my client has told me about the other spouse ("he says he just wants to be fair") is probably not true and I know I had better buy myself some industrial-strength antacid because I'm going to need it.

I believe people are drawn to the attorneys they want, whether consciously or unconsciously. When a prospective client comes in to see me and says, "I hear you're a real barracuda; I want to clean my husband out," I instantly know what I'm dealing with. That's a case I don't take because I will never satisfy her. What she wants is part of her husband's anatomy, and I'm not willing to be the surgeon. I will explain to this client that my business is to get the best deal the law allows and my goal is to do it in such a way that it can be concluded as reasonably and quickly as possible. I explain that although I am one hell of a good litigator, litigation is a last resort. If I don't get a response I'm satisfied with, I decline the case. I can only assume that when the same client goes to see the "Lawyer from Hell," she gets the reaction she wants. He may do some strutting and primping and bragging about track records and such, and that client is going to get (and pay for) precisely the lawyer she asked for.

Sometimes your spouse's lawyer takes a much more aggressive position than you expect. He may be telling you one thing ("I really want you to have the house") while his attorney is moving heaven and earth to get it sold out from under you. He may even tell you that he "can't do anything about it" because his attorney is telling him he *has to*. Nonsense. One of the things lawyers are paid to do is to take the heat for our clients. I understand that. I cannot tell you the number of times a client has said to me, "I really want to fight this because I think I'm right; but I don't want it to look like it is coming from me because that will make it harder for us to deal with each other about the kids, so I'm just going to say you're insisting I do it this way." If the thing the client wants me to do is consistent with my own goals and ethics, that's fine; if it isn't, I have an ex-client. But that process has also taught me that most people pick the lawyers they want and get the lawyers they deserve.

I have very little sympathy for a client who goes to an attorney, hires him under the premise that, "I hear you're a real shark" and then complains later that the "shark" turned on him. Excuse me . . . what did you think you were getting?

I have much more respect for the client who gets a second opinion because, "I thought my attorney was going to help us settle out of court, but he just seems to want to get into a pissing contest with the other side."

Sometimes a litigant hires the attorney from hell out of fear. She knows he is a jerk, but is so afraid of her spouse that she thinks only a jerk can protect her. I have already said that anyone can make one mistake. At the beginning of a divorce, you're scared, confused, being pulled hither and yon by conflicting advice from friends, relatives and, yes, even the lawyers you've consulted. You make the best choice you can under the circumstances and, part way into the divorce, find that you've chosen badly. That I understand. But if it happens more than once, I question either your judgment or your motives.

If you think your spouse might hire the Lawyer from Hell out of fear and want to forestall it, your best chance is to assure her that you really want to settle, that you want the divorce to be amicable and fair, and that you will do whatever it takes to see that it is. Then, *demonstrate* that you mean it by being utterly aboveboard and absolutely straight at every opportunity. Instruct your lawyer to copy and share all relevant financial data without being asked for it.

So, when your spouse hires the Lawyer from Hell and, more important, stays with him after a skirmish or two, my advice is this: Take a closer look at your spouse. Whatever representations he or she may have made about wanting an amicable resolution are not true. Each of us is responsible for the choices we make. If he has chosen someone who truly wants and intends to clean you out, and he doesn't either intervene or change attorneys, he is getting precisely the lawyer he wants and the case is being run according to his plan.

A final note on the Lawyer from Hell: If your spouse has hired one in your case, that is not the signal to go out and hire his clone to represent you. At the risk of sounding trite, two wrongs don't make a right. In this case, two wrongs will drive both of you to the poorhouse. Instead, keep playing the case straight and by the book on your side. It will be frustrating, of course, but when all is done, you will at least be able to like what you see in the mirror. The moral of this story is that just because your spouse has decided to be a jerk, you are not absolved from taking responsibility for your own choices and your own tactics.

CHAPTER 14

Mediation and Collaborative Law

THIS IS THE 21st century and you have choices about divorce that your parents didn't have. You are no longer compelled to march in lock step through the courts. It takes two to opt out, but there are less adversarial methods of resolving divorce issues than there were even a few years ago. This results from at least two factors. First, litigants are becoming much more sophisticated about finding less litigious and expensive ways to resolve their legal disputes. Second, for reasons on which I am only too happy to expound at length, our court systems are quite unsuited to the practical and expedient resolution of most family law conflicts, and with dwindling funding, those systems have become virtually dysfunctional in many cases.

The most popular alternative process is mediation. In mediation, you and your spouse work jointly with a specially trained individual to craft your own solution to your legal problem. Most people don't realize that the courts are often severely restricted in the kinds of orders they can make. They have to follow approved legal precedent, which may or may not result in the best solution for your family. No two families are alike and in mediation you are free to create the solution which works for yours. You can't mediate yourself out of tax consequences, and other strict rules imposed by the government such as mandated public policy, but you can deviate from traditional property or support provisions if other arrangements work better for you and your family.

Mediation and Collaborative Law

By definition, a mediator is required to be neutral. You and your spouse must both agree not only to the process of mediation, but to the individual mediator you choose. If either of you loses confidence in the process or the mediator, you may opt out at any time

Many people confuse mediation with both parties using the same lawyer. They are not remotely the same. In fact, I think it is unethical for a single lawyer to represent adversarial parties. It stands to reason: The attorney's job is to protect the rights and interests of his client. However, if there are two clients, and what helps one may by definition hurt the other, the lawyer is in the untenable position of choosing where to place his loyalty. A mediator, although very likely a lawyer, is not representing either party, but is rather helping the parties negotiate an agreement within the confines of applicable state law.

In mediation, you jointly consult an individual (usually an attorney, but not always) who is trained in family law mediation, which is an entirely different process from adversarial law, and requires a separate set of skills. Most mediators take ongoing training to hone and improve their skills. Although your mediator will probably be an experienced family law attorney, she does not give you individual legal advice, and it is always a good idea to have a consulting attorney to whom you can direct your specific legal questions as they arise during the mediation process You will also want to ask a consulting attorney about issues or proposals that you want to know about before discussing them in front of your spouse in mediation. In fact, your mediator may insist that each of you independently consult with your own attorney who represents only you, to be sure you understand the legal consequences of the agreement you are negotiating.

By periodically consulting with independent counsel, you can educate yourself on the potential legal pitfalls of a proposal that is being discussed before committing to it. Make sure you understand any resolution before you agree to it. And, of course, whatever discussions, offers and counteroffers may have been had in mediation, it isn't over until it is over. That means that before signing the agreement, each party has a chance to think about it, and consult with any attorneys, financial advisors, or anyone else whose input they need to make an informed decision.

The duty of the mediator is to assist you in reaching the agreement that works best for both of you. In order to do this, he will start out by leveling the playing field, and assuring that each of you is in a relatively equal bargaining position, with access to the information which you will need in order to make intelligent and informed decisions about your divorce. He will usually do this before any actual negotiation takes place. This means that if your spouse is promoting mediation because he thinks he can push you around better in mediation than in court, he is going to get a surprise. A good mediator simply won't let one party control or manipulate the process to the detriment of the other. If you feel that your mediator isn't keeping the field level, you can withdraw from the process at any time, or, if you both agree, select another mediator to finish the job.

Sometimes people act as advocates, trying to convince the mediator that their proposal is better than their spouse's. This is a waste of time and money. It is not the mediator's role to take sides; quite the contrary. You aren't going to sell the mediator on your position, and if the reason you want to opt out of mediation is that the mediator won't take sides, you have missed the point. You will be just as unhappy with the next mediator, who will also refuse to take sides, and you will be back in litigation.

The mediator works outside of, but parallel to, the court process. He may help you fill out necessary court forms, and may well draft the final written agreement after a deal is made. He will ask that you take this agreement to your consulting attorney or any other professional who may be assisting you before signing it.

Mediation offers numerous advantages over litigation. Among them are:

- It is private.

As I've indicated, courts are almost always open to the public. Although it is sometimes possible to seal court files or obtain a closed hearing, it is relatively rare. In mediation, however, all proceedings are closed and this can be a real benefit as it keeps your personal and financial business out of the public eye and only the final agreement is in the court file. The only people present in the mediation room are you, your spouse and the mediator. Sometimes people want their consulting attorneys present at mediation sessions, but most do not, preferring to do the negotiating themselves and then take proposals back to their attorneys to get some confidential advice. In some states, mediation is always confidential, which means that, even if you don't reach an agreement, no one can reveal what was said in mediation. There is a good reason for this. People will be more frank in discussing settlement options if they know that what they are offering to settle for now won't later be used against them in court. As a result, they are more likely to reach an agreement if assured of confidentiality.

- It is cheaper.

You may ask how that can be when you are paying the fees of an additional professional. However, even if there are two consulting attorneys, their roles are radically redefined once you enter mediation. Discovery (that is, investigation of the facts) is usually informal and coordinated by the mediator rather than the infinitely more cumbersome and expensive formal approach. The role of the consulting attorney is to advise you of your legal rights and the consequences of the agreements being considered. This requires much less of their time than litigation and its attendant court appearances do. And there is no incentive to over-litigate the case to be certain they have looked under every rock. The average cost of mediation is 25%, 35%, or even less of the cost of a fully litigated case. Thus, you and your spouse keep more of your marital estate for yourselves.

- It is quicker.

Formal discovery is not only expensive, it is slow. Time delays are built into the system, but they can be shortcut by the informal exchange of data contemplated by the mediation process. Also, interim issues can be determined in accordance with *your* timetable, not the court's. Mediators have more time to devote to your case than judges do. You won't have to wait weeks or months for a hearing and order for temporary support or interim custody, or take the risk that your case is postponed repeatedly because the judge ran out of time. Depending on how well prepared you are for your mediation sessions, how well you do your homework between sessions, how complicated your legal issues are, and how willing you both are to compromise, a complete resolution can often be reached in four to six sessions with a good mediator.

- It is creative.

This is probably the greatest single advantage of mediation. Most people don't realize that the judge's authority is often extremely limited. In a system based on specific statutes and legal precedent, the judge is likely to be bound to apply only one or two solutions to a legal issue. The truly elegant solution tailored to the facts of your particular situation may well be deemed "abuse of discretion" by an appellate court if it doesn't fall within the parameters which your trial judge is obliged to follow.

The truth is that on your worst day, you and your spouse can probably think of several better and more creative approaches to your legal problem than a judge is likely to be able to impose. Mind you, it isn't because the judge is unwilling, but you and your spouse will always have more time and wider discretion than the court to create the compromise solution that best fits your family.

Mediation and Collaborative Law

For the right couple, mediation is a humane and creative way to resolve family law problems. So, how do you know if you are a good candidate for mediation?

- Are you willing to educate yourself about your rights and obligations and take responsibility for your decisions? If not, you are probably better off turning your case over to an attorney and letting him negotiate it for you.
- Are you willing to consider non-traditional solutions to your legal problems, or would you rather just let the judge decide?
- Are you willing to do your homework and come to mediation fully prepared with all of the information you will need in order to make a decision?
- Are you willing to compromise? By definition, nobody gets everything in mediation, and each of you will have to be able and willing to compromise to get an agreement. If either of you won't, your mediator will probably spot that right away and tell you that you are not good candidates for mediation. If you are not willing to make concessions, rethink your course and review Chapter 4, "Recipe for the Divorce from Hell."
- Are you willing to put your personal conflicts and animosities aside long enough to craft a solution which works for your entire family, and reduces the conflict to which your children are exposed? If all you want to do is to rail against your spouse in front of a witness, you will be wasting your money and the mediator's time. That kind of conduct is also unlikely to promote a spirit of compromise. I'm always amazed at the number of people who will use their mediation sessions as a free-for-all to viciously berate their spouse, and then be shocked, *shocked* that that same spouse digs in and refuses to give them concessions that they couldn't win at court.
- Are you willing to be in the same room with your spouse? If not, some mediators will do what is called "caucus mediation," where

they meet with each of you separately and sequentially. This reduces the stress of having to deal directly with each other at a tense time over sometimes loaded issues. However, it also slows down the process and increases the time and expense.

It may be that you can settle some, but not all, of the issues in mediation. So be it. Even if there is a sticking point you need an attorney to negotiate for you or even judicial help with, if you can settle everything else in mediation, you reduce the cost of litigation and make sure that the judge's time is used efficiently. If there are only one or two issues, the court is more likely to be able to work you in sooner rather than later.

Finally, recognize that some cases simply are not suited to mediation. Mediation assumes first and foremost that both of you are being straight with one another, that you both are sharing information equally and no one is withholding relevant financial or other data. It assumes that neither one of you is trying to play games to obtain an unfair advantage. And it assumes that you are each committed enough to the process to compromise and reach an agreement even if not everything you wanted.

If you are honestly willing to do all of this, proceed:

Choosing a Mediator

As with any other professional, all mediators are not created equal. A great deal depends on the kinds of issues you are bringing into mediation. If your only dispute is about the kids, your mediator may be either an attorney experienced in mediating custody disputes, or a mental health professional with a strong background in co-parenting arrangements. Many therapists and custody evaluators are also skilled custody mediators. If, on the other hand, you are also mediating property or support, that presents different complications. In that case, your mediator will need to be an attorney who can spot lurking legal issues. Many therapists, while possessing strong mediation skills, simply won't have the legal background necessary to spot potential pitfalls in the property agreement being discussed. They won't know how to run the computerized support guidelines or recognize the red flags that will trigger a tax audit.

Similarly, attorney mediators have differing levels of skill. If the property at stake is a house, a pension and personal property, this is relatively straightforward, as long as the house isn't under water. However, what if you own a family business or one of you has stock options from employment? These can be very tricky issues, and you should find a mediator who has significant experience with them. Again, the mediator won't be representing either of you, but you need to have someone knowledgeable enough to spot complicating issues and know how to deal with them to avoid future problems. These may be issues you did not even know existed, but could be very detrimental if not identified and resolved.

Make sure your mediator is experienced in handling the kinds of specific issues your case presents. I once had a client come to me for representation after losing faith in her mediator, who, after hearing the parties discuss their very complex family business which was about to go public, exclaimed, "This is going to be fun. I've never done one of these, so I'll be learning along with you." The client felt guilty for leaving the mediation, but knew that her entire financial future was at stake, and she understandably didn't want to trust it to someone with no knowledge and experience regarding the key component of her marital estate. If that happens to you, find another mediator who *has* done one of those and won't be learning on your dime.

Do your homework. In any community, there are going to be some people who have proven track records as family law mediators. There is also a growing number of wannabes who have decided to become mediators because they can't make it in the world of adversarial law and think mediation is easier than going to battle in court. You do not want one of these. In choosing a mediator, you want someone who is into mediation because she is very, very good at it and not because she failed at litigation. The changing economics of the legal profession, coupled with increasing law school output and shrinking litigation budgets are causing more and more attorneys to find they simply can't make it in the world of adversarial law. They are often drawn to mediation as an alternative. Find out which category your prospective mediator falls into. Your consulting attorney will probably know who the top mediators are in your area. Another good source for a referral to a mediator may be your therapist.

How about searching the many websites where mediators advertise? It is just like finding an attorney on the web or in the yellow pages. That's a place to get the name of a person who you then investigate. It isn't a substitute for doing your homework. Many sites will list the names of anyone who pays a fee, with little or no screening. If you just pick someone from the list, you have no information about his skill and expertise. And here's a scary thought: When I described the Lawyer from Hell in Chapter 13, I had a very specific individual in mind. While surfing a mediation referral site some years ago, I saw a him listed. He described himself as a mediation-friendly lawyer who would keep clients out of court. Now, the person who was the prototype for my Lawyer from Hell is a predator who lives to fleece clients and only stops when they get wise and fire him or run out of money. Nevertheless, he was advertising on the web as a mediator who would promote settlement! Do your homework, and investigate each professional by the means I have suggested. Never rely on information of any type just because you saw it on the web.

Here's what you want to look for: The talents required of a good mediator are very different from those required by either a therapist or an adversarial lawyer. You may find an individual who happens to be good at both, but don't assume that it is so. A good mediator should be someone who is an effective listener and who can be creative enough to help both parties achieve most if not all of their goals. A good mediator is nonjudgmental and can achieve a balance of knowledge and power in the mediation process without favoring one side or the other, is familiar with the law as it relates to your case, knows what is likely to happen in court, and can spot red flags.

There are two basic styles of mediation, one proactive and the other relentlessly passive (you can tell where my personal bias lies). A proactive mediator will assist you to reach your own resolution. However, if you get stuck, or need suggestions on how to meet your goals, the mediator will suggest possible solutions, and will tell you what a court is likely to do in a similar situation. This is important because you need to know what the default is, that is, what a court would do, and what other alternatives are available, before deciding the mediation isn't working. In that case, you may be surprised to find out that the offer which was on the table in mediation was better than what a court could give you. Other mediators feel it is inappropriate for them to make specific suggestions, and will refuse to do so. While I respect their reasons, I believe couples in mediation usually need more guidance than they receive from a passive mediator. They don't know what their options are, or what a court is likely to do, and the mediator's experience can be an important resource in steering them to a reasonable solution.

After you have investigated mediators in your area, it is time to make an appointment for a consultation. Don't forget, however, that both parties must agree on the mediator. Each mediator has a slightly different way of doing things. I would caution you not to talk to the mediator individually until you have discussed it with your spouse. Doing so may make it impossible for you to get an agreement to use this individual. Remember, we're all human. If you are already afraid that your spouse (who you perceive is in a position of greater knowledge or power) is going to pull a fast one on you, you will be very nervous if he's already had a conference with the mediator he wants you to consent to. You will assume that he's already "gotten to" the mediator because it fits with your fear. Now, mind you, any professional, whether a mediator, custody evaluator, forensic accountant or anyone else who functions as a neutral in divorce cases in a professional capacity will tell you it makes not one whit of difference who calls him first. His job is to form his opinions objectively. But we are not talking about objective facts here; we're talking about fear. Therefore, if you want your spouse to agree to use a particular mediator, make the first appointment jointly. I also suggest that you and your spouse interview two or three of the top mediators before deciding which one to use. It is highly likely that you will decide that one is a significantly better match for you than the others, but you only learn that by actually meeting with them. This also ensures that both of you have had input in the selection and will increase the likelihood of a successful resolution.

If you want more information about mediation and how it works, check out the FAQs at www.pearcemediation.com.

Collaborative Law

Another growing alternative to traditional litigation is collaborative law. Some parts of the country are well ahead of others on this, but I'll tell you what it is, and what I perceive as its strengths and weaknesses.

In collaborative law, each of your attorneys agrees that they will NOT go to court. You will cooperate in exchanging all information, and commit to keep negotiating until you have reached an agreement. That means each of you, both attorneys, and your experts, if you have them, attend every meeting. If either of you decides to opt out of the process, you will have to find another attorney to represent you and pay her to get up to speed on your case, because your collaborative lawyer has committed to staying out of court.

Obviously, it takes two lawyers who have been trained in collaborative law and who are willing to make this commitment.

My complaint about collaborative law is that it *can* be very slow and is sometimes as expensive as full-on litigation. There are two reasons for this. First, in addition to paying your attorney to address the issues of your case, you are also paying your attorneys to talk about the process of collaboration. Each time you meet, everybody participates, including the experts. That means that you have meeting after meeting, where all the meters are running and there is no pending court date creating pressure to make a decision. The process can be abused by a party who doesn't want the divorce or is trying to starve the other side out to get a more favorable settlement. It can get extremely expensive and I have seen many cases drop out of collaboration when one side concludes the other is abusing the process.

Other than the desire to stop the bleeding of the ongoing expense, there may be little pressure to move off firmly entrenched positions in collaborative law because there is no deadline. Frankly, that looming court date is often just the motivation people need to start making concessions and reach an agreement. Without that pressure, some collaborative cases can feel as if they are going on forever. If you find yourself in that position, I would suggest that you consider scheduling a settlement conference with a skilled private settlement judge (if they are available in your area). That doesn't violate the agreement to not litigate, and can provide much-needed guidance in breaking a log jam. Of course, both attorneys and both parties will have to agree to it. However, since collaborative lawyers, like mediators, are paid for their time at the time of service, if you get tired of writing those checks, that in itself may be an incentive to start making some concessions, as might the thought of having to start the whole process over from scratch with another lawyer after you've invested months and thousands of dollars.

Now, the point is that I am all in favor of any process which keeps husbands and wives out of court and helps them reach an amicable solution to their legal problems. Anything is better than trooping down to the courthouse girded for battle against the parent of your children. Court is, and should be, a last resort rather than a first.

If the thought of going to court is repugnant to you (and by now it should be), there are several options available to you. You can retain an attorney to negotiate for you, whether formally or in collaboration or not. Most good family lawyers do, in fact, settle most of their cases without going to trial. You can mediate, with or without a consulting attorney (and I strongly recommend with). If you feel it is necessary, perhaps your attorney can participate in the mediation, Most people have a sincere desire to settle, but some simply can't come to an agreement unless they feel they have someone in their corner.

In any event, a resolution which you work out yourselves is always more nuanced than something imposed on you by a stranger who has only known you for an hour or two.

CHAPTER 15

Special Masters, Referees, Court's Experts, and Evaluators

THERE HAVE BEEN radical changes in recent years in the way in which cases are prepared and either resolved outside of court or litigated. As a result, there are a number of terms with which you will need to be familiar.

In the old days (and in some parts of the country, it still is "the old days"), in a so-called "complicated" case, each party would retain their own team of expert witnesses who would then march down to the courthouse and, as advocates, present "their" side of the case. This "battle of the experts" significantly increases the cost of trial and, all too frequently, leaves the court with very little more information than it had in the beginning with which to decide difficult issues. One "expert" says the family business is worth millions (and, of course, their client wants to be bought out at full value), the other says it has a liquidation value of $25,000, and the court has to decide what to do with that testimony.

The lunacy of this approach was particularly obvious in custody cases. Mom would hire her expert who would meet only with her and with the kids, and would testify that she was Mother of the Year. Dad would take the kids to his own expert when they were with him. His expert would then testify that Dad was Father of the Year and Mother (whom he hadn't even met) was psychotic or unfit. Each party's expert would only interview one side, so how *could* he have a balanced opinion? After all, if the standard for determination of custody is "best interests of the child," how can an expert witness who has only seen one party or who is in fact hired by and beholden to only one side be in the position of independence necessary to objectively evaluate the best interests of the children?

As a result, more and more of the really good custody evaluators began to insist that they would work only as joint experts or as the neutral expert appointed by the court. This preserved their independence and their ability to competently discharge their duty to represent the best interests of the children rather than the interests of the parent who was paying them.

This is now the standard procedure for custody and visitation evaluators, and the approach is becoming more common in other areas of the law as well.

In selecting expert witnesses and evaluators, it is important to consider not only their professional qualifications and expertise in the subject matter, but their ability to effectively testify in court. Whether for custody or financial issues, any evaluator or expert witness has to be able to withstand cross-examination and think quickly. She must be clear about her conclusions and the factual basis which supports them, and be able to defend those conclusions to the satisfaction of the judge. In other words, she has to be able to take the heat. Frankly, to be cross-examined in public by someone whose job it is to make you look like an idiot is not a very pleasant experience and not everyone can do it effectively.

Here are some definitions:

Custody Evaluator

This person is generally a psychologist, social worker or a marriage, family and child counselor. Someone who serves in this capacity should be trained in developmental psychology, and have extensive specific experience with blended families, a wide variety of potential custody arrangements, and the issues which impact children of divorced parents. They often maintain a private therapy practice in addition to court evaluation work. Sometimes they are called "forensic" psychologists. Forensic simply means someone who is familiar with the law and presents information and recommendations in a way that is useful to the court.

Some custody evaluators are affiliated with and in fact employed by the court. There may or may not be a fee for court-based evaluations. There is always a fee for private evaluators, and the judge will decide who will advance the fee (usually equally, or from joint funds) when the appointment is made. On the other hand, the attorneys may agree on an evaluator, since good family lawyers all know who the good evaluators are.

The custody evaluator will be appointed to interview and evaluate the family and make recommendations about the custodial or visitation arrangement which is in the best interests of the children. They may meet with the parents together and separately, each parent with the children, and the children themselves. They may talk to teachers, day-care providers, pediatricians, or anyone else who has information which helps them understand what each child needs. Generally they will prepare a written report summarizing their findings. Sometimes the report includes psychological testing of both parties (they should never test only one party) and/or they may test the children. Depending on the facts and the children's ages, they will want to interview the children. This is covered in greater detail in Chapter 20, "Custody Mediation and Evaluation."

The evaluator's task is to determine the attachments and relationships in the family, the characteristics of each member and how they fit in the family dynamic. Good recommendations will not be based on an arbitrary formula; they will be custom-tailored to the family involved.

This is a very narrow subspecialty of psychotherapy. There are any number of people who are superb therapists who simply do not make good evaluators. The most important distinction between the two is that the evaluator has to be able to step back from the therapeutic desire to help the family heal and make the hard decision as to which custodial arrangement best serves the needs of the children. This assessment function is critical in a custody evaluation. The evaluator must have significant experience in working with divorcing families. Only in that way can he anticipate the issues which his report must address and make appropriate recommendations. Though remaining independent, a good evaluator will try to convey her recommendation, and the manner in which it was reached, as therapeutically as possible. However, their role is not to do therapy: It is to make a recommendation for a custodial arrangement.

In virtually every case, at least one parent is not going to get what they want from the recommendation. Frequently, *both* parents object. This means that, by definition, the evaluator is going to anger at least one and maybe both parents. It takes a strong and talented person to consistently make good assessments and recommendations under these circumstances.

I have no respect for an evaluator whose primary approach is to "cut the baby in half" so as to please both parents. This does nothing for the children and prolongs the conflict. I refer custody evaluations to highly qualified individuals, and I look to the evaluator to make the hard recommendation.

In most cases, two knowledgeable and experienced family lawyers will be able to agree on a competent joint expert. At least in my jurisdiction, we both know that we are wasting time and money in trying to line up "our own" experts since the court won't listen to them. We also all know who the good evaluators are. No, this doesn't mean that I prefer the evaluator who always comes down on the side of my client. In fact, the evaluator to whom I probably referred more cases than any other was selected for precisely the opposite reason. I knew that I could trust him to do what was, in his opinion, best for the kids, regardless of what pressure Mom or Dad or Mom's or Dad's attorney applied. I respect that enormously. So, before referring a family to him, I would look twice at my own client, double check to make sure I hadn't misread the situation and I had the bad guy, and pick up the phone.

In any given legal community, there will probably be a pool of as few as two or three and as many as 15 or 20 custody evaluators with whom all of the family lawyers have had experience and whose credentials and expertise are well known. These will be people who are very comfortable in a courtroom and will have demonstrated an ability to make the hard decision and back it up. They will not be "hired guns" who will support whichever parent or attorney applies the most pressure or who pays the bill. We all know who those people are, too, and they don't get much respect either from good attorneys or from the courts. Now, bad attorneys love hired guns because they make them look good, but that's a different topic.

After an evaluation, most cases settle without having to go to trial. The reason is obvious. I always caution my client that if the report of the independent evaluator comes down against him, he will have a huge uphill battle at trial. This is not to say that the evaluator is always right or that defective reports can't be successfully challenged. However, one of the reasons it is so important to start out with a very good evaluator is that the court is going to find an independent evaluation much more persuasive than one which is commissioned after the fact by the party who "lost" with the independent.

I am reminded of a local family law judge who stopped me in the hall one afternoon after I had just finished trying a particularly difficult custody case, and commented, "Sue, you always bring me the hard ones." Of course I do . . . if it weren't hard, I wouldn't need a trial after the evaluation. I would have settled it.

There is another important benefit to having a joint custody evaluator. Kids have no business in a court of law, even in the judge's chambers. There is an old New Yorker cartoon where Mother has taken her little boy into the courtroom. She stands in front of the bench, leans over and admonishes him, "Now, honey, tell the nice judge what a son-of-a-bitch Daddy is." Very few judges will allow children in court and good evaluators are not going to ask children to choose which parent they want to live with. Also, older children often reach a point where they "vote with their feet." The good news is that the evaluator has more specialized training and has much more time than the judge to meet with you, your spouse, the children, and even talk to teachers and day care providers if appropriate, and therefore gather as much information as he feels is essential to make a good recommendation. Assuming you have a competent evaluator, you are going to get a much more thoughtful recommendation and a more thorough review of the facts than if you simply take it into court and let each party explain why they should have custody of the kids.

There is an exception to the "no kids in court" rule. Teenagers have their own, often very busy, lives and may have very strong opinions about where they want to live and with whom. This may have nothing to do with which parent they love most, and everything to do with where their friends, athletic activities, and school connections are. In recent years, the California Supreme Court established a commission to look into how family law is administered. They had hearings throughout the state and heard time and time again from teenagers who felt they were marginalized by the process and who demanded a way for their voices to be heard. It is now part of California law that children over the age of fourteen who want to express their opinion regarding their custodial arrangement must be given an opportunity to do so. Judges still don't want kids on the witness stand testifying "for" or "against" a parent. However, they are coming up with creative ways for kids to express their desires regarding timeshare and visitation schedules. I still think the best way for the children to be heard is through evaluators, but it is not the exclusive one, at least for older children. A word of caution: This shouldn't be used as an opportunity to bribe Jake to say what you want him to say because you've offered to buy him a car for his sixteenth birthday if he does. That kind of thing always comes out.

My comments have been primarily directed toward private evaluators. Most counties in fact have publicly funded evaluation departments, sometimes called Family Court Services or Conciliation Courts. The caution is that there are wide variations in the funding and administration of these offices, which directly impact the quality of the resulting evaluations. Some counties have substantial budgets which not only allow them to hire highly qualified people who are enthusiastic about their jobs, but also allocate the time necessary to do a thorough evaluation. Other counties are so strapped for cash that they simply can't offer competitive salaries to lure the truly good people and don't have the staff time available to do a complete evaluation. If you are facing a custody dispute, you should ask your attorney about the practice in your court so you can make an informed decision.

Forensic Accountant

A forensic accountant is usually a certified public accountant who testifies in court on financial, tax and accounting issues. In a divorce, these topics typically include the valuation of a business which is subject to disposition at trial, the availability of income for payment of support, or the tracing of separate and joint contributions into various assets. Sometimes the tax consequences of the disposition of an asset will be a key issue at trial. If any of these are potential problems in your case, your attorney will probably suggest consulting a forensic CPA. Again, this is a relatively limited pool of people who are not only highly experienced in divorce taxation (and, believe me, this is a real specialized area of tax law) but people who are also comfortable testifying at court. Therefore, it is important to find an accountant who not only knows divorce taxation (and more specifically the area of divorce finance relevant to *your* case) but who also has substantial courtroom experience.

I teach seminars for forensic CPAs, and am finding that lots of accountants are now trying to break into forensic work. It takes years to learn the nuances of divorce accounting. The person who does your tax return is probably not a good choice unless you happen to have your returns done by someone who also has a thriving practice doing divorce litigation support.

As with custody evaluators, there will probably be a relatively small pool of highly respected forensic accountants in your area. They will all be very busy. There will be a much larger pool of part-time or "wannabe" experts and, with luck, some rising stars who will work at lower rates because they are trying to build their professional reputation.

If your divorce is likely to include issues of business valuation and division, the valuation of stock options, partnership buyouts and the like, your attorney should be talking to you about consulting an accountant. Find out who the top local experts are. You will want to know what they do, what experience they have and why your attorney thinks one would be more appropriate than another for your case.

If you or your attorney suspects the tax returns are fraudulent, you may need someone who can review them and advise you. If your or your mate's income situation is highly complicated, for example, if large amounts of income are routinely derived from capital gains, the exercise of employee stock options, or unusual business transactions, you may well need a forensic accountant to sort it all out so that the court can make an appropriate support order. More and more frequently now, accountants are retained to determine the marital standard of living for purposes of ongoing spousal support or alimony. Finally, the property division may create, in and of itself, tax consequences to you or your spouse. As with any complex financial litigation, you should be advised by a forensic CPA, whether or not you intend to use this person at trial. It is simply part of evaluating a complicated financial situation and making sure that you are making good decisions regarding settlement and/ or trial.

Suppose you find you simply can't afford one of the top forensic CPAs, but you really need expert assistance in your case. You do have a couple of options.

First, you may be able to get by with a limited evaluation from the expert. This means that rather than doing a full blown "by the book" business evaluation, you limit the areas they look into or ask for a "ballpark" or range of values based on certain assumptions. Of course, you have to be sure you are comfortable with the assumptions used. This generally results in the expenditure of significantly less time by the expert, and a resulting lower total fee. You may also ask if there is an associate in the expert's office who can do the work under supervision at a lower hourly rate.

Alternatively, ask your lawyer who the rising stars are in the next generation of experts. You may be able to find someone who is newer to the profession, charges a lower hourly rate, and whose enthusiasm makes up for limitations of experience. Someone who is young and building a reputation will want to do an excellent job to generate future referrals. Don't confuse this person with the "wannabe," however. The person I'm referring to here is not merely dabbling. He's striving mightily to enter the ranks of the top forensics, and wants to do it as quickly as possible. He will benefit professionally from doing a super job in your case, and he may do it at a reduced rate, because it is a way to advertise his competence to the judge (who may appoint him in other cases), and to the other attorneys who may be sitting in the back of the courtroom when he testifies. I've found some great young forensics this way.

Discuss all of these aspects with your attorney, along with the possibility of using a joint expert to control the cost.

The idea of joint experts is a little later in coming to the financial arena than in custody. I have seen a definite trend in recent years in favor of either "joint" or "court's" experts. Some judges will blatantly tell litigants not to bother retaining their own separate forensic CPAs because the court is going to appoint its own expert. If your court is one of those, don't waste your money on "your own" expert. If the court's expert disagrees with yours, guess whose opinion is going to carry the greatest weight with the judge? Again, most experienced family law attorneys will seriously consider a joint or court's expert. If the other side refuses to agree on a joint expert, you may be able to file a motion with the court asking the judge to appoint an independent expert rather than have the duplicate work and expense of two separate evaluations.

A word of caution: Once you are armed with this information from your initial contact with your prospective new attorney, *don't* call the expert yourself to "sound her out." Doing so will taint her for a joint appointment. This means that if you decide that you would like to have her do the work, chances are she won't be independent anymore because you talked to her before she was jointly retained. Even if you didn't get any particularly useful information from her or she from you, your spouse may be so paranoid that you might have tainted the expert's neutrality that they refuse to agree to her appointment. Therefore, don't ever call a prospective forensic evaluator or expert, whether for custody, visitation, financial or any other matters, until your attorney has instructed you to do so. The legal culture varies widely from jurisdiction to jurisdiction and the last thing you want to do is find out that you have just discovered the absolutely perfect person who understands your case and will do the evaluation for a fraction of what everyone else is charging, only to find that he can't accept the appointment because you have already talked to him and he is therefore no longer "independent."

There is another reason you shouldn't contact the expert yourself. Some lawyers want to insulate their expert from discovery by the other side. It is called "attorney work product" and you don't want to inadvertently waive this potentially important protection.

Special Masters and Referees

These are terms which may or may not be used somewhat interchangeably in your jurisdiction. If your attorney uses one of them, ask him to define it for you.

Generally, a special master or a referee is someone who is deputized by the court to make certain factual findings, or at least make a recommendation to the court on a complicated issue. This is different from an expert witness who will evaluate the situation and then testify as to his conclusions. He is giving an opinion, but he doesn't have decision making power. In contrast, the court's power may be delegated in large degree to a special master or referee. The special master makes a specific recommendation, which carries much greater weight with the court than the opinion of an expert witness, and may even be legally binding.

Special Masters, Referees, Court's Experts, and Evaluators

There are a number of situations where a special master or referee (and I am going to use the term special master to refer to both) is a very good thing to have. Generally, they are used to gathering and assembling information which is too voluminous, time consuming or complicated for the judge to do. There may be tricky tracing or accounting issues which need to be resolved before the judge can make a ruling. There may be facts which need to be investigated and reported back to the court. These people usually have specialized training in the factual or legal issue they are assigned to investigate. They can devote significantly more time to a complex issue than the judge can. Therefore, if you have an issue which requires two days of hearing time to adequately present the facts, it may be a good idea to use a special master. They can usually fit your case in their schedule faster than the court can, which significantly speeds up the process.

For example, suppose you have a highly complex family-owned business which constitutes the primary marital asset. The value of the business and the determination of who should get it in the divorce depends entirely on the trier of fact (that is, the person making the decision) having sophisticated knowledge of the specific industry in which the business operates. Now it is just possible that your family law judge, before being appointed to the bench, had a flourishing business valuation practice, and therefore understands the legal nuances. However, it is much more likely that he was a district attorney prosecuting drug dealers and doesn't know a Schedule C from vitamin C. Now, I'm not saying that former district attorneys do not make good family law judges; in fact, some of the best family law judges I have seen started out as criminal lawyers. That being said, one doesn't learn overnight how to read a tax return or spot a phony balance sheet. With the best intent in the world, the brightest judge will not see all of the implications of the evidence being presented if the subject matter is new to him, especially if the evidence or the law is complicated. Some industries have very unusual business practices, and a judge who doesn't know what they are might make a significant mistake in evaluating the business. Therefore, in many cases, I will ask the court to appoint someone who is an expert in these areas to make the decision instead of the judge. If you are considering asking the court to appoint a special master, find out how it is done in your county. Some courts are so preoccupied with appearing to be fair and impartial that they put all the possible candidates on a list, and simply appoint whoever is next on the list to your case. I recoil in horror at this practice. Some of the people on these lists are terrible. Even if they are good, their expertise may not be a good match for your issue. Anyone can hold himself out as an "expert," and some of these self-proclaimed experts are people I wouldn't appoint to take my dog for a walk, much less make the decision on a key asset that is critical to my case.

In some jurisdictions, the special master can only report her findings to the judge, who then must review them before making the final decision. However, as a practical matter the special master often has all but judicial powers. This can be wonderful, and in most cases I think it is. It can be dreadful if the person to whom the power is delegated is biased or is not as sophisticated or knowledgeable as he represents. Therefore, it is important for you (or more particularly for your attorney) to know who is likely to be appointed special master and whether that individual's background and training qualify him to evaluate the evidence and make an appropriate recommendation.

In my county, there is a small pool of accountants whom the courts routinely appoint for this type of work. I am advised that in other states, the practice is growing but not nearly as advanced as it is here. Whatever your jurisdiction, if this sounds like your case, ask your attorney about the practice in your local court.

Evaluators, forensic experts and special masters are all valuable resources in proper cases. They can also be misused when judicial power is improperly delegated. All in all, however, they significantly streamline judicial proceedings. They have the advantages of specialized training and expertise as well as significantly more time than the judge. As a result, they can resolve a complicated problem more efficiently than a traditional hearing. You will pay for their expertise, however. Frankly, I would rather have a competent expert take as much time as necessary to make the right decision, rather than the most brilliant judge in the world try to decide too quickly on too little evidence because they lack the specialized knowledge or there simply isn't enough time to explore it thoroughly.

There is an emerging field for special masters in high-conflict custody and visitation cases. Some parents choose to fight about every facet of their children's lives long after the divorce is over. In some cases, the court will appoint an individual (usually a custody evaluator, but sometimes an attorney experienced with custody issues) to be a special master for post-divorce disputes involving the children.

There are generally two situations where custody special masters are appointed. It is sometimes important to have someone in place to make a quick ruling as issues come up, and there isn't time to wait for a slot on the court's calendar some weeks or months hence. A special master can usually act must faster than a judge. In the other situation, the parents are in such high conflict that they are constantly trooping down to the courthouse to fight over every little thing. Appointing a special master as the first line of resolution ensures that every conflict doesn't result in the filing of a new motion and a series of court hearings. Instead, the order will provide that neither party may raise a non-emergency issue involving the children with the court until they have first taken the issue to the special master. Sometimes the special master has the power to make a binding decision. In other circumstances, the special master prepares a written recommendation, which must be approved by the judge to become effective. In either event, it is a powerful tool for keeping litigious families out of court over relatively minor issues. Of course, the parties are ordered to pay the fees of the special master, which also has a chilling effect on making a federal case over how Matt's hair is cut.

Much of a custody special master's work is now done by email or conference call, which makes it more efficient than face to face meetings, especially if the issue is who is going to take Olivia to dance lessons, or why you haven't paid your share of the wrestling fees.

Here's a final note about custody special masters. If one is appointed in your case, it is not a compliment. It is the Red Badge of Failure. It means the court is putting a professional referee in place because you (the parents) are not capable of effectively managing your children and yourselves on a day to day basis.

Parenting Coordinators and Co-Parenting Counselors

Many parents have difficulty learning how to effectively work together in joint custody. They may not need as firm a hand as families who are assigned to special masters or referees, but still need help from a qualified professional. A new subspecialty of custody mediators is emerging to help these parents. These individuals serve as parenting coordinators, and are sometimes called co-parenting counselors. They are usually (but not always) therapists with a background in custody mediation or evaluation. They are familiar with the problems which arise in joint custody and blended families, and experienced in helping parents find solutions to those problems. This is a less intrusive role than a special master, who usually has decision-making authority. A parenting coordinator will work with the parents to help them learn to co-parent with each other to make their custody arrangement work for the children. They will teach parents communication skills and help establish ground rules for joint decision making. This is intended to be a relatively short-term intervention designed to teach parents the skills they need to deal with each other effectively for the benefit of the children in a post-divorce context. They may work intensively with parents at the beginning of a joint custody arrangement while they are working out the kinks and learning to co-parent cooperatively. Then, after patterns which work are established, they will occasionally be consulted as problems arise. Some high-conflict parents who start out with special masters "graduate" to parenting coordinators as they hone and develop their co-parenting skills.

PART III

What About the Kids?

CHAPTER 16

Kids Aren't Property

ONE OF THE most painful realities faced by any parent contemplating divorce is the certainty that for large blocks of time in the future, your kids will not be with you. This is true whether or not you are the primary custodial parent. The children have been with you since birth, and the fear that they won't be in the future can stop you in your tracks. *Don't let that fear cause you to turn your children's lives into a battleground.*

Countless parents have said to me, "I won't settle for less than 50/50 custody; that's *my* right." Nonsense. This isn't about *your* rights. It's about your child's.

Kids are not fungible possessions which can be divided, such as pots and pans, bank accounts, and place settings of sterling flatware. Kids are people, small and highly vulnerable people. You brought them into the world and it is your responsibility to protect and nurture them. Nowhere is that more important than when you are divorcing their other parent. A divorce turns your children's world upside down and threatens their sense of security to its very core. They are utterly powerless and don't understand why this awful thing is happening. How you, as parents, handle your responsibility to them will greatly influence whether your children come through the process healthy, well-adjusted and feeling loved, or so scarred that they turn into miserable parents themselves and repeat the same dysfunctional patterns with their own children. You owe it to your children to protect them and give them a sense of security, as well as to model for them how grownups handle difficult challenges.

There is a huge difference between "I'm entitled to 50% time with my children" and the real truth, which is that the *children* are *entitled* to two parents. This simple fact escapes all too many parents and their children pay the price. It's the kid's right, not Mom's or Dad's.

I would like to say that the divorce process can make good parents out of bad ones, but that is only occasionally true. Sometimes divorce is a wake-up call to parents who have been largely absent from their children's' day-to-day lives. They suddenly realize what they and their children have been missing and educate themselves about how best to assume an active and positive parenting role. I always encourage this, no matter how belated their change of heart, as the children can only benefit. The good news is that even if you haven't been Parent of the Year in the past, you have a second chance. You have an opportunity through the process of divorce to create a new relationship with your children, to love, nurture and support them, not because it is your right, but because it is theirs.

So what happens when someone actually does decide, in the throes of a divorce, to start being a better parent? The other parent all too often is outraged, convinced that this is just a diabolical plot to take "their" children away from them. It is amazing how often the parent who has been the primary caregiver is angry and resentful, bitterly complaining that the former partner (who "didn't give a rip" about the children before) is suddenly insisting on being involved in their lives, and turning into an active, engaged parent. As though that is a bad thing. This parent will complain endlessly that the very person who was too busy to attend soccer practices and ballet recitals now insists on coaching the team and schlepping tutus to dance lessons, treating the turnaround as a dirty trick. Of course, these are the same people who want gold stars for having done it all without help in the past. I submit that the parent who has been carrying the burden of these activities should be grateful that the children will benefit because the other parent has decided to step up, however tardily.

Joint custody is designed to provide kids with two active, engaged parents. This spirit is lost when parents become obsessed with marking calendars and counting days and hours (even sleep and school hours!)

in order to calculate their exact percentage of time with the children. Sometimes this is a smokescreen to increase or reduce the child support, but more often it's just to keep score. Many state legislatures have quite deliberately tinkered with child support guidelines to reduce or eliminate the financial incentive to fight over time with the kids. They have done this by adjusting the incremental reduction in child support as the noncustodial parent's percentage of timeshare increases. Some states give no financial credit at all for timeshare. In others, the support will still be reduced somewhat as timeshare becomes more equally divided, but not proportionally. The net result is that a noncustodial parent who wants more time with the children may suffer a financial hardship because the increased responsibility and cost are not necessarily reflected in reduced child support payments. The states which have adopted this philosophy do it intentionally. They don't want parents fighting over custody to save money on support, and if that means that the higher earning parent bears a greater proportion of the financial burden, so be it. The result is that almost-but-not-quite equal custodial parents don't always get the financial breaks they probably should. On the other hand, only a jerk would fight for custody just to save a few bucks on child support, although a distressing number do precisely that.

When I hear someone say he has "27%," or "33%," or "36%," timeshare it's a red flag. There is an agenda working, and it has nothing to do with the kids. Not once have I heard a kid worry about whether they spend 24% or 28% of their time with Dad or with Mom, but I've had to litigate it when it made a difference in the child support or the parents were entrenched in keeping score. I once had a case where everyone agreed what the custodial schedule was. They even had prepared a calendar for the following full year which allocated every single day between them. Nevertheless, I had to have a special master appointed to calculate the actual timeshare percentage because Dad was holding out for a fantasy number that bore no relationship to the actual schedule because it saved him money on child support. True, the percentage of timeshare is important to some parents because they want tangible, quantifiable evidence that they are still actively involved in their child's life. It's never the child's agenda, though. Kids couldn't care less about percentages; what they are interested in is the love, care and attention they receive from their parents.

Many custody conflicts are traceable to a fear that if you don't have custody, you won't see your kids. I have found that some custody fights can be avoided at the outset simply by making certain that the lesser time parent knows that there will still be frequent and continuing contact with the children. That reassurance reduces the likelihood that they will pursue custody for defensive reasons. Many parents know in their heart of hearts that the children (at least at this stage of their development) are probably better off living primarily with the other parent. Nevertheless, they fight for custody out of fear. In these cases, the litigation can sometimes be averted if they are assured that they are not giving up their rights forever, that they will still get frequent contact with the children, and the timeshare arrangement will change as the children mature and their needs change. If they can be sufficiently reassured, a custody dispute may be averted.

This is a good place to point out that what used to be called the "tender years" doctrine, that young children always go with the mother, is dead in most states and on the way out in the rest.

It is important to note that custody orders are never permanent. The courts and the custody evaluators who make the recommendations realize that children's' needs change as they develop. Each child is unique, and individuals within a single family may have vastly different needs at various stages in their development. Recognize that custody is a fluid and elastic concept. The sooner you and your spouse can accept this fact for the sake of the kids, the better it will be for all of you.

You and your spouse will be parents of these children forever. Don't make the children choose between you. If you don't know how to tell your children you're getting a divorce, see a therapist and get some suggestions from an expert. Let your children know in every possible way that you love them, that you care for them, that you are not divorcing *them* and, most important, that the divorce *is not their fault*. There are now many helpful books, pamphlets and videos available which contain excellent suggestions for how to explain divorce to kids and deal with their inevitable fears and questions. Research these and implement the suggestions you find there. Some good ones are listed in Chapter 45, "More Resources." If you and your spouse are having difficulty working out what you want for your kids, utilize the tools on uptoparents. org. They have a wonderful protocol for helping parents jointly evaluate their children's needs.

Make a deal with your spouse that money issues will never, repeat *NEVER* be dragged into discussions of "kid issues" and "kid" conversations. I cannot state this strongly enough.

One of the most useful techniques I have found is for the parents to agree on a code. If either party starts a conversation, text or email with "This is a kid issue," or "This is a kid conversation," it's absolutely *verboten* to mention money. I don't care if the support check is two months late and the electricity is about to be turned off; I don't care if there's an offer on the house and you need to decide right now whether to accept it and how the proceeds are going to be divvied up; I don't care how irresistible the temptation is to rehash for the fiftieth time the "how dare you leave me and what are you doing with that slut" conversation — resist the impulse. This rule has no exceptions. When the code is used, it means that "kid" issues are discussed first and, to the extent that you can, they are discussed dispassionately and calmly. If there are other pressing matters to be discussed, hang up the phone and call each other back or start a new email or text string on non-kid issues. It may sound silly, but this technique is successful because it is a very tangible, physical reminder that bleed-through between kid issues and money issues is not acceptable.

Despite the obvious benefits to the kids of having two parents jointly involved in the ongoing and inevitable issues of child-rearing, there are very practical benefits of this technique to the parents as well. Neither parent will be dissuaded from discussing a legitimate parenting issue for fear that it will trigger a rehash of the marital history. It is more important that each of you feels free to call the other to report that Jason is getting a "D" in math and we have to do something about it, without fear of repercussions. Otherwise, the call is not made, the conflict escalates, and no plan is made to help Jason with his math, all to the detriment of the child.

It works like this: Assume Jason's math grade comes in, and Mom knows that Dad should be told so they can address the issue constructively and consistently. However, every time she calls Dad, she has to listen to him berate her for leaving him. Not surprisingly, she doesn't want to hear it again, so she doesn't call. Dad finds out after Jason flunks math. He then feels that Mom is abusing her custodial power by shutting him out of Jason's life and keeping legitimate information from him. He concludes that the only way to be sure he has ongoing input in Jason's education is to go after custody himself. Or perhaps he doesn't start a custody proceeding, but begins hounding the school for direct information, which makes the teacher, principal and, yes, Jason, feel they are caught in the middle of a dispute that is not of their making. You can see where I'm going...

The ante increases when the call which isn't made is about the fact that Jake is being cyber-bullied or Emma is cutting herself. These can be life-threatening. Work on communication with each other for the sake of the kids.

Use the same rules with email and texts, which have become both a blessing and a curse to divorcing parties who have difficulty communicating verbally. Keep emails to the point, and don't use them to vent. Emails about kid issues should be short, succinct, and limited to the topic at hand. And *please*, make sure your emails to your spouse and your attorney, or emails to friends which might contain details about your divorce are passworded so that your kids can't get access to them. Don't leave your password lying around, and change it frequently. I recently had a case where we couldn't figure out how the kid was getting all the dirt in the divorce, since the parents swore they had "never said a *word*" to the kids about it. They didn't have to. One of them was clever enough to leave the emails on the computer, hidden just well enough that the child, who was way too invested in the conflict, could easily find them. Don't do it. And remember, too, your kid's computer skills may be much more sophisticated than your own.

And while all this is going on, don't forget that your kids are experiencing totally ordinary developmental issues which may account for their behavioral changes. Developmental stages are just that, and not the other parent's fault. If you and your spouse were still together, Brooke would still be acting out at this phase, so don't automatically run to the courthouse asking for a reduction in contact with the other parent because your child is behaving differently from the way he did a year ago. He's growing, even in the middle of your divorce. Guess what. . . ? A 15 year old is going to be 15 (oh, joy) whether or not Mom and Dad are divorcing. Recognize that, and don't assume the problem is the other parent. Instead, use it as an opportunity to try to work cooperatively for the benefit of your child, perhaps with a co-parenting counselor.

Suppose your spouse is fighting for custody solely to get a break on support or to pressure you to concede property issues in exchange for the custodial arrangement that you both know is in your children's best interests. I would like to say that I have a magic answer for this one. The process of divorce does not of itself turn bad parents into good ones, though some marginal parents do wake up and learn from their mistakes. However, we rarely see a complete personality change. Someone who was a self-absorbed, manipulative and controlling parent prior to the separation is not likely to become a model one simply because the two of you are no longer together.

You may, in fact, have the opposite problem. Rather than trying to take the kids away from you, the other parent may simply be absent. The courts cannot legislate good parenting. Be real. It's not the divorce that caused the problem. If your mate was cold, narcissistic and inattentive when you were together, she is unlikely to turn into Mother of the Year afterward. You can't force her to be meaningfully involved in the children's lives. In that case, my guess is that you would have been raising the kids by yourself even if you had stayed married.

I can only offer you this observation: This is the person with whom you chose to have children. Obviously when you made that choice (or at some time since) you had to face the reality that you were going to have to go it alone. That's the truth. The consolation is that there are many highly responsible adults who only had one parental role model. If it's a good one, one is all it takes.

Terrible Reasons to Start a Custody Fight

- I'll save money on child support because I can raise them for less money than the support guideline calls for.
- I won't have my children around "that woman."
- I have more money and can provide the fancier home.
- I don't approve of her morals.
- Fear of what your friends will say: "What's wrong with *her*? I heard she doesn't have custody of her children!"
- I'm remarried and we have a new family now, so the kids don't need the old one.

Many custody fights are traceable to all the wrong reasons. The parents may be motivated by a continuation of the marital issues, usually power and control or hurt feelings, vengeance, rejection, humiliation and the like. They may feel they can achieve financial gain, i.e., an adjustment in support in relation to timeshare. Or maybe they are just keeping score and control of the kids is the current sporting event.

Your spouse may have done any number of terrible things. He may be sleeping with someone else; his house may be a mess; he may cheat on his taxes. All this may have little or nothing to do with parenting skills. As strange as it may seem, an individual can in fact be mentally ill, and still be the better (indeed, sometimes exemplary) parent, if the illness is under control and doesn't negatively impact parenting. A competent mother with controllable OCD is far better than a manipulative jerk who only sees the kids as tools to be used to further his individual ends. Your mate's conduct may mightily offend your sensibilities, but if it does not adversely affect the children, so what? The issue is the impact on the kids. On the other hand, if your spouse is flaunting her boyfriend in front of the children and the *children* (as opposed to you) are having a hard time accepting it, that's legit. If you're simply suffering from sexual jealousy yourself, go see a therapist and deal with it there.

Suppose your spouse's home, while not toxic, is a pigsty. Well, I'm sure it's going to come as a great surprise that many perfectly well adjusted people were raised in log cabins with dirt floors. A little clutter was never at the top of any kid's list of complaints. If you know that your spouse can provide a warm, loving and safe environment for your kids, whether or not it would win Martha Stewart's approval is irrelevant.

The issue of social pressure and sexual stereotyping is insidious. This was brought home to me years ago when I returned to the office after having won a particularly difficult custody case for my client (the father). A longtime employee (female) from another department immediately asked me, "What's wrong with the mother?" I was insulted at the implication that the only reason a father would win custody was that the mother was somehow defective. After I recovered from the slam at my legal skills, it occurred to me that this comment came from someone who had been around the legal business for years and (I felt) should have known better. It taught me that social and sexual stereotypes are very deeply ingrained.

I hope we are getting to a point where a mother who knows in her heart that the kids are better off with Dad will feel freer to let that happen rather than subject the kids to a battle for fear of what the neighbors will say. Think about this: The better parent may well be the one who can be honest enough to admit that the kids really need the other parent more and let them go, rather than subject them to a bitter custody fight. That parent is really putting the kids' needs first.

How to Avoid the Divorce from Hell

Instead of plotting a power play for the kids or obsessing about what's wrong with your spouse, focus on your children. Redirect the energy spent vilifying your ex into planning an outing with your kids. The last I heard, it didn't cost a lot of money to be a good parent. It does, however, require effort. Go for a bike ride, build a model plane, or just *listen*. You'd be amazed how many people who have lived in the same house with their kids for years never learned how to listen to them. Attend a parenting workshop. There are lots of parenting resources online. Get creative. And above all, get real. An 8 year old may like nothing better than to go for a hike with you or just hang with you and have your undivided attention. A 16 year old is probably not going to want to hang with a parent when he can be out with his friends, but you can still be available to him. Remember, too, that "custody" is a relative term when applied to a teenager: Often, the only thing it really means is that he's texting his friends from your house rather than the other parent's and that your refrigerator gets cleaned out first.

A final word on joint custody: If you are demanding equal custody of your kid, and you don't even know the name of his teacher, his favorite TV show, who he is rooting for on American Idol, his best friend, his favorite Harry Potter character, his pediatrician, or the other details of his day-to-day life, you aren't going to have much credibility with the court or the custody evaluator. Get to know your kid.

CHAPTER 17

Custody and Access

THERE IS A great deal of variation in the terminology which is used to describe how much responsibility each parent has for the children. The old terms were "custody" and "visitation" where one parent was the one with the responsibility (and the power) and the other merely "visited" with the child. Many lower-time parents felt the term "visitation" denigrated their relationship with their children and marginalized them as parents. Some parents tend to equate "custody" with possession, which can subtly reinforce the idea that children are things and not people.

Urged on by mental health professionals, many states have gotten away from such loaded labels and are not only using gender neutral terms, but words which underscore the fact that both parties remain parents of their children with important roles to play in the child's development. I've defined the various terms as I use them in the Glossary.

Among the labels which are gaining favor are "timeshare," which carries no negative or positive connotation whatsoever about power and control and underscores the concept that the parents continue to share the children. Another is "access" which recognizes the importance of parental involvement in the child's life.

Where the term "custody" is used, it may be called "physical custody" or "legal custody." The former refers to where the child lives. The latter designates who has the authority for the key decisions in the child's life, such as religious upbringing, schooling, and health care. Check to see what terms are used in your state and whether they are defined by statute.

I favor terminology which provides that Parent A has physical custody at certain times, and Parent B has physical custody at other times. Even if the percentage of Parent B's time is only twenty percent, it still underscores the importance of the relationship, both to the parent and to the child. And when it comes to legal custody, that is generally a nobrainer. Unless the parties are so firmly entrenched in mutually irreconcilable opinions ("I've enrolled him in Catholic school during the week," versus "He's going to Hebrew school when he is at my house," or a bitter dispute about whether or not to vaccinate) that one parent simply has to be designated as the decision maker if any decision is to be made at all, both parents should be involved in all the major decisions about the children.

Most states encourage some form of shared custody, although it is defined differently. Some have restrictions on "split" custody, where the children in a family may have different schedules with each parent. Some states have preferences for joint custody. Review the definitions in the glossary, and find out what the rules are in your state.

I am firmly convinced that some form of shared or joint custody arrangement is almost always in the children's best interests, at least where the parents are reasonable and responsible.

Joint Custody

I find there is a great deal of confusion about what joint custody does and does not mean.

In the first place, it does not mean that every parent has a "right" to 50% timeshare. It represents a recognition that it is generally in the children's best interests to have frequent and continuing contact with both parents. That may mean 30% timeshare or 50% or some other number, as long as both parents are actively involved in the children's day-to-day activities and share decision-making authority. Most states favor the active involvement of parents in their kids' lives and try to encourage it. Many parents are able to work remarkably well with each other where the kids are concerned, even after a divorce. And there are numerous resources, books, and online services which help parents do just that. If you want or already have joint custody of your kids, take advantage of some of these as they are listed in "More Resources," Chapter 45. Since new ones are being added all the time, check out my website, www.privatefamilylawjudge.com. I post new ones as I discover them.

Some parents can't give up the need to keep score, even in joint custody. Don't get sidetracked counting days and hours to figure out the exact percentage of time you spend with your kids, and above all, don't start counting sleep and school hours to prove your point. Remember, also, that whether you call it custody, timeshare or access, it includes *responsibility*. When there is a problem on "your" time, you have to deal with it. Before insisting on 50/50 timeshare, think carefully about what you will do when the school calls and says your child is sick and you need to come and pick him up. If you can't take off work to do it, it is your responsibility to have someone else available who can. And although it is often a good idea to offer the other parent "right of first refusal" if you are unavailable at times when you are scheduled to have the children, that doesn't mean that you can simply foist any problem that arises on your watch onto the other parent. It may be equally inconvenient for the other parent, and if it is on your time, you have to have a Plan B.

People sometimes assume that if there's equal time, there will be no child support; that is not necessarily so, unless both parents also have equal incomes, and sometimes not even then.

- If you want joint custody, you'll need to carefully discuss the implications with your attorney. Consider the following:
- You may well end up paying close to the same child support, notwithstanding the fact that you have to provide a home for the children as well.
- Can you really make room in your schedule for the children's demands? Can you take off work when they are sick, or pick them

up and take them home if the school calls? Who is going to take them to the orthodontist? Soccer practice?

- What about extracurricular activities? Can you really get them to their lessons and soccer matches? Be realistic.
- Recognize that if you have joint custody, you will have much more day to day interaction with your ex-spouse over the kids than if one of you had primary responsibility. If you have joint custody, you'll be communicating with each other all the time. Can you put your own differences aside in order to do this for the sake of the kids?

Children require time and attention. If you're not used to being the primary care giver, your life is going to change radically. Lose 10 points if your response is, "I'll just hire an *au pair* and a cook."

It bears repeating that joint custody doesn't necessarily mean equal time. Even equal time doesn't necessarily mean one week on, one week off, although that is becoming more standard in many parts of the country, after the children reach a sufficient age to handle the transitions. If you are considering joint custody, take stock of what the children really need on a day to day basis. What lessons do they have? What extracurricular activities? Is there a particular schedule which better lends itself to their situation? Many couples who negotiate 50/50 timeshare are motivated more by being "fair" with each other than determining whether that is the schedule that works best for the children. Little kids don't react well to constant shifts in where they sleep or in bedtime routines, and will have no concept of what it means to say, "Daddy will see you again next week." For them, it is important to have frequent, perhaps even daily, contact with each parent, even if only for brief periods. One way to do this is for the lesser time parent to pick them up from daycare every day to drive them home, stopping at the park along the way and having time with them there.

Even for older kids, a week is a long time to go without seeing a parent. You may want to schedule some midweek contact during the other parent's week. And of course, telephone, texts, Skype, webcams and email can help keep the relationship current. Some kids are simply more adaptable than others, and some kids really need to have a home base, even though they want to spend substantial periods of time with each parent. And if your kid is one of those, don't take it personally. If they don't do transitions well, it may be important to limit the frequency of exchanges. Whatever arrangement you work out must be tailored to your children's needs, and not dictated solely by some arbitrary sense of "fairness" between you and the other parent. Remember, children aren't property; they are very special people.

I have seen true 50/50 custody work beautifully, but it requires two committed parents. More often, it turns out to be 60/40 or something akin to that. Don't be too concerned about the precise amount of time. It is far more important that the children have frequent contact with both parents with as little disruption of their lives as possible. The idea is that they feel they have two homes, not that they are bounced back and forth between houses with no roots in either. If you work together for the sake of the kids, it will all balance out in the end.

Someone may suggest an arrangement to you which is called "birds' nesting." This means that the children stay put and the parents move in and out of the house at regular intervals. I have never seen a court order this, but have occasionally had parents work it out themselves. It is very difficult to do successfully. If it works at all, it seems to work best for an *extremely short* period at the very beginning of the separation, while you're trying to sort out the financial separation, or while the house is being sold. It requires two parents who are absolutely committed to respecting each other's privacy. If either of you is not, it is doomed from the start.

You may be considering split custody. This means that each of the kids has a different schedule. Children have different needs, and sometimes that means that one comes more frequently or stays longer than his sibling. This arrangement can even be advantageous from time to time, as each child gets one-on-one time with each parent. It needs to be carefully tailored to your kids' needs, however. Just as kids need both parents, research indicates that they need their siblings, even if they wouldn't admit it on pain of death and fight like cats and dogs when they are together.

If you're considering joint custody (and except for situations involving abuse, or where geographical distance makes it impractical, I recommend that you do), spend significant time and effort on the scheduling. Make sure that you and your spouse are putting the kids' needs first. One of the best places to start is a website called UpToParents.org. You and your spouse can log on separately and use an interactive protocol to prepare a set of goals for your children. It is helpful, thoughtful, and creative, and very much designed to help parents reduce conflict around the kids and flesh out workable arrangements for dealing with their children. Try it.

And if you're having trouble keeping track of the transitions, appointments, schedules, play dates, etc., try Cofamilies.org or OurFamilyWizard.org.

CHAPTER 18

Access Games, or How to Ensure Your Kids Will Resent You Forever

THERE ARE COUPLES who, once they have divided the property and determined the level of support, can't resist continuing to fight with one another. They may still be trying to obtain that pound of flesh they think they should have gotten. Or perhaps they can't let go of the tie with their mate, feeling that *any* relationship with each other, even a hostile one, is better than none. If they have children, there is a ready-made battleground. Even after custody is decided and an order is in place, there are a million ways in which they can push one another's buttons to continue the war. When they do, the children pay a horrendous price. The best timeshare ("access") order is a flexible one. When I see an order that says "Reasonable access on suitable advance notice" which *works*, I know I am dealing with two responsible and adult parents. On the other hand, the more detailed the order has to be, the more likely it is that the parents have a separate agenda that has nothing to do with the kids. I once saw a negotiated timeshare agreement that ran to eight pages (single spaced) and in addition to the usual recital of time and location of drop off and pickup, delineated in exhaustive detail who could attend parent/teacher conferences and back to school night, how many hours each parent had with the child on Halloween (and whether those hours were before or after dark and with or without costume) and countless other micromanaged terms. I immediately knew that at least one (and in this case, both) of the parents couldn't care less about the kid. It was an endless power struggle, not a timeshare schedule. Not surprisingly, after working under this order for a couple of years, one of the parents moved across country and essentially abandoned the child. I shudder to think how that kid turned out. To parents like this, the kid's needs are irrelevant. They are nothing but the turf which the parents have selected as the current site on which to conduct their ongoing war with each other.

I'm going to give you a whole list of things not to do to your children around visitation and access. Before I do, there are a few things which you need to understand.

First, recognize that your children are going to want to see the other parent. This is not a betrayal or rejection of you. Even if they are furious adolescents who are taking out their rage over the family breakup on one of their parents, at some level they probably want contact. They are just too angry to admit it. If you are the primary caretaker parent and the other has been absent, don't get your feelings hurt if the children suddenly express a desire to spend more time with your ex. It's healthy and is not a reflection on the care and the love that you have given them. It is likely that they will need extra reassurance that both parents love and will protect them. Don't turn it into a loyalty issue. It does not mean that they love you less, but rather that they have needs which, as good as you are as a parent, you cannot meet. This is the reality. You cannot completely fill the roles of both father and mother to your children, try as you might. Just pick one and do it the best you can.

If you are the parent with primary custody, don't get too excited about the fact that the kids are a little nervous and upset or crabby when they come back from the other parent's home. Don't go running into your attorney's office on Monday morning complaining that the kids should spend less time because they returned tired and whiny. They will. The upset is often caused because the lower-time parent feels that time with the kids is so limited and precious that they try to cram too much activity into a short period and the kids return tired and cranky. This usually diminishes as they settle into a routine and realize that they won't lose their kids just because they don't have primary custody. If the kids continue to return upset, that is usually caused by the fact that each transition between households underscores again the reality that Mom and Dad don't live in the same place anymore. They may become depressed at each transition. The cause of the depression, however, is that a transition, *any* transition, is necessary at all. Don't use this normal reaction on the part of your child to try to restrict the other parent's time. Recognize it as a normal process and deal with it as best you can. Reassure your children that whatever happened between you and the other parent, you both love them very much and want the best for them. Research shows that the better the *parents* deal with transitions, the less likely kids are to be stressed by them. Be matter of fact, timely and courteous, and don't make a big deal of transitions. The more normal you can make the transitions, the less your kids will struggle with them. The more you are able to reassure the other parent that you support the children's relationship with both parents, the less likely they are to feel they have to "buy" their children's affection with activities and toys. Many parents take the stress out of transitions by doing them at a public place. If you're meeting at Denny's or the skate park, it can be turned into a fun event.

As hard as it is, keep your kids' needs first. They can't be with both of you every Christmas. You are going to have some lonely Christmases when you would give anything to be watching them open their presents. You won't be there. On an equal number of Christmases, the other parent will be experiencing the same loss. Do the sensible thing and have two Christmases (or birthdays or Hanukkahs or whatever). Make sure that whatever the timeshare arrangement, to the extent that it is possible, the kids are with Dad on Father's Day and with Mom on Mother's Day. This only makes sense. I know a growing number of kids who have the benefit of joint Christmases and other holidays. Not everyone can pull it off, but if you can, your children will be thrilled. Check out www. bonusfamilies.org for some tips.

Above all, let your children know that it's OK to want to spend time with the other parent and that you don't view it as a betrayal. It's OK to let them know you'll miss them and will be glad when they come back. It's not OK to make them feel guilty for wanting to go. You don't have to say anything to them to communicate how you really feel; kids know when a parent doesn't want them to see the other parent. So don't get all sanctimonious about it and declare, "I've never said a *word* about how I feel to the kids," when you have been conveying it every way you know through pursed lips, rolled eyes, sighs, sarcastic asides or conversations with your friends in their hearing. Please do your kids a favor and let it be safe for them to let you know they love both of their parents and not just you.

Failing all of the above, if you really want to make sure that your kids are going to resent you forever, here are some suggestions:

- Promise your kids some rare treat and then blame the other parent for the fact that it didn't come off. "I was going to take you to the water slide last weekend, but your Mom wouldn't let you go." Or do the reverse, when you know the kids are already committed to go to the other parent's house, let them know that you had this wonderful opportunity to take them someplace special but couldn't because, "The judge says you have to go see your Dad."

- Arrange soccer, summer camp, or some other rigidly scheduled activity for the only time in the summer when the kids can visit the other parent at a distant location.

- Send only ill-fitting, torn and crummy clothes to the other parent's home. Or, if you are the lower-time parent, refuse to return the good clothes and send only the crummy ones back. Or, buy good clothes for the children but insist they leave them at your house and only wear them when they are with you.

- Don't let the children take their favorite toys with them or, if you are the lower-time parent, buy all sorts of great toys and video games for them, but insist that they can only play with them at your house. This may mean that they want to show up at your house more often in the short term because of all the cool stuff you have for them there, but don't flatter yourself: It has nothing to do with *you*.

- Make them leave their special things at your house when they go to the other parent's house. This sends a clear message that their "stuff" isn't safe with the other parent.

- Create a scene at each transfer. Use the opportunity of the children being picked up or dropped off to berate the other parent about the girlfriend, the support check, or some other unrelated issue. This will guarantee that the kids have a real knot in their stomachs long before the transfer takes place.

- Dispose of your kid's pet while he is visiting the other parent (yes, I have actually seen someone do this). He is going to be scared to death to ever go on another visit for fear that his new pet will go down, too. Imagine how he is going to feel when he comes running into the house looking for Snuffles only to find out that Snuffles bit the dust three days ago because you couldn't stand having him around. That's one that will have your kid in therapy till age 45.

- Use every holiday, every birthday party, even the school pageant as an opportunity for a confrontation. Suppose Jake is very proud to be in the school play. How is he going to feel when he is torn between wanting to have both of his parents there to see him perform and knowing that if they do, there is going to be an embarrassing blowup in front of his friends and their parents?

- While the kid is with you, give him a weird haircut that Mom won't let him have, dye his hair blue, let him get a tattoo, or get his ear or eyebrow pierced. You get the idea.

- Prevent them from participating in their favorite activities because it's "your" time. It may be that being on the All Star team or in the soccer playoff or dance recital is the most important thing in your child's life right now. Kids live in the moment and believe the entire universe revolves around what they are doing. If there is a special event scheduled for a week from Saturday, and that happens to be "your" time, the quickest way to alienate your kid is to refuse to give up "your time" and the "family outing" you planned so he can play in the All Star game or participate in some other important event. If you want guaranteed long term resentment, this is a good recipe.

- Then there are all of the obvious things: Don't have the kids ready at the appointed pick up time. Don't show up for the scheduled visit because "I got held up at the office." Cancel at the last minute. Return the kids late. Send your new mate (whom your ex detests) to pick up or drop off the kids. Don't be home at the appointed time when the kids are returned. Some parents are so unable to control themselves at transitions that the court is required to order that the delivering parent wait in the car while the child walks up to the house to be greeted by the other parent. Imagine how little Matt is going to feel walking that no man's land between hostile, warring camps each time a transition to the other house is required.

Parental Alienation

Much has been written about "parental alienation syndrome." Current research has generally discredited alienation as a syndrome. Some children do get turned against one of their parents, but it isn't as simple as it has been portrayed.

Even in intact families, children may well be more attuned to one parent than the other. They may have similar personality styles. If you have an anxious kid, he is more likely to be attuned to the more structured parent than the laid back, disorganized one. That doesn't mean he doesn't love both parents and want to be with them. It just means that he feels more comfortable with the style of one than the other. The fact that your child wants to spend time with the other parent doesn't mean he has been alienated. One very articulate 14 year old child who was asking me to change the joint custody order from a week on/week off schedule to one with a home base with one of his parents said to me, "The other house just feels more like home." This wasn't a criticism of his other parent, but a validation of that child's legitimate feelings.

Sometimes kids align with a parent. They may feel that one parent is being treated unfairly, and become protective. As I discuss in the next chapter, it is a really bad idea to lean on the children for emotional support. Alignment doesn't mean that the child has been alienated, although it does raise questions about whether the aligned parent is setting appropriate boundaries.

Sometimes children reject a parent entirely. This may be the result of alienation, or just his toxic relationship with that parent. I once represented a mother whose eight year old daughter simply refused to go to her father's house. My client had tried everything to get the little girl to visit Dad as scheduled. Each transition was a nightmare with the kid hiding, and then having to be forced into the car. Finally, the case ended up back in court. Dad claimed that the child had been alienated. The family was sent to a first rate custody evaluator who interviewed the child, with and without her father in the room. The child was quite articulate about how her father never listened to her, constantly interrupted and talked over her. When the child and her father met with the evaluator together, Dad did just what she accused him of, ignoring her, talking over her, telling her she didn't mean what she was saying, and essentially devaluing her. The evaluator pointed this out to the father, calling his attention to the fact that even though he knew he was being observed, he was doing exactly what the child complained of. Dad defended his conduct and didn't think there was anything wrong. He was "being a parent." At the hearing, the evaluator testified that the child had not been alienated, and had very mature and well thought out reasons for not wanting to spend time with her father, which reasons were supported by his own clinical observations during the joint sessions. He recommended no contact unless initiated at the child's request. Note that the result would have been different if the child reported that she didn't want to see Daddy because, "He's a bad man for leaving Mommy," or because she knew Mommy would be lonely without her. The child described very specific behavior which demonstrated that the father didn't care about *her* or treat *her concerns* seriously, and that specific behavior was repeated and defended by the father in the presence of the evaluator. The court concluded that any alienation that occurred in that case had been caused by Dad himself.

At the extreme end of the continuum is the parent who will consciously and deliberately embark on a course of alienation designed to turn a child against the other parent. This has absolutely nothing to do with love for or protection of the child. The parent who would consciously do this is *not* motivated by concern for the child. Alienation is the ultimate power and control battle, and despite the protestations of the alienating parent, has absolutely nothing to do with the child's welfare. It is always about the alienating parent's need for exclusive control or revenge against the other parent.

I once refused to accept a case for a prospective client who continually referred to her former husband (the father of her four year old) as "Hitler." When I cautioned her that it was most damaging to a child to hear his father referred to in this way (even at his tender age), she assured me that she *never* used the term in front of the child. Baloney. The word tripped so lightly off her tongue (and she clearly thought it was so clever) that I knew she was lying to me. Hitler was who she thought he was, Hitler was who she told everyone else he was, and that was the message the child received. I am sure the four year old had no idea who Hitler was, but he knew it meant somebody really bad.

An evaluator once told me about interviewing a nine year old girl who referred to her father as a "limp dick." Now really, where do you think a nine year old got that?

Less extreme is the parent who, although not consciously trying to alienate the children, seeks to interfere with and restrict the amount of contact the children have with the other parent. Except in cases where there is a legitimate fear of verbal, physical, or sexual abuse, this is indefensible. There is also a very practical reason not to do it; it tends to backfire. If a child's access to one parent is restricted, two things tend to happen. First, on the limited occasions when the lower-time parent actually has the children, he goes out of his way to make the visit as fun and memorable as possible for them ("Disneyland Dad" and "Marine World Mom"). Because the visits are so infrequent, he wants to make them as special as he can.

This gives the children an unrealistic image of the other parent. They tend to fantasize that life is always fun when they go to see Dad, and Mom is the one who nags them to brush their teeth, stop texting, and do their homework. Frankly, if Mom wanted the kids to get a more realistic picture of who Dad is, she would make sure that he had some tooth brushing and homework time as well. That tends to end the fantasy very quickly. Unfortunately, many parents don't see it this way. They are so afraid that the children will love the other parent more that they can't help consciously or unconsciously conveying the message that the other parent is bad.

Parents usually assume that if their kid resists being with them they are being alienated. If you are in that position, consider the reasons. Is it possible that your child would rather be with his friends than with either of you? Is it possible that you need to learn how to listen better and more effectively? Are you forcing your new mate down the kids' throat when what they really want is more one on one time with you? Have you been spending your custodial time focused on your new step children instead of giving quality time to your own? Have you been involving your child in your continuing battle with the other parent? If you grill Emma on everything that happened in the other house each time she walks in the door, don't be surprised if she prefers not to be subjected to the interrogation and finds excuses not to come. Some parents in this situation turn themselves inside out trying to come up with spectacular treats for visiting time, to bribe the kids to want to come. I think it is important to do everything you can to see that the time together is pleasant. However, if they are only coming over because they want the goodies you have promised them, that doesn't do anything to mend or improve your relationship with them. Concentrate instead on improving your parenting skills, learn to listen to and talk to your kids, develop common interests and activities you can do together, and build the relationship from the ground up.

What if it really is alienation? Fortunately, a good professional will probably spot it easily. Alienated kids have all sorts of reasons why they hate the target parent. However, unlike the eight year old I mentioned, those reasons have *absolutely nothing to do* with their own relationship to the other parent. Their reasons are not age-appropriate, and are usually based on accusations of misconduct of which they cannot possibly have firsthand knowledge. If your kid is refusing to visit the other parent because he's not paying you enough support, or because she left you for someone else, the problem isn't the other parent; it's you.

And if you are so consumed with rage at the other parent that you are tempted to interfere, here's a warning: Alienated children come back. (Check out YourSocialWorker.com and under Divorce Articles, find the article entitled "Keeping a Child From the Other Parent Can Backfire.") You may succeed in the short term. However, there is a fundamental human need to know our origins. When kids get older, they tend to want to track down the missing parent, to see for themselves who that parent is. When they find out that the other parent isn't the uncaring ogre you portrayed, and had been regularly sending cards and presents which you intercepted, guess who they are going to turn on? You. And rightly so.

So, if your spouse wants more time with the kids and abuse is not an issue, the best way to give your child a dose of reality is to let her spend some "real world" time in the other parent's house. Let her stay long enough to acquire a few chores and restrictions there. You may be surprised to find she appreciates you a great deal more when she comes back.

The High Conflict Divorce

This leads us to another topic. Conventional wisdom used to say that divorce was always bad for children, and they were always better off in intact families. Research indicates that this is not necessarily so. We now have some longitudinal studies of children of divorce which have seriously challenged this assumption. A number of talented researchers, notably Constance Ahrons and Mavis Heatherington, have followed children of divorce for decades as they grew, through college, their own relationships and parenting their own children. (See references to their books in Chapter 45, "More Resources.") These studies have reached some interesting conclusions. They find that divorce itself is not the determining factor in whether children will grow up well adjusted or profoundly scarred. Instead, it is how the children *experienced* their parent's divorce. Children of parents who were able to work together to protect the children from conflict, and who were able to cooperatively co-parent, or at least disengage enough not to have a war, do very well indeed. Even children of very conflicted parents *may* do well, *if* the parents are able to successfully shield the children from the conflict. It's the children of high conflict parents who were unable to insulate them from the war who have the greatest difficulty as adults. That means it isn't the divorce itself which is the determining factor, but the amount of conflict to which *the children* are exposed. Interestingly, it doesn't seem to matter *what* the conflict is about. As long as there is high conflict which the children experience, those kids are at risk, regardless of the subject over which the parents are fighting. And it stands to reason: In most high conflict cases, the war is endless. That is, as soon as one issue is resolved, another one pops up and the battle continues. That's because the conflict isn't really about the disagreement *du jour*. It's that the parents simply aren't ready to stop fighting, and if it isn't one thing, they'll find another. Those children are at high risk for emotional problems, both now and later in their own relationships. That alone should be reason enough to refrain from the tactics I'm talking about in this chapter. You're not doing it for your ex. You're doing it for your kids.

Minor's Counsel

Sometimes in a hotly contested custody dispute the court will appoint an independent lawyer to represent the child. If a judge appoints counsel for your child, it is not a compliment. It means the judge does not believe that either parent is representing the best interests of the child. It means the judge believes that the parents are operating on their own agendas and it is necessary to separate and protect the child's interests from those agendas. If a case has deteriorated to the point where a lawyer for the child is necessary, that is a good indicator that one or both parents lack perspective on their kid's needs, are overly invested in the conflict to the detriment of their child, or may even be downright unbalanced. It is not uncommon for the parents in these conflicts to lack boundaries and be unable to see the possibility that their child's needs and their own are not the same. One or both parents are likely to be extremely unhappy with the position minor's counsel is advocating. It stands to reason: if they were being reasonable, even if they didn't agree, the court wouldn't feel that an independent professional was required to protect the child from the advocacy of his own parents.

Minor's counsel is a very specialized corner of family law practice, and the lawyers who accept these appointments often take extensive additional training. In some states, minor's counsel may be called *guardian ad litem* ("guardian for the litigation"). Some courts have funding for minor's counsel, but most order the parents to pay the child's lawyer.

Parents are often confused about the role of minor's counsel. They often think it is the job of minor's counsel to represent the kid's preferences and tell their kid to instruct "his" lawyer to advocate for what he wants. If the child is of sufficient age and maturity to express an opinion, his counsel will want to hear it. But the lawyer's responsibility is to advocate for the child's best interests, not the child's wishes. They are not the same thing and may be wildly divergent if the child has been overinvolved in the dispute between his parents or aligned with one side. If the minor's counsel believes that what the child says he wants is not in his best interests, he will say so.

Access Games, or How to Ensure Your Kids...

A lawyer who is appointed to represent a child does just that: she represents the best interests of the child or children, not the wishes of either parent. She has access to the child's teachers, daycare provider, pediatrician, and anyone else who has information which she believes will help her form an opinion as to what is in the child's best interests. She may meet with each parent or with the parent's lawyers.

It takes a very special breed of custody lawyer to serve as minor's counsel. In addition to having a keen desire to protect children, he must be well versed in custody litigation as well as the stages of child development, a broad range of custodial arrangements, and must be able to take the heat.

It also takes great fortitude and considerable skill to serve as minor's counsel. By definition, they are stepping into the middle of what is already an ugly fight. They know that at least one and probably both parents will be difficult to deal with, and even their own client may be hostile. It is a thankless job on many levels and the people who do this work are truly dedicated to protecting kids, even from their own parents if necessary.

The judge is going to give great weight to the recommendations of minor's counsel.

So, if the court appoints independent counsel for your child, you need to be clear on what her role is. Don't call her and demand she do what you tell her because you are paying her. She won't. She doesn't represent you. It doesn't help your case if you call and berate her, write her nasty letters and emails, or otherwise pressure her to adopt your world view. Don't instruct your kid (her client) to give her orders. Instead, this is the time for you to be courteous, thoughtful, and reasonable as you discuss your child's needs with her. This is your chance to show her that, though the case is one of high conflict, you are truly looking out for your kid. Paying her to listen while you berate and vilify the other parent is a waste of her time and your money. Instead, check out the suggestions in Chapter 20 about preparing for a custody evaluation, think through your reasons why you believe your proposal is the best *for your child* and be prepared to back that up with child-centered reasons.

The bottom line is that if the court is going to give your kid's lawyer's recommendations considerable weight, you want to impress her with how you are putting your own kid's interests first.

CHAPTER 19

Leaning On the Kids

VERY FEW DIVORCING parents would consciously and deliberately add to their children's pain. However, all too often parents turn to their kids for emotional support. This may start as a perfectly innocent way of reassuring the kids by saying, "We're all in this together." Even though one person has left the family circle, the rest of us are all interdependent and care about each other. It can unfortunately segue into the children being used as emotional and psychological props. These patterns are no less damaging because they are unconscious.

As with so many other issues raised in this book, this is one to be discussed with your therapist. My goal is simply to alert you to the danger and highlight the extreme and unfair burden it places on your children.

Whether it begins as circling the wagons in a time of mutual trauma and stress or for some other reason, don't get into a situation where your kids are taking care of you, either emotionally or physically. They have enough to deal with simply getting through the process and their own developmental stages themselves, and it is *your* responsibility to be the grownup.

You should not be discussing the divorce with your children and certainly should not be placing them in a position of choosing sides. I have had this discussion with many clients. I usually get a wide-eyed protest, "Do you expect me to *lie* to my children?" In a manner of speaking, yes. If you consider it a lie to refrain from telling the children what an unregenerate jerk you think the other parent is, then lie. I would prefer that you simply tell them the part of the truth that is healthy for them to hear; that is, that you love them, that the other parent loves them, and this has nothing to do with them, it is between Mom and Dad. That is not a lie. If you perceive that you are lying to them if you do not share the intimate details of why and how much you loathe the other parent, so be it. I call it being a mature individual and a responsible parent.

As the adult, it is your responsibility to determine how much of the truth they are ready to hear. Depending on the age and maturity of your child, you can "dose" the truth. This means you should be guided by what the child wants to know (rather than what you want to tell him). This in turn is determined by the child's interest and curiosity. If the child asks a question, answer it in a general and age-appropriate way. The key here is to reassure the child that the grownups are in charge and taking care of things. They don't need to know how the grownups are doing it. They just want to know they are still safe. Chapter 45 on "More Resources" has some good information on how to talk to your children about divorce, as well as books and handbooks written for children of various ages.

I don't care of your kid is 17½ and is practically grown up herself. Don't lean on her. A kid who becomes your caretaker during this trauma will be paying a high psychological price for years to come.

It won't help *you*, either. You will be substituting a dysfunctional parent/child relationship for a dysfunctional marital one, which is hardly the optimum way to promote your own journey toward emotional health.

Don't by word or implication indicate to your children that they need to "stay home and take care of Mommy." I once had a case where the mother was so needy that she kept her elementary school age children home from school on days she felt particularly depressed and would actually write in the school excuse that she needed them today for emotional support. You can imagine what I did with that when I subpoenaed those notes to use in the custody trial.

Finally, if your child asks you questions you don't feel you should answer, don't ever be afraid to say, "That is private and I would rather not talk about it." Children understand privacy, and expect it themselves. It is much safer to err on the side of circumspection than to risk the psychological damage which inevitably results from the over involvement of the children in their parents' conflict.

CHAPTER 20

Custody Mediation and Evaluation

MOST COURTS WILL require that you attend custody mediation of some kind before proceeding with a formal hearing on custody. There are several good reasons for this. Many parents can come to an agreement with the help of a trained mediator. If that happens, there is no need for a trial, and that court time can be used for other parents who can't work it out themselves and need a judge to set the rules. In some jurisdictions, mediation serves a dual purpose. Mediation can either be confidential or recommending. If it is confidential in your court, that means that nothing which is said in mediation can be used in court. In other courts, the mediator can recommend an appropriate custody and access order, even if the parents don't reach an agreement.

Some mediators are affiliated with the courts. They are funded publicly, although there may or may not be a charge for mediation services. You may also have the option of hiring a private mediator. This will probably cost more than the public mediator, but you will have greater control over the amount of time you get and the qualifications of the mediator. As with mediation of property and other issues, you cannot unilaterally select a private mediator, (and you have no choice when it comes to a mediator provided by the court). The decision on a private mediator must be a joint one and both parents must agree. Also, don't start calling mediators to interview them before agreeing to their appointment. If you do, they may no longer be neutral, and may be unable to take your case as a result.

Even after divorce, many parents agree that before either of them can bring a dispute involving the kids to court, they will be required to enter into good faith mediation to try to resolve it there first. Agreements which the parents work out themselves, with or without a mediator, tend to work better than orders which are imposed over objection. They can be tailored to the specific (and changing) needs of your family and your kids. Both parents participate in reaching the agreement, so they are both invested in making it work, and are more likely to perform on their commitments. Research shows that people are more likely to abide by an order they participated in reaching than one imposed by the court.

If you are going into mediation, discuss the process with your attorney. Ask about court based mediators and private ones. Who would be best for your kind of case? What can you expect it to cost? Who would your attorney recommend? Find out whether mediation is confidential or recommending in your jurisdiction. You may feel comfortable being much more frank in mediation if you know that what you say can't be repeated or used against you in court. If you are in a recommending jurisdiction, you will want to pay particular attention to the suggestions of the mediator. Since he is going to repeat them to the court, which will likely give them considerable weight, this is important information for you to have.

In mediation, you and your spouse work out the custody and access arrangement which will be implemented for your family. By definition, mediation involves compromise, so don't go into the process drawing lines in the sand and insisting it be your way or the highway. It is helpful to get rid of preconceptions before starting mediation. Among them are:

- Mothers always get sole custody unless they are unfit, and always get custody of young children.
- Fathers who don't get a full 50% custody either wussed out or were the victims of gender bias.
- The kids should be able to decide where they want to live.

After you've eliminated these, and any other preconceived ideas of how it "should" be, start thinking about what your kids (not you) need. Think about their personalities. What makes them feel secure? Remember, there may be different answers for different kids in the same family. What kinds of needs must be accommodated? What scheduling problems will need to be addressed? What are your strengths as a parent? Your spouse's? (Yes, really). What are the realistic work and other commitments of each parent? How will these impact the timeshare with the kids? Are there ways in which you can build flexibility into the schedule? A trained mediator will have lots of experience helping parents work out answers to these questions, but can't do so as effectively if you haven't done your homework and thought about it in advance. *Then* discuss it with your mediator.

As with custody evaluation, make a list of all of the considerations you think the schedule will have to address, so you can build in as many as possible. This is a much more effective use of your time than making a list of all the "evidence" that your spouse is a jerk and you're a long-suffering saint. Mediation isn't about proving someone right or wrong; it is about working out a solution to a common problem that everyone can live with. And that's the operative term. You may not love it, but can you (and especially your kids) live with it? An agreement between the parents which solves as many problems as possible, which is focused on the kids' needs and not the parents,' and which the parents can live with, is *always* better than an arbitrary schedule imposed by a judge after a few minutes of court time. The video "Who do those judges think they are?" at UpToParents.org is a good reality check on this.

Prepare for your mediation as thoroughly as you would prepare for court. If you do, you stand a much better chance of staying out of court altogether. And remember, the biggest indicator of future trouble for kids is the level of conflict between their parents to which they are exposed. By working out your own solutions and staying out of court, you are taking a big step in the direction of putting your kids on the path toward healthy adulthood.

Custody Evaluation

Sometimes you just can't work out an acceptable schedule in mediation. That means that a judge will have to decide. Of course, the judge will need evidence on which to base that determination. This may well mean that a professional custody evaluator is assigned to your case. As with mediation, this may be done as part of a court-based service, or you may jointly agree to a private custody evaluator.

If you have gotten as far as having a custody dispute assigned to an evaluator, there are a number of things which you can expect.

First, a private evaluator will generally (but not always) have more time to spend with you, your spouse, and your kids than an evaluator provided by the court. Some courts have wonderful family court services or similar adjuncts available free or for a nominal charge. Others can do only a very limited intervention, and some are downright dreadful. Some are so overworked that the evaluation process doesn't start for six to eight months after your separation. Frankly, an "evaluation" which doesn't even begin until the parties have been living in separate households for months is not of much use. Patterns have already been established and may be hard to change. You may not be able to afford a private evaluator, and as a result have little choice. However, if you can, and your court evaluators are heavily backed up and understaffed, I suggest that you seriously consider a private evaluator.

Who should you select? First, you should probably defer to your attorney on this. Your attorney will (or should) know who the good evaluators are and be able to give you reasons based on professional experience. The individual should have a thorough grounding in child developmental psychology. Most are psychologists, but many superb evaluators are trained in social work (usually with at least a master's degree) or as marriage, family and child counselors. I would suggest that you not be overly concerned with the letters after an individual's name. The level of experience and the respect which their opinions are afforded by the local courts are infinitely more important.

How to Avoid the Divorce from Hell

If your case is going to require psychological testing, that will have to be done by a qualified psychologist. It can be accomplished either by the evaluator doing the testing himself (if he is qualified), or by appointing a separate psychologist to conduct the tests and report the results to the evaluator. I have found either approach to work perfectly well. If psychological tests are administered, both parents are tested. Therefore, if you go into your evaluation insisting that the other parent has narcissistic personality disorder and therefore must be psychologically tested, prepare to be tested yourself and to deal with the results of your own testing, which may not be what you expect. Psychological testing is incredibly invasive and before you insist on it you may want to "be careful what you wish for."

If tests are administered, they will probably be standardized tests such as the MMPI (Minnesota Multiphasic Personality Inventory), Rorschach, etc. Some evaluators routinely test the parents in every evaluation. Others believe testing is unduly intrusive in an average custody dispute, and should only be done when one or the other of the parties exhibits some indicia of mental illness. I have a personal bias against wholesale testing in garden variety custody disputes. In the first place, the tests used were not created or normed to highlight the issues raised in custody disputes. I also don't think the information added to a competent clinician's observations justifies the level of intrusiveness, but it is always the evaluator's judgment call.

It doesn't make one whit of difference whether your evaluator is a man or a woman. Many of you will assume that a woman would tend to favor Mom and a man would tend to favor Dad. That has not been my experience. As with lawyers, it is most important to have the best possible person for your case, and I couldn't care less about the gender of the evaluator. I would, on the other hand, be interested in any demonstrated biases. I would reject an evaluator (as well as a judge) who was in the midst of a hotly contested custody fight himself. At the same time, I wouldn't arbitrarily reject someone because of a stated bias. For example, a very fine custody evaluator of my acquaintance is quite up front about the fact that he prefers joint physical custody and that is his starting point. Now mind you, joint custody doesn't necessarily mean 50/50, but instead means that the children have frequent and continuing contact with both parents. Nevertheless, the same evaluator has on more than one occasion recommended not only sole custody to one parent, but limited or supervised contact with the other, simply because the facts of the case were egregious and too much exposure to the other parent would be seriously damaging to the child. Therefore, I know that although he starts an evaluation with the assumption (and hope) that joint custody will work, I also know that he will make the hard decision if it is in the best interests of the child.

An additional consideration is whether your attorney has worked with the proposed evaluator before. This does not mean that someone she has worked with will favor her over opposing counsel. However, your attorney will generally have familiarity with the evaluator's work, know how she likes to conduct her evaluations and can therefore do a better job of preparing you. Remember, the key is to get as much relevant information as possible in the evaluator's hands. There are any number of evaluators to whom I regularly refer who have recommended against other clients of mine in the past. I am more interested in the reasons for his recommendation than whether he rolled over as soon as he realized I was in the case. If he'd roll over for me, he'd roll over for someone else as well. Some evaluators can be intimidated by lawyers. I would reject them out of hand. I know an evaluator who can be counted on to agree with the last person he talked to. No referrals from me there. Likewise, evaluators who routinely try to cut the baby in half so as to keep everybody "happy" (and as a result nobody is happy, least of all the kids) are equally unlikely to get referrals from me. Your attorney will know which is which and can make a recommendation. I've said elsewhere that not all attorneys are comfortable with custody work. This is another reason to make sure that the attorney you select does a lot of custody work if you expect that to be an issue. A lawyer who specializes in valuing and dividing family businesses may not have the experience to make a good custody evaluator recommendation.

Each evaluator is going to have his or her own style and preferred procedure. Some will want to start by meeting jointly with you and your spouse. Sometimes this is because they don't want either of you to feel that the other one obtained an advantage by meeting with him first. Certainly, I would expect that any evaluator is going to want to see you and your spouse jointly at some point during the evaluation. Frankly, the interaction between the two of you when you are in the same room is going to be very different from your interaction with the evaluator when you meet individually. Since the joint interaction is what the kids are most likely to experience, and so many people go through major personality changes when they get in the same room with their ex, this interaction is valuable information for the evaluator to observe.

The evaluator will generally want to meet with each of you individually at least once and sometimes a series of times. Depending on the ages of the children, he may want to meet with the children individually with each parent to see how the children interact with each of you. He may do a home visit to each household and may want to talk to day care providers and teachers. It generally is not helpful to give the evaluator a long list of your friends (a judge I know calls them "Friends of the Bride and Friends of the Groom") to attest to what a saint you are and what a jerk your spouse is.

Your attorney can tell you about the style of the evaluator who has been appointed for your case. Here are some general rules, however, which you would do well to consider:

- Experienced custody evaluators can smell a programmed kid a mile away.

These people have seen everything and if you think that you are going to score points by programming Jenny to say what you want her to say, think again. There are ways in which kids talk and there are ways in which adults talk, and it is very difficult for a programmed kid to come across as natural. If your child tells the evaluator that Daddy isn't paying his support, or had an affair, or is narcissistic, it isn't going to go well for the Mom doing the programming. This is information which shouldn't be shared with children.

- Evaluators are not going to ask your child to choose between her parents.

Doing so puts a tremendous burden on children and is considered therapeutically unsound. Instead, the evaluator will be much more interested in the substance of your relationship with the kids than with whom the kids would prefer to live. For example, if your child spontaneously expresses a desire to live with Dad, they are going to want to know why. If the reason is that the kid feels more comfortable with Dad because he feels Dad really listens to him, that points to a different result than if it is because Dad doesn't believe in curfews, or Dad has promised him some treat if he gets custody. Evaluators are much more inclined to want to know to whom the kid turns in a crisis and why. They want to know what activities he does at your house and with the other parent. If one parent tends to park the children with a sitter or in front of a video game or YouTube, whereas the other one actually spends time talking with them, helping them with their homework, doing activities together and the like, that is going to leave a much more favorable impression. They may ask the kid who is more likely to help with the homework. If one parent sets all the boundaries and the other lets them run rampant, this will factor into the evaluation. The evaluator will want to know what you do when your kids are with you. And if you took the kid to the park or the aquarium for the first time in eight years the weekend before your first meeting with the evaluator, don't think that isolated instance will make your case for custody after years of indifference. The evaluator is looking for patterns.

- The evaluator may or may not want to know why the marriage broke up.

If it is relevant to the kids, they may want to explore it. However, if it is clear that your agenda is to prove how unfit your spouse is because he elects to be unfit with someone else rather than with you, that isn't likely to score you many points. You will undoubtedly have a great deal of information you want to convey. Make sure that it is relevant to the kids and their needs and not simply venting about how you've been wronged.

- Focus on the kids.

If you appear at the custody evaluator's office with an entire case prepared against your spouse, demonstrating by chapter and verse what an unregenerate disgrace to the human race he is, you are unlikely to get the result you want. If, instead, you can illustrate through concrete examples how his indifference to the children's needs has caused ongoing harm or distress *to them*, you will be more likely to make your point. What matters to the evaluator are the children's attachments. A chronicle of your spouse's wrongs against you will at best waste the evaluator's valuable time on extraneous matters, leaving you less time to convey the information which truly is important. At worst, it will convince the evaluator that you really aren't that interested in the kids, and are fighting custody to keep the battle with your spouse alive. It may well signal the evaluator to look for signs of alienation.

- The evaluator needs to see who you are.

You are not being judged as an individual. What is being evaluated is how you interact with the children and the kids' needs and attachments. You are who you are. If you don't think who you are is going to play well with the evaluator, this isn't the time to invent a whole new persona and try to convince the evaluator and the judge that it's real. It won't ring true. Instead, work on changing who you are into the parent you would like to be. There are lots of free parenting courses online and through community organizations. You and your kids will benefit.

- When you go into a custody evaluation, prepare for it as carefully as you would for a trial. That's exactly what it is.

It is infinitely more difficult to get around an unfavorable evaluation because you didn't get the proper information to the evaluator than it is to do it right the first time. Many clients have consulted me over the years for a second opinion on a "bad" evaluation. More often than not, they come in with a long list of information which "proves" the evaluator was wrong. When I ask them if they gave this information to the evaluator, they usually say no, because they didn't know it was going to be important until they saw the final report. They often didn't present the information to the evaluator in the first place because they were too busy castigating the other parent, or buried it in so much venom that they lacked credibility and the evaluator blew it off. Do yourself, your kids, and the evaluator a favor. Spend some time and thought on your children's attachments, their needs, and the ideal time sharing plan including child-centered reasons *before* you meet with the evaluator. Don't just wing it, assuming that of course you know what is right for your kids because, after all, you're the parent. Think about it. Consider what would be best for your children and be prepared to explain your reasons. Your thoughtful reasoning will pay off. The evaluator will thank you, and your children will thank you.

Here are some questions to ask yourself as you prepare for an evaluation:

- What are my children's individual needs?
- How do Caitlin's needs differ from Jake's? What comforts each of them and keeps them grounded and feeling safe?
- What are the significant developmental issues in each child's life right now? Their most important activities?

- What are the critical components the timeshare arrangement must include for each of the children? Why? What is the ideal arrangement for these particular kids? Why?
- What does your spouse contribute to the children's needs?
- What important needs of the children are left unmet by the arrangement proposed by your spouse? Why? Why does your proposal work better *for the kids*? (Not you.)
- How do you anticipate the kids' needs changing over time? How would you propose to adjust the arrangement to address those changing needs?
- Be prepared to remain child-focused at all times. A custody evaluator told me of an evaluation she had conducted. The father, a high powered business attorney, was insisting on 50/50 custody. He didn't know the names of the children's teachers, their best friends, or favorite videos and books, had never attended a parent-teacher conference or a trip to the pediatrician. To top it off, during the 90 minute joint appointment with his children and the evaluator, he kept taking business calls on his cell phone. The evaluator asked him how he was going to give the kids his attention for 50% of their lives when he couldn't even give it to them for the 90 minutes during which she was interviewing him with the children (at a time when he knew he was being judged on his attentiveness and attunement to the kids, no less). He got huffy and accused her of being biased against dads.

When all else is done, remember one thing: If you believe in your heart of hearts that you are a *slightly* better parent than the other and it looks as though a custody fight is ensuing, consider carefully whether it would be in your children's best interests to leave them with the other parent, subject to liberal access, rather than to make them a battlefield for the war between their parents. The children are going to be uncertain enough during your divorce. They don't need the additional apprehension of not knowing from day to day with whom they will live, where they will go to school and how often they can see their friends or the other parent. When I see a parent who will walk away from a custody fight for the good of the kids, while ensuring him or herself a lasting place in the kids' life and development, I know I've got a good parent as my client.

CHAPTER 21

Blended Families

IN THESE DAYS of serial monogamy, the issue which arise in blended families is one which is inspiring countless graduate theses and keeping thousands of therapists in business. The therapeutic issues are far beyond the scope of this book. It is, however, important to address the practicalities.

The typical scenario goes like this: A couple is divorced. (H-1 and W-1). They have three children (C-1, C-2 and C-3) of whom they have joint custody. After the divorce, each remarries (H-1 marries W-2 and W-1 marries H-2). Perhaps W-2 and H-2 each have children (C-A and C-B go with W-2; C-X, C-Y and C-Z go with H-2). Sounds complicated, doesn't it? Then consider the fact that H-2 and W-2 each have former spouses who also need time with the kids and may also have blended families. Now try to arrange a timeshare schedule that works for everyone.

If you think arranging timeshare between W-1 and H-1 creates problems, you have no idea what the foregoing, quite common scenario presents in the way of complications. Is it better for each family to have weekends off while we coordinate the timeshare weekends (i.e., everybody is together at the same house on the same weekend and everybody is away on the same weekend)? Or is it better to have each set of children have their own "quality time" with their own parent, that is, without stepsiblings? If so, when do the parents get a break? What do you do with school vacations? You obviously have to start coordinating summer vacations in about February and what the hell do you do about the holidays? How do you ensure that you alternate each kid's birthday and what about Mother's and Father's Days? Unless both parties and the other two ex-spouses are all extraordinarily adult, cooperative and sensitive, you are going to have problems. Conflicting soccer games are going to be hell and heaven help you at graduation. Fortunately, there are tools to help you do it, including computer programs and web-based services such as Cofamilies.com and OurFamilyWizard.com, which can manage these complicated schedules.

The reality is you have chosen a new mate and that mate comes with baggage, a former spouse, some children, and a whole lot of history. The fact that you love him is part of the package, but it may not always be easy.

You may find that your little stepdarlings refuse to eat at your house because you don't make their favorite dishes the same way Mommy does. They may blame you for the breakup of their family. Then there are conflicts between the stepchildren in each family. All these possibilities come with the territory. There are therapists who build their entire practices around the issues of blended families. If you recognize your situation here, you might want to search one of them out.

In this situation, you will be well advised to practice patience, flexibility and compromise; rigidity simply won't work.

Coordination of schedules is only one of the problems facing blended families. Discipline is one of the biggest stumbling blocks. How does he feel about your disciplining his kid? What is going to happen the first time the kid says, "I don't have to do what you say; *you're* not my mother." Is your mate going to back you up or throw you under the bus? It's better to work this out between the adults before you get into a confrontation in front of the children. One way to do this is for the parent and new spouse to have a session or two with a co-parenting counselor to work out the kinks before they have to respond to a crisis in the moment.

Anyone who deals consistently with blended families will tell you that there is no single right answer. However, it is critical that you and your new mate talk honestly about how you are going to handle these issues and reach agreement with respect to each of your children. If either of you is perceived to show favoritism to your own children over the other's, be prepared for problems in the relationship. If neither of you can be flexible, you are in for lots of conflict.

Fortunately, much work has been done on this subject since the last edition of this book. Numerous resources are listed in Chapter 45 on "More Resources." One of the best is Ex-Etiquette for Parents, a wonderful book written by two women who are the current and former wives of the same man. Although things started our rocky for them, they worked it out, and then wrote it for others, so that they could share their considerable experience, tact and wisdom. Check it out, and take their advice very seriously. It is golden. You can find them online at bonusfamilies. org

PART IV

Support and Maintenance

CHAPTER 22

Support, or "Which Bills Shall I Pay This Month?"

A SIGN USED to be prominently displayed in one of our local family courts. It read:

NOTICE TO LITIGANTS: INSOLUBLE FINANCIAL PROBLEMS CANNOT BE RESOLVED BY THE COURT

Unless you and your spouse are both fortunate enough to be highly paid professionals, support is likely to be an important issue in your divorce. If you have children, support is guaranteed to be significant.

There is more awful truth about support than just about any other area of divorce. Start with the economic reality that there is almost never enough money to go around in the first place. Most intact families need two incomes just to make ends meet. Then the pie is split in two, dividing the available funds between two households. Add to that governmental tinkering with mandatory guidelines and the inevitable emotional overlays attendant to spousal support ("alimony"), and there is more than enough ugly truth for just about everyone's taste.

Payors and recipients of support will never see eye-to-eye on these issues. I use the gender-neutral terms of "payor" and "recipient" advisedly. We are more frequently seeing fathers as custodial parents and high-income mothers who pay not only child but spousal support to their former mates. This so-called role reversal brings up all sorts of biases and stereotypes:

How to Avoid the Divorce from Hell

Incredulous successful woman client, after being told how much spousal support she'll have to pay: "You mean I'll have to pay alimony to *him*?!" Yes, indeed, dear. I guess you overlooked this possibility when you were fighting for equal career opportunities and breaking through the glass ceiling. It goes with the territory of success. Speaking for myself, the trade off was well worth it.

I have had more clients go into shock over support than any other issue in divorce. Not only are the issues financially difficult and legally complicated, but they hit you right where you live. A support order can literally determine whether or not either party can live with dignity.

So, let's get started. Here are some of the truths that everyone needs to consider:

If there wasn't enough money for a single household, it's not going to be pretty when you try to stretch it over two.

In good times, American consumers quite consistently live beyond their means. Most middle-class couples routinely spend every nickel they make and then some. With the poor, of course, it isn't a choice; there *never was* enough money, so it's not surprising that they face even worse poverty at divorce. In recessionary times, everyone suffers when what was one household with a single set of expenses becomes two. Even high income families are not immune. A huge number of high income professionals carry thousands of dollars in consumer debt with no immediate ability or plan to pay it. For them, divorce sometimes means bankruptcy, despite their incomes.

If you're the average, middle-class family, you and your spouse have between you a house, two cars, a pension and some miscellaneous furniture. You may have an IRA or two, probably some bank credit cards, several store credit cards and a home-improvement loan. You are barely managing the minimum payments on the consumer debt and have little ability to reduce the principal. You probably have to scramble twice a year when your property taxes are due. When the kids need orthodontia, it's a real shock, and you haven't even begun to think about how you are going to pay for college.

Support, or "Which Bills Shall I Pay This Month?"

Then you separate. When you try to support two households on the same income and no longer have the economy of scale of a single mortgage, single light bill, telephone bill, etc., there will not be enough money to go around. Something is going to give. The first to go are entertainment and vacations. Then the property taxes will go unpaid and, well, you see where I'm headed. At this point, your attorney may be suggesting you consider selling the house or filing for bankruptcy to eliminate the debt burden. And even bankruptcy may not be an option with current restrictions on the discharge of credit card debt or a house that is under water.

The most important information for either a payor or a recipient of support to have at the beginning of a divorce is precise data regarding their cost of living. Your attorney will probably give you a questionnaire to complete, listing all your living expenses. She may caution you that most people substantially underestimate these expenditures. Accordingly, you should review a full year (or two) of check records and bills in order to obtain an accurate figure. Don't forget the credit card bills, because a large component of clothing and entertainment is frequently buried in these, as well as in Christmas and other gifts. If you can, compile this data *before* you consult an attorney. If you're within average norms, you will probably be shocked at how much you really spend.

Your attorney will then tell you about the support guidelines in effect in your state and most likely will run a computer program that projects a support figure based on your family income. This is going to be your second shock. If you are the recipient, you are going to say, "But I can't live on that . . ." This is true; your bills are in fact higher than the guideline support you can expect to receive. It is also quite irrelevant.

As a recipient, you need to know that the court is not going to simply add up your bills, arrive at a grand total, add a component for income tax, and tell your spouse to pay it. Unless you happen to be one of the very few super-rich, there will not be sufficient funds to pay the sum total of your bills and allow your spouse a reasonable standard of living as well.

How to Avoid the Divorce from Hell

As a payor, you are not going to have a clue how you will live on what is left over, at least in the short term. (Lose 10 points if you say, "Then *I'll* take the kids; I can raise them more cheaply.")

You need to know that courts have little discretion over child support, though there may be more latitude where spousal support or alimony is involved. Whatever the mechanism by which the support is set, several things are likely to happen. First, the support may well be paid by wage assignment. If so, an earnings withholding order will be sent directly to your employer with instructions to cut a check to your spouse each time they pay you. Don't get all embarrassed. Wage assignments used to mean that you probably had defaulted in your support in the past and there was a "Deadbeat Dad" connotation. That isn't the case anymore. In fact, many states make wage assignments mandatory. Employers hate it, but the legislature isn't going to lose much sleep over them. After all, the enforcement of support orders, especially child support orders, is strongly favored by public policy. If you don't pay your court-ordered support, enforcement procedures are becoming ever more draconian. Tax intercept programs are proliferating, whereby a lien is imposed on your income tax refund, thereby "intercepting" the money and applying it to the support arrearage before you ever see it.

Many states now have licensing penalties as well. For example, if your work requires that you be licensed and that license must be periodically renewed, a notice of arrearage can be filed with the licensing board which will prevent renewal of your license until the back support is paid. This can also apply to driver's licenses. I'm not sure I understand the logic behind this one. The presumption seems to be that the money to pay the arrearages does in fact exist, and all we have to do is turn the thumbscrews enough and it will be produced. While that may be true in some cases, sometimes the money just isn't there, and this tactic isn't going to create it out of thin air. It obviously puts pressure on payors to raise the funds in the interim, but if they can't, where's the sense in putting them out of work, guaranteeing they can't pay the next installment, either? This is about as practical as throwing them in jail for nonpayment. Unless you're using jail to send a message, or as a deterrent to defaulting on support, contempt really serves no useful purpose. If the payor is sitting in jail, he is not making money which can then be used to satisfy the support arrearages.

Years ago I had a client who was screaming at me to throw her husband in jail because he was paying most (but all) of the child support for her seven or eight children. The husband was a wage earner who clearly was trying to spread the money too thinly. I explained how jail wasn't a useful collection process since he wouldn't have any money coming in if we were successful in having him held in contempt, but she was adamant. When I won the contempt action she insisted on, he was jailed, and of course missed the next support payment because he didn't get paid for the time he didn't work. I received an irate phone call from the same client, screaming that she hadn't been paid and demanding that I *do something about it!* Presumably she got the revenge she wanted by humiliating him, but it did her no good in the long run. It certainly didn't get her light bill paid.

On the other hand, you might argue, "They can't get blood out of a turnip." True, they can't. But they can make sure the turnip doesn't have much of a life. Technology has made enforcement procedures much more effective, and there is huge federal pressure on the states to collect unpaid child support. States with poor track records may actually lose federal funding, a fact which makes them very creative indeed. Also, unpaid support accrues interest in most states. While some states use market rates as the legal rate, others charge a different "legal interest" rate, that is, the interest on legal judgments. Don't assume they are the same. In California, the market rate may be 3%, but the legal rate is fixed by law at 10%. Yikes.

Truth: Support is likely to leave everyone unhappy. Accept that fact and try to reach a compromise both of you can live with, however uncomfortably.

CHAPTER 23

Support Guidelines

WHEN YOU FIRST consult an attorney, you will probably be told that mandatory guidelines for child support are now being imposed on the states as a condition of receiving federal funds. The actual guidelines vary dramatically from state to state. Although a few states have caps on child support regardless of the payor's income, the more common situation is that the formulas applied are steadily taking a larger and larger percentage of the payor's income, making for very unhappy payors.

The goal behind guidelines was to standardize support so that couples in similar financial circumstances received comparable support orders. Guidelines have generally achieved that goal, albeit at the expense of the judge's discretion to tailor an order to the specific needs of an individual family. If you are the recipient of support, your award is going to be very similar to the one received by anyone else who has the same incomes as you and your spouse. It may be totally unfair if you have significantly higher fixed expenses than the norm, but the award may not take that into consideration. So be it. That is the price paid by individuals for overall consistency in support orders.

The final support figure is likely to be based upon a computer program. You would be well advised to learn as much as you can about whatever guidelines or computer programs are used in your jurisdiction. Each of them varies because they are based on different tax, input, and even cultural assumptions.

The underlying philosophy varies radically from state to state, and this issue is very much in flux as new federal mandates are being implemented. If you have the choice of filing for divorce in one of two or more states, you might want to research the variations between them before deciding where to file.

There are, however, certain common denominators. Guidelines are generally driven by taxes and income. The computer will want to know how many children you have, with whom they primarily reside, and (usually) the incomes of both parents. It may then want to know about those expenses that are tax-related, such as home mortgage interest. Some guidelines consider after-tax consequences of the payment or receipt of support, and others don't. They may or may not be interested in the percent of time the children spend with each parent, or how much the parent with primary custody earns. They may want to know how many other children the payor is responsible for supporting. Generally, the computer will *not* make allowances for non-tax-related expenses such as utilities or consumer debt. This is an area where you have to ask your lawyer exactly how the guidelines work in your state because the variations from state to state make a huge difference. For example, some states don't even consider the custodial parent's income. This can be totally unfair when the primary parent is a highly paid executive and the lesser time parent is a wage earner.

The computer will then apply the local guidelines and spit out a combination of child and spousal support or, occasionally "family support," which lumps them both together for tax purposes. In some states, the result will be mandatory with limited exceptions; in others, only the child support component will be mandatory. Some jurisdictions don't even have alimony guidelines. Some states put a cap on support in high income cases. A few put a cap on child support regardless of how much money the payor has.

There is an interesting twist in the relationship between tax and support in some of the computer programs. If you run the program without regard to your mortgage interest payment, you will get one amount for support. If you then remember that you actually have to pay $1,500 per month of tax-deductible mortgage interest and plug it in under the recipient's column, the support will go down. *"What?"* you shriek. *"I just added a bill that I have to pay and my support goes down?"* Precisely. This is because the mortgage interest is deductible on your tax return, and therefore the computer will say you don't need as much money because you'll be deducting the mortgage interest and as a result you will pay less in income taxes at the end of the year. The reverse is true if you are the payor of support. If you run the program once without your mortgage interest and again with it, your support figure will increase, because the computer calculates the tax benefit of the deduction and decides you will have more money left over after taxes to pay support. *"But how do I pay my mortgage between now and next April 15?"* you ask. The computer sits there silently blinking at you.

After going through this drill with the prospective recipient of support, we begin the following exercise: First, my client will tell me, *"But I can't live on that."* This is, of course, an obviously true statement. They can't live on it if they continue their current spending patterns. I then point out how much is left for the payor and ask how a second household can be sustained on the remainder. One of two things happens at this point. Either I can tell by the stricken look on my client's face that the message has gotten through, or she laments, *"But it's not fair . . ."* We're talking reality here, not fairness.

There's a popular myth that pops up all the time. My client will ask, *"But there are four of us and only one of him, so shouldn't we get four-fifths of the income and he gets one-fifth?"* Nice try. The answer is no, since in the average middle-class family, the one-fifth left over would leave the payor living in his car (if he still could afford one). Also, though some payors may not believe it, the court really does want to leave them with an incentive to go to work.

When the intact family was barely getting by on the available income, the standard of living in both separated households is likely to slip, at least initially, while the finances are being sorted out.

If you are fortunate enough to be at the very early stages of planning for a divorce, I strongly suggest that you minimize the nasty shocks of your first visit to your attorney by doing the following:

- Become intimately familiar with your family's cost of living and know precisely where the money comes from and where it goes.
- Identify all the assets and debts, including current balances for each. Find out which debts are secured and unsecured and what other resources, such as CDs, savings accounts and IRAs might be utilized to liquidate the debt.
- To the extent you can, get your financial house in order before you split the sheet. If you're not worrying about how to pay the consumer debt, you will be much more likely to keep food on the table and a roof over each set of heads.

Questions to ask your lawyer

After having done your homework, consult with your lawyer. Since support philosophies vary so widely from state to state, I cannot predict what is likely to happen in your case. I can, however, suggest some questions to ask your lawyer:

- Does your state have a support guideline? (They all should by now.)
- Are the guidelines mandatory or discretionary? If discretionary, what factors in your case could cause the support to deviate from the guideline?
- If the guideline amount is mandatory, are there hardship or other mitigating factors which might allow an order which deviates from the standard? If so, what are they? Do they apply in your case?
- Does your state award spousal support or alimony?
- Is that part of the guideline calculation?
- What are the factors which are used to calculate the guideline support? Do the courts consider income only, or are your expenses relevant? If so, which ones? What information does your lawyer need from you in order to accurately predict the guideline calculation?

- Does the guideline consider the recipient's income, or only the payor's?
- How do the guidelines treat children of prior or subsequent relationships? Are they considered at all?
- Are the spousal support guidelines treated the same as child support?
- Do the guidelines consider the income of the payor's new mate? The recipient's? If so, is all of the income considered, or only part of it? How do they treat the expenses of the stepchildren? Children of the new marriage?
- How do the guidelines treat seasonal or fluctuating income? Bonus income?
- Are non-cash items such as employee stock options available for support? Are the value of company cars and other perks added into the income before calculating support? How do they treat voluntary 401(k) and similar payroll deductions in calculating support?
- Is the amount of support tied to custodial time? How does that work in your state?
- Does your state expect custodial parents to work outside the home? Do the courts impute income to someone who is not working to capacity?
- Can you get child support for children in college?
- How often is support reviewed? Do the guidelines provide for cost of living adjustments? What is the standard used (e.g., Consumer Price Index)?
- Is support ordinarily paid by wage assignment? How does this work in your state?
- Is there a cap on support in your state? What is it?
- What if you object to the guideline amount? (Everyone will . . .)

It is obvious that end results can deviate dramatically depending on the answers to these and similar questions. Ask them, and be sure you get answers you can understand.

CHAPTER 24

Choices — Part II

YOUR PLACE IN the support scheme is largely the result of choices you made years ago.

Every day of our lives, we are making choices, and living with the resulting consequences. It's an absolute fact that the choices we make when we believe we're going to be married forever are different from the ones we would make in contemplation of separation and divorce.

At the time you had your family, you and your spouse may have been utterly committed to the importance of the children having a full time parent at home. You may have followed up that philosophical commitment by giving up your schooling or career to stay at home with the children.

These decisions are going to have far-reaching impact. If you are the wage earner and chose, for the good of your children, to support a stay-at-home spouse for 7 or 10 or 15 years, that decision is going to have financial consequences. Now that you are separating, don't expect the parent who has been assisting in the kids' classrooms and schlepping them to soccer practice and lessons to suddenly become a brain surgeon or go out and earn six figures. Even if your spouse was a straight-A student in college and had a highly promising career prior to the birth of the first child, the choice to stay home for all those years means the training and contacts are stale. It's going to take time. And be fair. If it was OK with you for your spouse to stay at home with the kids while the marriage was intact, my guess is that a judge is going to find it is OK for that same pattern to continue after the separation, at least for a while. You are going to pay support for now. Period.

How to Avoid the Divorce from Hell

If you're the one who opted to stay home with the kids and give up the promising career, I'm sure that at the time you made that decision you thought it was the best for yourself and your family. In most instances, that doesn't mean you are going to get so-called "lifetime" support (more about that later). The courts are likely to pressure you to pursue education or training consistent with your abilities, the job market and your children's needs.

Don't expect family law judges to be overly impressed with the argument, "But I *can't* work; I have children." Elsewhere in this book I have advised individuals contemplating divorce to sit in a courtroom and watch the divorce calendar for a day or two. In no area is this more instructive than in the area of support.

Most judges handle dozens if not hundreds of cases every week. In most of these, the litigants don't have enough money to support one household, much less two. In the vast majority of cases, the family simply can't afford the luxury of one parent staying at home with the children. Except for the very poor, where public assistance may be an option, and the rich, where it isn't needed, most families require two incomes simply to get by. Working may well be an economic necessity. The judge may in fact share your philosophical belief that it is better for children to have a stay-at-home parent. The reality, however, is that in many households, the money simply isn't there.

Don't overlook the possibility, also, that the judge herself has small children, children with whom she'd like to spend more time. When you say, *"But I can't work; I have children,"* she's not going to be moved by your arguments. *She* has kids and she works.

Suppose you are the bright, college-educated recipient of support, and suddenly find yourself forced to consider career and training opportunities. Don't waste your time railing against the gods for the failure of your expectations. Instead, take this opportunity to decide what you would really love to do, what is practical, considering your age, talents, education, and economic circumstances, and devise a plan for becoming as financially independent as you can. What skills do you have?

How might they translate into income? Even if you haven't worked for pay outside the home, you may have significant talent and experience acquired in volunteer work. If you've successfully organized the community festival for the last five years, you probably have many skills which could directly translate into a career. Think about this. You're not doing it for your ex. You're doing it for yourself and your kids and for your own protection because you never can tell what your financial future holds.

Be realistic. This isn't the time to say you always wanted to get a Ph.D. in art history so you could become a docent at the local museum, or you've always wanted to be a ballerina, so you've decided to start training at age 44.

But more about sensible career choices later . . .

The Myth of "Lifetime Support"

I have counseled countless support recipients to never use the term "lifetime support" because it doesn't exist. They don't listen.

In most states, the courts recognize that in a "long term marriage" (defined as anywhere from seven to 20 years in duration) one party may have foregone career opportunities in order to concentrate primarily on domestic responsibilities. The courts recognize that those choices (and the choice was, of course, made by both parties to the marriage) have resulted in a diminution of earning capacity. They will grant long term support in such cases. In California, we refer to a spousal support order that continues "until death, remarriage or further order of the court." Those words do *not* mean for life. They mean just what they say: Until somebody asks the court for a different support order and convinces the judge that a change in the amount of support, or even outright termination of support rights, is appropriate.

If you are the recipient of support, you should assume that at some time in the future the payor is likely to ask the court to either reduce or end your support order. The courts may entertain motions requesting that they admonish recipients of support about their duty to maximize their own earning potential and become as self-supporting as possible. So, after six or seven or eight years of spousal support, you may be hit with a motion to either reduce or terminate your support payments. You will then probably be utterly shocked because, of course, you thought you got "lifetime support." There is no such thing.

Assume that your spouse is going to ask that your support be reduced or eliminated at some point in the future. If you choose to ignore that reality, you will be in for a nasty surprise.

There are long term marriages where support does, indeed, last for a very long time. Even length of marriage, however, is no guarantee against future vicissitudes. If you doubt this, just think of all the 55 year old executives whose company has merged with another, and as a result have been downsized out of the management positions they thought were secure until retirement. Or the victims of the dot.com bubble bursting. Or the recession. Or the people whose retirement plans were looted by company executives.

I have seen many cases in which a couple was married for 30-35 years. The wife never worked outside the home and had absolutely no marketable job skills. She made no effort to obtain an alternate or backup source of income. When the husband retired, his income was reduced and he went back to court to reduce his support obligation as a result. It is tragic to see the number of couples who have made no plan for that eventuality. Perhaps in the divorce, the wife decided it was important to her to keep the house, so she traded her interest in her husband's pension for his interest in the house. When retirement time comes, the husband's income is reduced. He seeks a modification order which is granted because, of course, he now has less income than he did when the original support order was made. If the wife never considered that possibility, she may well lose the house because there was only enough retirement income to support one household. Too many people are being reduced to a poverty level at stages in their lives when they have limited options, simply due to lack of prior planning. Even if she is still convinced that keeping the house was a good financial move, that wife would have been better served by having a plan for what she would do when retirement hit. And what if the house value has declined in the interim, as so many have, and she's not in a position to sell it? Few judges will think it fair that the husband who bought his wife out of the retirement plan should then be required to turn around and give her, as alimony, part of the pension which he bought in the property settlement. And don't forget: In an intact marriage, retirement at some time is inevitable. If you were still together, your income would have been reduced at retirement in any event. There is simply no reason to expect that the recipient's income stays the same after the payor's is reduced.

If you have a so-called long term marriage (and check with your attorney for the definition in your state), and receive spousal support, do yourself a favor. Don't even think the words "lifetime support." Recognize that support can always end, whether by court intervention, death or disability. Assume that sooner or later you may have to support yourself, in whole or in part. There is no excuse for not considering the possibility and making a contingency plan.

As a footnote, I would suggest that you not respond the way one of my clients did when I gave her the foregoing speech. She was bright, talented, and educated and had an enviable country club lifestyle. When I pointed out to her that although I had negotiated a great support order for her, even her highly-paid and guilt-ridden executive ex-husband was likely to successfully move to reduce her alimony in the future, she said "Well, if that happens, I'll just have to find another man to marry me."

There's a word for earning your living that way. And what happens when husband No. 2 loses *his* job?

CHAPTER 25

—— 〜 ——

The Payor's New House

SUPPOSE THAT YOU are the payor of support. At the early stages of the divorce, you were probably living at a mere subsistence level. Too much money was coming out of your paycheck for you to live comfortably, but somehow you managed to keep body and soul together and move up in your job. The studies show that in the years immediately following divorce, the high-income earner (i.e., payor) tends to recover much faster from the economic divorce than the recipient of support does. The recipient may be in the same house as during the marriage, but the overall standard of living tends not to improve as quickly.

So here you are three or four years after the divorce, and you are now getting back on your financial feet. Perhaps you've even remarried and started a second family. Then the dreaded process server arrives at your door to serve you with an Order to Show Cause to appear in court on a given day and present your case why your support payment should not be increased. There are many nasty surprises awaiting you when you return to your divorce lawyer's office.

Your income has most likely increased significantly since the divorce. Therefore, even if the guideline formula has remained unchanged, you will probably be facing an increase in support simply by reason of your higher current income.

After I've told you what the new support number is likely to be and revived you from your faint, several things will be happening.

By now, your new wife (who accompanied you on this visit for moral support) may be threatening to divorce you, because in some states her income is also considered in setting support for your ex-wife, and she retches at the thought that she is working to help support *that woman.*

You may be thinking about the new house you just bought or the new boat that you won't be able to pay for if your support order is increased. Sorry. Judges are not inclined to reduce guideline support by giving the boat a higher priority than supporting the kids or the ex.

Don't expect to get very far with the argument that you now have a new family to support, so you can't afford to support the "old" family to the extent of the guideline order. You chose to have the first family, and then with full knowledge of your responsibilities to them, you chose to have a second. Many support calculations will give you a deduction for the children of the new marriage, but the deduction rarely exceeds the amount of child support you are paying for children of the first family.

This is not the time to threaten a custody fight because it would be cheaper to raise them yourself than to pay the support to your ex. Instead, refer to Chapter 16, "Kids Aren't Property," and lose 10 karma points.

Instead of railing against fate and the unfairness of it all, there are a few positive steps you can take.

First, step back and look at the situation realistically. If you've bought a new house and a new boat and the kids go back from visits with stories of all the toys at your place, don't be surprised if your ex-spouse files a motion for increased support. Ditto if you are bragging on Twitter about the European vacation or posting pictures of it on Instagram. If your support order hasn't been modified in the last year, and you haven't suffered an involuntary loss of income, the support order is most likely behind your own income. Don't be angry at your ex for filing the motion; she probably has no economically viable alternative. She may still be living below the marital standard of living which you enjoyed when you were together.

What if you really can't pay increased support because of all the consumer debt you've taken on? The reality is that child support has priority over every other debt except taxes, and you can't avoid an increase by making the argument that you really need that money to make the payment on your VISA card.

How to Avoid the Divorce from Hell

Second, if you didn't do it at the time of the initial divorce, look at the practical suggestions for buying out the support rights or building work incentives into the support order (See Chapter 27, "Buy Outs and Employment Incentives").

Third, recognize that you are much better advised to periodically agree to cost-of-living adjustments in conformity with your increasing income (adjusted, hopefully, by the recipient's retraining efforts) without recourse to court. The adjustments that you and your ex work out between you are likely to be more favorable than those that the courts would impose, and you save the attorneys' fees consumed by fighting the modification request.

One of my smartest payor clients would periodically consult with me to give me his updated income figures and have me run a guideline calculation to see what he would be paying if his ex-wife took him back to court. It was always a *very* big number. Instead of hiding income, he did the sensible thing. When the kids needed something extra, he paid for it. He periodically agreed to voluntarily increase the amount of child support he was paying. As a result, he ended up paying less than he might have under the new guideline calculations, but more than the original order. His ex-wife was satisfied that the kids were taken care of, and didn't take him back to court to get an increase in child support, which might well have triggered an increase in alimony as well. He didn't incur the cost of paying me to fight a request for an increase, and didn't run the risk of paying his ex-wife's attorney fees to bring the motion. Now that was one smart payor.

A final word on alimony: Unless you and your spouse specifically agree otherwise (and there are tax implications you should discuss with your attorney before doing this) it ends when the recipient remarries. Hope your ex finds love. Not only will she be happier, and less likely to be fighting with you, but your alimony will end.

And if she does get remarried, send a nice wedding gift . . .

CHAPTER 26

The Standard to Which I'd (Like to Have) Become Accustomed

MOST STATES HAVE provisions for spousal support or alimony tied in some manner to the marital standard of living. In practice, this isn't as significant as it might seem. Marital standard of living is frequently irrelevant because after dividing the available income in half, it is not going to be sufficient to support two households at that level. If you fit into this category, the following discussion is going to be largely academic. Moreover, unless you are fortunate enough to be married to a multimillionaire and there's money to burn, your standard of living is likely to change after divorce.

The definition of marital standard of living is vague in the extreme. While most of us have a general idea of what it means ("I want to live as well after the divorce as I did before"), it is very hard to quantify.

Some courts simply look to your joint tax returns to see what your combined income was in the years immediately prior to separation, and attempt to extrapolate the marital standard from that. Others will look to subjective indicia of marital standards of living. What type of neighborhood did you live in? How many and what types of cars did you drive? How often were they replaced? How often did you go on vacation and where? Did the children attend private schools? Did you belong to a country club? How often did you go out to dinner and where? How much did you spend on an average restaurant meal? Where did you shop for clothes? How much did you spend on them annually? Did you routinely save money as a family and if so, how much?

How to Avoid the Divorce from Hell

Whether you are the payor or recipient of support, these are questions which you should be asking yourself. Document the answers to the extent you can, since the information is elusive and subjective at best and can quickly become stale. You will never have access to better information on your standard of living than you do at the time of your marital separation.

Ironically, the marital standard of living itself frequently doesn't become relevant until long after the divorce is over. Typically, at the initial separation there is insufficient money to support either of you at the marital standard. Therefore, the question was moot then and nobody bothered to gather and preserve the evidence. In most cases, it takes several years for the parties to recover financially from the economic shock of the divorce. After a few years, the payor is making more money, and the recipient goes back to court in order to get increased support based on the increased income. The recipient then has a double burden. She must first establish what the marital standard was, and then she must prove that the current support order is inadequate to sustain it. By this time, evidence is probably gone and it may be impossible to reconstruct so long after the fact.

In most cases, there is very little that you can do other than simply gather whatever information is available to you at the time of the divorce and hope that you will have what you need later if it becomes necessary to prove your case.

If you are a recipient, you need to preserve whatever evidence and documentation you have which will demonstrate that your current standard of living has deteriorated since the separation. Generally this is going to mean a detailed review of records of the last year or two of the intact family. You may never have an opportunity to use this information, since it only becomes relevant if the payor's income level increases enough to justify an increase in support during a period when the court still has jurisdiction to order it. However, since it is so difficult to reconstruct this information after the fact, it is a good idea to simply assemble it and tuck it away in case you ever need it.

The Standard to Which I'd (Like to Have)...

Digital media have made this easier to do in recent years. Scan photos from your expensive vacations. Ditto the menus from your favorite restaurants (note how frequently you used to eat there). Credit card bills and check registers contain a wealth of information on how much you spend on clothing, entertainment and personal grooming. Annotate them now while you still remember what the charges were for and scan them to a thumb drive. Include car leases and registrations showing what kinds of cars you had and how often you replaced them.

Payors should do their homework as well. You should also accumulate information to document the marital standard of living. If your income increases dramatically, you want to be able to argue that you should not have to pay more than the marital standard, even if you now have sufficient income to do so. When a court is called upon to make a support order, the parties are required to file a financial affidavit of some kind demonstrating their income and living expenses. Different jurisdictions have different rules, but in California this is required to be on a Judicial Council form called Income and Expense Declaration. We have all seen them come in: The prospective recipient of support files a declaration under penalty of perjury which states that the essential family expenses exceed the family income by thousands of dollars per month. Sometimes this is in fact true when people have been living on credit cards. More frequently, it is wishful thinking. When one of those inflated financial declarations is presented, the payor should review the actual family records and determine the true expenses by referring to (and preserving copies of) source documents, compiling and averaging them. The last thing you want is for an inflated declaration filed at the time of the initial separation to become the "standard" for a later hearing on modification of support just because it happens to be in the court file. This can occur if you simply assume it is ludicrous on its face at the time it is filed. The judge who will be making the decision on a modification hearing five or six years later has no way of knowing whether the original declaration was true or not. Accordingly, both sides need to do their homework on this issue, and neither can afford to simply dismiss it unless you know as a matter of fact and law that the court is only going to have limited jurisdiction in the future to modify or award alimony.

Note also that the marital standard of living may be irrelevant when it comes to child support. In many states, the recipient who is seeking spousal support or alimony cannot receive support above the cap established by the marital standard of living. Not so for children. If the payor's income goes through the roof after the separation, the children may well be entitled to ride the upward income spiral and enjoy the standard of living of the higher income parent, regardless of whether it substantially exceeds the standard of living which existed prior to the parents' separation.

Ask your attorney the precise meaning and interpretation of these issues in your state and don't assume you don't have to pull the evidence together now because it isn't going to come up until later.

The "Ball-Soxer"

Many years ago, a former legal assistant coined a phrase that I have always found amusing. One day she returned from lunch railing about long lines of "ball sox people" at the grocery store. I had no idea what she was talking about. She was referring to a particular type, very common in our affluent suburban community — a woman who was married, educated, unemployed, had 2.3 children and drove a Volvo station wagon (nowadays a Range Rover), played tennis three mornings a week and invariably showed up at the grocery store in her tennis outfit. My legal assistant had just been trying to make a quick trip to the store on her lunch hour and found long lines of "ball sox people," wearing their little tennis dresses with tennis socks, hence the term. Her complaint was that she, like everyone else who worked for a living, had only limited time to go to the store and run errands. In her view, "ball sox people" could go to the store any time they wanted all day long and it was unfair of them to create long lines during the lunch hour when working people were in a hurry.

The Standard to Which I'd (Like to Have)...

This phrase stuck and spread through my office to describe a particular type of client. She was generally married to a successful and highly paid executive. By the time she consulted me about a divorce, the children were probably teenagers and she was relatively free of day-to-day and hour-to-hour parenting responsibilities. She finally had the time to engage in the social activities she enjoyed. She could meet friends for lunch, play tennis or golf several times a week, and probably belonged to a country club.

When she came in for the initial consultation, her primary financial concern was generally that she wouldn't have to go to work.

I can see her logic. Who in their right mind would not prefer that life to taking rusty job skills into an iffy job market? If I had it, I wouldn't want to give it up either. On the other hand, as someone who has always worked for a living, I have limited sympathy with the concept that she gets to retire at 38, and he (and the rest of us) have to work to 65. I said that very thing to one of these prospective ball sox clients on a day when my fuse was short. As you might imagine, that was a professional relationship which did not go far.

It is going to be quite difficult to sell a court on the argument that an intelligent and able-bodied recipient of support should not have to do something to contribute to her own expenses. This is particularly true if she has been an active volunteer, organizing charity functions or running the local thrift shop. Just because someone doesn't get a paycheck doesn't mean they don't have skills and experience that an employer would pay for. The world of online business has also created many opportunities which were not available a few short years ago. There are very few people who truly have no marketable skills or who, by reason of physical or emotional disabilities, are completely incapable of working. Additionally, most states require that both parents contribute to the support of their children to the extent of their abilities. It's not just a one way obligation.

And if you're divorcing a ball-soxer, stop complaining. She probably made a great corporate wife and hostess as you were moving up

191

the ladder and it suited you to have her available. You weren't required to worry about the kids' school, lessons, doctor's appointments and extracurricular activities, and if you got the opportunity to take a business trip to a fancy resort on the company's dime, her job might have prevented her from accompanying you. If you're honest, you'll probably admit that you didn't want her to work while you were together, as the demands of her job might have conflicted with the demands of your job or the needs of the kids. It worked for both of you then, and you're going to pay for your choices after divorce, at least while she updates her education and training.

CHAPTER 27

Buy Outs and Employment Incentives

ONE AREA WHERE you can be creative is the spousal support buy out, which should be seriously considered in appropriate cases.

A spousal support buy out occurs when the payor of alimony pays the recipient a lump sum of money or transfers an asset in exchange for a permanent waiver of spousal support. This only works for spousal support and not for child support and is recognized by federal tax law.

There are some rules you need to know if you are considering such an arrangement. First, courts don't have the jurisdiction to order it over the objection of one of the parties. You and your spouse can agree on a buy out and, if so, the courts will enforce your agreement, but they generally cannot impose such an order on either of you.

If you are considering offering a buyout of spousal support, you don't just add up the number of monthly payments that you are likely to pay over the probable duration of the support order and assume you'll pay all of that up front. You certainly need to be able to estimate the probable amount and duration of spousal support in order to frame a reasonable offer. You should factor in the likelihood that the recipient will become reemployed or remarried. You also have to weigh the risks of significant fluctuations in your own income during the likely duration of the support order. We used to assume that income generally trends up over time. The recession has taught us otherwise. Once all of these components are weighed, you should be able to estimate a range of predictable amounts and durations for a support order. The next step is to reduce the total of your estimated monthly payments by an amount equal to your federal and state income taxes. The reason for this is that alimony paid "periodically," that is, on a monthly or other regular basis, is taxable to the recipient and deductible to the payor. Alimony which is paid in a lump sum is not. Therefore, since it is tax-free to the recipient and not deductible to the payor, it should be discounted for the tax benefit to the recipient. It is then discounted again for the present value of future dollars. The discount factor is always an estimate based upon current interest rates and market conditions. You can go to a CPA or a financial planner to do these calculations, but an experienced divorce attorney can probably give you a ballpark estimate.

Recognize that these lump sum payments are always gambles for both parties. The payor is gambling that the recipient isn't going to get married soon and therefore terminate the spousal support obligation before the projected duration. He is also gambling that his income is going to increase, and therefore he would be at risk for increased support payments in the future. If he assumes continued upward spiraling income, and he later gets laid off, he doesn't get his lump sum back, so he has to be comfortable that the risks are justified by the probable benefits.

The recipient is gambling that she is going to be able to meet her reasonable needs from the lump sum plus the interest it generates and that her costs of living are not going to significantly increase.

Interestingly, in the mid-80's, we assumed the payor's income was going to continually escalate and as a result, many high income payors were offering extremely generous lump sum alimony buy outs. With the economic turnaround of the late 80's and early 90's and the number of executives suddenly out of work, it became clear that the recipient made the better bargain in many of these deals. Similarly, during the stock market bubble of the late 90s, there was a sense that the sky was the limit. Many payors made extremely generous deals to buy their way out of a support obligation, including projected future employee stock options, only to find that they had no recourse when they found themselves unemployed and holding worthless stock. The recent recession has reinforced this lesson. While alimony buy outs may be useful tools, they carry risk on both sides and the downside can cut either way. Consider and weigh the risks and benefits carefully.

There are some obvious advantages and disadvantages to support buy outs.

For payors:

They know precisely what they are obligated to do. They can make financial plans and know there won't be any nasty support increases in the future. They know that they can maximize their earning potential with absolute impunity (except as regards child support, of course) and needn't worry about the ex finding out about the big raise or the bonus and demanding a piece of it. They don't have to pass up buying a house or a new car for fear the kids are going to tell the ex, who will then file a motion for an increase in alimony. They don't have to worry that their social media postings about how well they are doing are going to become Exhibit "A" in a support increase hearing. Even if they have to borrow the money for the buy out, they are paying interest on a fixed term and know precisely when the obligation ends, as opposed to having an indefinite term and amount in an open ended support order. The longer the underlying marriage and the less economically self-sufficient the recipient is, the better the gamble is for the payor. The exception to this is if their ex is secretly planning to get married soon, in which case alimony would end in any event.

For recipients:

They are in charge of their own finances and their own life. They are responsible for budgeting and investing. Because they got the money up front, they needn't fear the ex suddenly losing his job or becoming disabled. If they are planning on getting married again or starting a lucrative new career or internet business in the relatively near future, this can be a very good gamble indeed.

In appropriate cases, I always encourage clients to consider a buy out, recognizing that it is always, but always, a roll of the dice. Fortunately, however, it is frequently a good one.

If you can't afford a complete buy out, consider some form of non-modifiable support or employment incentives.

Most jurisdictions allow alimony to be treated as "nonmodifiable" in some respects. That means that you and your spouse can agree to restrictions, both as to amount and duration of alimony, which can give each of you important incentives.

Some of the possible restrictions are:

- Alimony will continue at a specific level for a fixed period of time and can be modified only in the event of the recipient's death or remarriage prior to the end of the fixed period.

Such a restriction is designed to give the recipient an incentive to get a job. She can earn as much as she is capable of without fearing that her alimony will be reduced based on her increasing income. The whole idea is that during the period of nonmodifiability, she has an incentive to maximize her earnings. The payor typically pays more than he normally would in exchange for the restriction. The trade off is that he knows exactly how much he is going to have to pay and for how long and can maximize his own income without fear of increased support payments. When the fixed period expires, if this has worked as planned, there is a track record of provable earnings for the recipient, which will be evidence in the subsequent hearing.

- Alimony will not be modifiable unless the recipient earns more than a specified level of income.

Such an order is also designed to give the recipient an incentive to maximize her income. For example, if the vocational evaluation indicates that she can be expected to earn $1,500 per month and the payor wants to give her an incentive to do that, he may agree to an order which says that her support won't be reduced for a specified period of time unless she earns at least (for example) $2,000 per month or some other number that is high enough to create an incentive. This means that she knows she can be employed for a while, building her career without having to worry about losing alimony. It enables her to get on her feet in a new job or industry and she develops a track record of employment which can be used as evidence in later modification proceedings. One would not want this type of order to go on indefinitely, however. It is important that it be either fixed for a finite period or, at the very least, set for a court review at a specific date in the future.

Again, in agreeing to such an order, the payor is gambling that the recipient will take advantage of the incentive, get a good job, and therefore, when he requests a hearing to modify the support downward at the end of the moratorium, he will have evidence that she can, in fact, earn money at a predictable level.

- Alimony will remain at a specific level for a fixed period of time and can be modified only if the payor's income exceeds X dollars or drops to less than Y dollars.

Such an order is designed to discourage interim modification hearings for relatively small variations in income. For example, if the parties really don't want to go back to court every year based upon the payor's cost of living adjustments and have to relitigate everyone's finances, they may establish a range within which they will agree not to go back to court. For example, if the payor's income is $60,000 per year, they can agree that they will not go back to court unless his income exceeds $80,000 or falls below $40,000 during a specified period. Both parties take a risk here as the payor is going to have to pay more than state guideline support to get the restriction. He, of course, is gambling that his income is not going to go up more than $20,000 a year during the moratorium and that he is also not going to take a major cut in pay which still leaves him over the $40,000 a year modification threshold. The recipient is getting a bit of a break on interim support in exchange for giving up her right to take him back to court over small incremental increases in his income. It is designed to reduce interim litigation, save attorney fees and, again, give both parties some predictability in their income levels.

- Alimony will drop to specific levels at specific dates in the future (generally leading to an ultimate termination of support).

This is called a step down order. When such orders are made, both parties are assuming that the recipient's re-employment and/or training plan is going to proceed according to schedule. It can be a risk for the recipient but as long as proper homework has been done (more about this in Chapter 28, "Vocational Evaluation") the risk can be minimized.

Finally, there are endless permutations of the foregoing restrictions which creative lawyers can build into support orders. You might have one type of support order for the first two years during the recipient's early retraining and then switch it to a step down or limited nonmodifiability. The goal here is to tailor the support provisions to the facts of your case in such a way that the risk to both parties is minimized. Any order which limits the risks of financial reversals and reduces the need to repeatedly return to court is worth considering.

In the proper case, you can have a support order which not only closely approximates the facts of life and the changes in your respective situations, but saves thousands of dollars in attorneys' fees which can then be spent on something much more fun than going to court.

CHAPTER 28

Vocational Evaluation, or What Do I Want to Be When I Grow Up?

MANY STATES PROVIDE for either mandatory or discretionary vocational testing of parties who are asking for alimony. If you have been ordered to undergo vocational testing, don't panic. It can be an invaluable opportunity.

When representing the recipient of support, I never force the opposing party to get a court order for vocational testing of my client. I know that the court will order it anyway if asked to, and it would be a waste of legal fees to fight it. Also, I happen to think vocational counseling is a good thing. If I represent the prospective recipient of alimony, I generally suggest that my client beat the other side to the punch and start vocational testing and career planning without being asked. I'm fortunate to have one of the most competent career evaluators in the state practicing in my county, and would send my clients to her myself.

There are several reasons for this. First, what can it hurt to know what you're good at? You may find that you finally have the opportunity to follow through on your aborted career plans, not only with official sanction, but at someone else's (read: your ex's) expense. Also, in these uncertain financial times, no one should assume that they can indefinitely rely on an outside source of support for the necessities of life. To recipients, the evaluation process can be a real eye-opener. How exciting is it to find out you have aptitudes and abilities you didn't know about? And you might rediscover your self esteem along the way.

Finally, if you are one of those individuals who, because of educational, physical or emotional problems truly can't ever be expected to be gainfully employed, you'll have a very competent witness in your corner. The vocational evaluator can testify to the precise conditions and circumstances which demonstrate your unemployability, thus relieving you of the onus of seeming to be dogging it.

My advice to payors of support is to get the vocational evaluation, and to the extent finances allow, support your spouse in training into a realistically attainable career.

There are countless resources out there. Excellent books about career choices abound, and most community colleges have reentry programs specifically designed to brush up stale work skills, learn new ones (especially essential computer skills), and assist people in retraining and reentry into the workforce. Many if not most of these courses are available online, so you can proceed at the pace that works for you and your kids.

After you've identified something you're interested in, do your homework. Talk to people who are already working in the field you are considering going into. You will be surprised at how willing people are to answer honest questions if you tell them why you want to know. Find out what drew them to this career. What worked best for them? How did they prepare themselves? What would they do differently if they had it to do over? Did it turn out to be what they expected? What do they like most about their career? What don't they like? How flexible is it (if that is one of your issues)? Is their income level what they thought it would be? What advice would they give someone who is just starting out? These are called "informational interviews" and can be immensely helpful in giving you a reality check on the career path you are contemplating.

Then find out what you would have to do to obtain the necessary qualifications. What programs are available locally? Online? How long will it take to complete your training? What do the available programs cost? Is any of your prior training or education transferrable? How long will it take to get established once you've completed training? What is the demand for these skills in your community? What do the jobs in the field pay? To start? With experience? What are the opportunities for advancement? Do the requirements of the career (travel, flexibility, hours, etc.) meet your needs?

Several years ago, court reporting was a hot reentry field. There were years where it seemed every recipient client I had was being steered into court reporting school. They had all seen fancy brochures from reporting schools detailing how easy it was to become certified in a matter of months, and touting the vast sums to be earned on a part time basis with flexible hours. Now, I happen to know that court reporting is a very demanding career. It is physically and mentally taxing, and only a rare individual breezes through the training and certification process in the minimal time advertised in the reporting school brochures. I also knew there were good job opportunities for those who could qualify. I talked to the reporter who took all of my depositions and asked her if she would be willing to spend a few minutes with some of my clients telling them the facts of life about the business. My goal was not to dissuade them from an appealing career, but to be sure they were realistic about their goals and expectations of the rewards on the other end. She was quite helpful and gave my clients invaluable information. As a result, they made better decisions.

Be realistic. Your support order will likely be based on the career assumptions you make, so you had better be sure they are actually attainable. It is tragic indeed to find that you agreed to limited support based on false assumptions (or advertising brochures) because you didn't investigate the program. Just because somebody else became a hot shot realtor making six figure incomes in three easy months doesn't mean that you will. If you don't speak Spanish and think you can become a Spanish teacher in two short years through an immersion course, find out if that is realistic. (Hint: This is from a real case and it isn't). Remember that you have other commitments, don't underestimate the time it will take, and don't waive future support based on brochures for training programs which are painting the picture in multiple shades of rose.

Do your homework. If you need something to take your mind off the divorce and the emotional trauma after separation, I strongly suggest that the investigation and career planning are good ways to occupy your time, and they will pay dividends in the future.

Retraining

Suppose you are a payor who can't raise the cash for a buy out, but you still have significant risk for long term alimony. You had a long term marriage and your spouse has limited marketable skills. There are some practical things you can to do minimize your risks.

If you, as the payor, have risk for long term support at more than a marginal level, I strongly suggest that you invest in your soon-to-be-ex's financial and business future and get her to invest with you. I do not recommend that you press her to go out and get the first low-paying, entry-level job she can find. This is particularly true if you have a good income yourself and are likely to get hit with a significant support order.

In a long term marriage where the income is sufficient, I believe the payor is much better off striking a bargain to pay full (or even slightly higher) support for a fixed period now, or even to pay part or all of the education costs, in exchange for a termination of alimony thereafter, rather than insisting on an immediate reentry into a low-paying job which lacks opportunities for advancement.

At separation, payors often try to pressure their spouses to take the first job available. I don't believe I have ever told a recipient to turn down a job or refuse to go to work in order to stick the ex with the maximum support order. What I have told them is not to get a dead-end job so that they are locked into that as their "career." Instead, they should consult a career counselor, look seriously at their aptitudes, abilities and the job market and come up with a realistic plan for training which will maximize their potential income and job satisfaction and which the court (and hopefully their ex) can buy into. They will be better off.

In the typical case, the recipient of support is not employed. She (and frequently, but not exclusively, it is she) has primary responsibility for the kids. If she's trying to go to school to develop marketable skills, deal with the kids and work at a part-time job, the stresses frequently become overwhelming. If something has to give, I guarantee you that what gives is going to be school. She probably can't afford to quit the job because her support order was predicated upon her receiving that amount of income. She obviously can't put the kids on the back burner, and so the training simply doesn't happen. Therefore, she's left in a marginal job and never has quite enough income to meet her basic needs. Every time you have an increase in pay or buy a new toy, she's going to be taking you back to court for more support. This doesn't mean that she's a leech; she probably has no financial choice in the matter. It is an economic necessity for her. And since she isn't making much money, you may be paying her attorney fees as well as your own for the privilege of opposing her request for an increase.

On the other hand, if you can both bite the bullet for a reasonable period of retraining and pay her full support so that she doesn't have to work during the training period, she can focus on her studies. You would then have a date certain when the support would end, or at least step down to a more reasonable level. In the long run, you won't be looking over your shoulder for the process server.

I must admit I have a much easier time selling this concept to recipients than payors, but I keep trying. Hope springs eternal.

Recipients have a different set of considerations. This is their opportunity to get the training they never had and I believe they should take full advantage of it to become as self-supporting as they potentially can be.

There's an added psychological benefit to all of this. Once they re-enter the job market and begin developing confidence in their abilities and pride in their work product, I have seen people who were profoundly depressed make major leaps in self-esteem. This is particularly dramatic if you had a spouse who constantly told you that you really weren't very bright and there wasn't much you could do that would be of value to anyone else. It's a great vindication to know that not only is there something you're good at and that you enjoy, but someone is actually willing to pay you handsomely to do it.

I once had a client who had been married to a high level executive for many years. She was very bright, but had never been able to develop a career of her own, because they moved around the country every few years to further his. After divorce she retrained in an industry she loved and moved up quickly through the ranks. Several years after the divorce she called to tell me she had received a very attractive promotion with a large raise. She was excited about the prospect. The problem was it required a move across country. Even though her kids were grown and launched, she wondered whether she should take it. I only asked her one question: "Would Ray (her ex) have taken the promotion?" That's all she needed to hear. She happily accepted the job and, last I heard, was one of the top producers in her company.

Above all, whether you are the recipient or payor of support, recognize that you are where you are because of choices you made. There were choices in the past that brought you to the point of being either financially dependent on someone else or responsible for someone else. There are also choices you can make from here on out that will either contribute to independence and self-sufficiency for both of you or keep you (as one of my colleagues phrased it) "chained to the carcass of a dead marriage." Think about it.

PART V

Fear and Loathing, or Karma 101

CHAPTER 29

The Paramour

MANY OF YOU are reading this book because you made a conscious choice to divorce. Others are reading it because you suddenly found out your spouse is having an affair. The existence of a "significant other" adds layers of complication to an otherwise relatively straightforward divorce, and completely mucks up a complicated one.

First, let's get the emotional context straight. If you're the one who was left behind, you may be suffering from hurt, rejection, abandonment, humiliation and yes, fear. You may be fantasizing about hit-men. All of these feelings are perfectly natural as long as you don't act on them, let them push you into making bad decisions, and deal with them in therapy.

If you are the one who left the relationship, you may be feeling guilt, remorse and sadness, all tinged with the exhilaration of starting a new relationship. You, too, may need therapy to ensure that you don't give away the store out of guilt.

Each role presents unique problems. It is beyond the scope of this book (and the author's expertise) to tell you how to deal with the emotional issues in a therapeutic sense. It is important, however, that you keep emotional issues contained and not allow them to contaminate the other, relatively unrelated elements of the divorce process.

I always hear warning bells when a prospective client starts referring to her spouse's "paramour" (a word I've heard only from women and never from a man). The term is so loaded that I know from the beginning she is going to have difficulty in separating the emotional content from financial and child issues.

How to Avoid the Divorce from Hell

Here are some things to do if you are the one who was left.

- Read *How to Survive the Loss of a Love* by Peter McWilliams, et al. Take it to heart, as it is one of the more constructive books I've seen in this field.
- Join a support group. If you can afford it, find the best therapist you can to address these issues in their proper setting.
- Give yourself time to get over the shock. Don't make irrevocable decisions about selling the house, or moving back to Kansas to be near your family until you've had some time to heal and gain perspective.

Here are some things to avoid:

If your spouse met the new flame at work, resist the impulse to report it to management or otherwise stir up additional trouble at the office. In the first place, management almost certainly knows about the situation and is trying to figure out how to handle it in such a way that the adverse impact on the office is contained. Additionally, if you're financially dependent on support payments and your spouse loses a job because of your intervention, where does that leave you? You'll pay a high price for blowing the whistle on the affair. I'm always amazed at the number of people who have to be dissuaded from creating trouble at their spouse's office, as though they'll somehow benefit by getting their breadwinner (i.e. payor) fired. I've seen it happen, and it isn't pretty.

Don't withhold the kids from the other parent as punishment for choosing to be with someone other than you. While it may feel good in the short term for you and the kids to circle the wagons against the common enemy of the new flame, in the long run the kids are going to suffer. Similarly, don't call a family meeting to announce to the kids that the other parent is an "adulterer" and will "go to Hell" as a result.

Don't take petty revenge on his or her personal property. I've seen some very creative stunts, all of which were satisfying in the moment and ultimately counterproductive. I have seen people:

- Cut the zippers out of all his custom-made suits.
- Melt down her jewelry into one gorgeous glop of gold and platinum, studded by various indistinguishable gems.
- Throw his clothes in the driveway and repeatedly drive the Mercedes over them.
- Take his favorite book and methodically cut a heart out of each page before returning it to him.

All of these make great stories in retrospect and are fun in the telling, but believe me, it's almost impossible to get the divorce back on track afterward. It's OK to fantasize about all of the foregoing and whatever else your fertile imagination may lead you to conjure up. It's not OK to act on your fantasies. If you're seriously considering scorched earth, watch the movie *War of the Roses*, with Kathleen Turner and Michael Douglas, and think again.

If you are the one who left the marriage, you have a different set of problems. You are probably suffering from acute guilt. Remember that acute guilt, painful as it is, is infinitely preferable to self-destructive guilt. That occurs when you let your guilt feelings drive your financial decisions. As with any of these issues, you will be best served by finding the best therapist you can and, if recommended, getting into a support group.

Try to keep your divorce as separate as possible from your new relationship. How fair can it be to the new love of your life to have you constantly obsessing about how much you loathe the ex?

There's also a list of things for you to avoid:

- Don't force your new lover down the kids' throats until they're ready.

In the urgency to get over the most painful part of the process, many parents announce to their kids, "Now we have a new family." Forget it for now. The kids don't *want* a new Mom or a new Dad. They want the old ones to get back together and put an end to all this nonsense. Be sensitive to your children's needs and reactions, and if they are not ready to accept the new lover (and they probably won't be right now), plan on having some solo weekends with your kids. They will benefit and so will you, particularly if you haven't spent a great deal of one-on-one time with them in the past.

- Don't give away the store.

There are always certain parameters within which a divorce settlement is relatively equitable. Parties suffering from the throes of guilt frequently give far more on support or property than they know they should in order to assuage their own guilt or attempt to buy forgiveness from their spouse. DON'T. If you are tempted to do so, put the property settlement on hold until you've had a chance to deal with the emotions and can make clear and clean financial decisions. I guarantee that if you settle the case too quickly while you are still in "guilt" mode, you will resent yourself (for being such a chump) and your ex (for taking advantage) for the rest of your natural days.

A colleague of mine is fond of saying, "Guilt has a very short half-life." That is absolutely true. Give yourself the time to deal with your emotions properly before you allow them to contaminate your business decisions (and yes, money decisions in the context of a divorce are business decisions whether they feel like it or not). I can assure you that the "wronged" party who is the recipient of the guilt-induced largesse is not going to feel any more forgiving of you if you overpay, and you are not going to buy the gold stars you want. Quite the contrary, the recipient will be accustomed and feel entitled to the overpayment, and resent you mightily all over again when you try to reduce it to a more reasonable level.

The nastiest divorces I have ever seen resulted from just this dynamic. The party in the position of financial power, in hopes of assuaging his own guilt or easing the transition for the other, pays far more temporary support than the courts would order. He is hoping that his wife will be less angry with him for leaving, or be grateful for his generosity. She won't. She'll assume she is entitled to what he offered, and probably ask for more. At some point, either because the guilt half-life has expired or the money has run out, a restructuring is required. In the meantime, the recipient has gotten used to the income and feels wronged all over again when it is reduced to a more appropriate level. You will never get any credit for having given too much early. All you do is create false expectations that you will continue to pay excessive amounts, coupled with renewed resentment when you decide to stop.

This isn't just true for support payments. Don't concede the property too quickly if you are operating in guilt mode. Support can be modified in the future. Property division cannot. If you give away too much property out of guilt, once the guilt half life has expired, you will try to recoup your mistake by grasping on to anything else that hasn't yet been conceded. It may be too late to fight over the house, but now that you are aware of how one-sided the agreement you made is, you may be tempted to do scorched earth litigation over the as yet undivided furniture. Don't. Do yourself a favor and do it by the book, fairly, honestly and openly, but by the book from the beginning.

CHAPTER 30

Mother Teresa and Attila the Hun

A HIGHLY RESPECTED family law judge of my acquaintance has observed that in his many years on the bench, he has never seen Mother Teresa married to Attila the Hun. Now, I *have* seen Mother Teresa married to Attila as well as Lucretia Borgia married to St. Francis of Assisi, but it isn't nearly as common as most people going through a divorce would have you think.

This is not to say that there are not truly abusive relationships and truly one-sided power struggles. Remember, this book is addressed to the 90% or so of well-meaning couples who simply want to get on with their lives without being married to each other.

Recognizing that it takes two to make a divorce, just as it takes two to make a marriage, here are some things you should avoid:

Client to attorney:

> *"My wife is an unfit mother/drug addict/alcoholic so she shouldn't have custody."*

If she has been routinely caring for the children for years with your approval, don't expect a great deal of sympathy here, especially if there's more than one child. If there is only one, and after the birth of that child you realized she wasn't cut out to be a parent, so be it. But if you then had more children with her, or left the one child in her primary care, what does that say about *you* as a parent? Either you were too stupid or dense to realize your kid was in danger, or you realized it but didn't care enough to intervene while it was convenient to have your wife provide child care. What is your excuse for leaving the kids with her? And how well do you expect it to play with an experienced family law judge? I used to ask this client if his wife was taken unfit after the first, second or third child. It is unlikely that she became an inadequate parent overnight simply because you decided to get a divorce.

*"My husband is **so** violent. He should only see the children on alternate weekends."*
or
"I'm afraid my husband is going to molest the children, so he should only have them one overnight a week."

Say what? Where is the logic that says he's only violent on week nights, so weekends are OK, but week nights are not. If you say it is fine for your children to be with their father 20% of the time, but not the 35% he's requesting because he is *so* violent, the court is going to wonder how you know which 15% is the violent time. The judge is going to assume (correctly) that you want some weekend time free to pursue your own social life but to otherwise deprive him of the kids, and violence isn't really the issue at all.

If you have real evidence of molestation, visitation should be supervised. If you're willing to let the kids stay overnight with him at all, you are either not very concerned about their welfare, or you are using the implied suspicion as an ill-considered weapon in the custody fight. Either way, you have no credibility.

Here's another cautionary note. Research has shown that allegations of sexual abuse which arise out of custody disputes are false as much as 85% of the time. Don't *ever* make such an allegation for tactical reasons. You are guaranteed the Divorce from Hell if you do.

How to Avoid the Divorce from Hell

"My husband is so crooked . . . I don't want to use this unless we <u>have to</u>, but he's been filing false tax returns for the past twenty years."

Lose 10 points.

Don't expect sympathy if you willingly signed the tax returns and looked the other way during all the years the filthy lucre was illegally flowing into the family coffers. He didn't suddenly become a criminal just because he's now spending the money on somebody else. It suited you just fine to have the extra income as long as you were the beneficiary. Moral indignation and righteous outrage are very poor form under these circumstances. Also, if *you* knowingly signed the false returns, you may be guilty of tax fraud yourself.

If he truly has been engaging in tax fraud for the last 20 years and you have "the goods" on him because you were aware of every detail, what does that say about your own morals? Why did you sign the tax return? I have asked this question of many clients. Their usual response is, "I had no choice," or "He made me do it." Nonsense. Most of the time, the party who offers to come forward with the goods is operating out of the same larceny as the soon-to-be-ex. What she really wants is to use the information to get a better deal for herself. It is called "blackmail," a crime in most states . . .

Suppose you are fantasizing about the withering cross examination your attorney will subject him to when he pulls out the fraudulent tax return in court. Don't be surprised to have a friendly IRS agent come knocking on your door. Your court hearing and case file are open to the public, and may even be available online. Moreover, many judges consider that the oath they take to support and uphold the law requires them to report tax fraud when it surfaces in divorce court. The bailiff might even decide to turn you in himself to snag the reward from the IRS. This cross examination you're fantasizing about may just land you and your spouse in tax court, faced with thousands of dollars in penalties and interest, or worse, charged criminally with tax evasion.

I know of very few cases where someone was physically restrained while being forced to unwillingly sign a fraudulent tax return. If you signed the return knowing it was fraudulent, you made a *choice* to do so, however reluctantly. You may have found the alternatives (such as blowing the whistle on your spouse, or precipitating an argument or even a divorce) to be unpleasant, but they were alternatives nonetheless. It may have bothered you to do it, but you obviously weren't distressed enough to make an issue of it.

And if you knew he was forging your name on the return, why didn't you do something about it? You have the same legal obligation to file an accurate tax return as any other taxpayer.

"I know he's hiding money on me and I know how he's doing it, because he did it to his first wife while we were living together during their divorce."

Really? If he financially cheated his first wife as he was divorcing her, what on earth made you think he wouldn't do the same to you?

I know that in the first throes of love, we all think this is the relationship to end all relationships. Moreover, if the soon-to-be ex is making your lives a living hell, it is easy to unite against a common enemy and collaborate to minimize income, hiding assets, etc. But don't kid yourself that the person who would do this *for* you would not do it *to* you.

I recognize that divorce frequently brings up anger and bitterness. At a time when you can't stand being in the same room with the other person, those character traits that in the past were merely irritating become wholly intolerable. However, as you are expounding on the fact that the man with whom you shared many years and several children is without a single redeeming quality, imagine the impact on your listener. Your attorney will not be the only one who wonders why, if he is so terrible, you stayed with him all of those years and why you chose *him* as the father of your children.

Hearing this diatribe, most people will (quite correctly) interpret it as hurt feelings and rejection. While some people do spontaneously change their characters (the proverbial mid-life crisis, which is blamed for more ills than Al Qaida) your spouse is a person to whom you were powerfully attracted at one time. He didn't become somebody different overnight. If he is an insensitive, devious jerk, he probably had all those charming traits before. What changed is not his fundamental character but the fact that you found out about his secretary.

I used to routinely say to these clients, "I'll bet you wish you'd seen this side of him before you married him." They would nod and agree that he is a pathological liar, and *no one* could have seen this side of him, he hid it so well for all those years. In all my years of practice, I only got one honest response to this observation, when my client told me, "Oh, I saw it; I just never thought he would turn it on *me.*"

Ask yourself, as you are trashing the character, morals and probable parentage of your spouse, what does that say about your own judgment?

So think twice before you publicly vilify your former mate. And, even if everything you're saying is absolutely true, remember one more thing. This person is and will always remain the parent of your children and the children don't need to hear it first, second or fourth hand. Every kid is entitled to believe that Mom and Dad are wonderful and neither parent has the right to take that away. And if the other parent isn't wonderful, they'll figure it out for themselves at the appropriate time.

CHAPTER 31

Threats and Ultimata

IN ANY EMOTIONALLY charged situation, we are all tempted to say things we shouldn't. Whether you are on the giving or receiving end, avoid the following statements. Alarm bells should go off if you find yourself either saying or hearing any of these:

- *"I'll be fair with you as long as you don't see a lawyer."*

Say *what* . . . ? If you don't see a lawyer and find out about your legal rights, how can you ever know if the proposal you're being offered is a fair one? It is axiomatic that when you and your spouse are in the process of separating your finances and your property, your interests are no longer aligned with each other. Why on earth would you allow the person who is divorcing you and who would directly benefit from your loss to be the sole source of information about what you are entitled to?

- *"If you leave me, you'll never see the children again."*

See Chapter 16, "Kids Aren't Property." For reasons more specifically outlined there, any parent who holds the kids ransom out of revenge or for retaliation should lose custody. Period. More subtle, but equally damaging variations on the foregoing are, "The kids will hate you for this," or, "If you leave us, the kids are going to be so devastated, they'll probably end up on drugs and it will all be your fault."

How to Avoid the Divorce from Hell

- *"I can't stand living in limbo any longer. It's either her or me. Choose right now!"*

I have spent a great deal of time dissuading people who don't really want a divorce from delivering this ultimatum. Never, *NEVER* give your spouse an ultimatum unless you are prepared to have it accepted. It only gives the fence-sitting party the permission he has been looking for. He can then shift the guilt and blame *you* for forcing the issue. I know it is hard to live in limbo. Waiting for the other shoe to drop is torture. You feel utterly powerless and have no control over your own future. You are probably saying, "I don't care what happens; I can't stand this uncertainty." That's not a reason to precipitate a divorce you don't want. Limbo isn't comfortable. Although it has been many years since I read my Baltimore catechism, my recollection is that as bad as limbo is, hell is worse. Before you give an ultimatum, be sure you're prepared to accept and live with the consequences of either answer.

- *"I want to file for divorce to show him that I'm really serious this time."*

I have also spent a lot of time talking people who don't really want a divorce out of filing papers just to send a message. The only reason to file for divorce is that you affirmatively want a divorce: Not because you want to send a message, not because you can't stand being in limbo anymore, and certainly not because your friends are shaming you into it. ("How can you put up with that? *I* never would.") If divorce is inevitable, you have the rest of your life to do it. However, once that paper is filed, a public record is created and a die has been cast. If anyone tells you that it is as easy to dismiss an existing divorce as it is to refrain from filing it, they are wrong. More often than not, the divorce develops a life of its own. People then get polarized into saving face, etc. This is not to say that couples can't reconcile after they have filed for divorce, but it is much harder than simply putting things on hold until you're each sure of your feelings.

CHAPTER 32

How to Be Inducted Into the Jerk Hall of Fame and Lose 10 Karma Points

- Hold the baby pictures and family videos ransom and refuse to share or scan them.
- Fight for furniture that was long in your spouse's family on the theory that it was "a gift to both of us," or because you're the one who refinished it.
- Claim that the jewelry you gave your wife for birthdays and anniversaries is "an investment" and she should pay you for half its value in the property division.
- Forget" to give your kid the phone messages, cards, letters and (yes, it does happen) gifts from the other parent.
- Fail to show up when you're supposed to pick up the kids so they are left looking expectantly out the window and wondering if you forgot them.
- Consistently fail to return the kids on time.
- Hide money or run up the credit cards in anticipation of separation.
- Tell your kids you can't afford to buy them anything because Mom "has all the money."
- Tell your kids you can't afford to buy them anything because, "your Dad didn't pay the child support."
- Withhold the kids if the child support is late.
- Refuse to let the kids see the other parent because she's "living in sin."

How to Avoid the Divorce from Hell

- When the kids come back from the other parent's house, pump them about your spouse's living arrangements, purchases, friends and social activities. Better yet, make them feel guilty if they don't voluntarily report to you. An even more creative way to do this is to constantly text your kids when they are with the other parent, insisting that they report back to you in real time. ("What are you doing now?" "Where's your father?" "Is someone else there?" and, best of all, "Do you feel safe?")
- Make your kids choose between parents.
- Send only old, torn or ill-fitting clothes when your kids go to the other parent. Or, better yet, don't return the clothes at the end of visitation. Or, return the kids dirty, sick and hungry. Or don't let the kids take their favorite toy to the other parent's house . . . you get my drift.
- Drag your children into court so they can see for themselves what a jerk the other parent is
- Insist the kids should be with you every Halloween because it is your birthday.
- Don't let your kids go to Mom's on Mother's Day because, "They have a new mom now."
- Argue with the other parent about *anything* at the kids' soccer game.
- Make sure your new spouse is involved with the kids' activities (coach, team mother, etc.) to the exclusion of the other parent.
- Discuss the problems you are having with your ex at back to school night, with the teacher, or with the parents of your kid's friends.
- Post or discuss your spouse's faults, your divorce conflicts, or anything else regarding the divorce on *any* form of social media.
- When the kids are with you, plan activities (dinner, movies, games, etc.) for the same time as the scheduled phone call from the other parent.

- Forget to tell the other parent about the school activities you received the notices for.
- Tell your kids "secrets" they have to keep from the other parent.
- Offer the kids some rare treat if they will tell the judge or the custody evaluator that they'd rather live with you.
- Show the kids communications from your lawyer or court filings as "proof" that the other parent is the "bad guy."
- Make your kids messengers for your nasty communications with each other.
- Buy your kid the super violent video game that you know your spouse objects to him playing.
- Tell the kids that though they've spent part of every summer with their cousins on the farm with Mom's parents, they can't go this year because their mom is leaving you.
- Play roulette with the school fees for the sports or other activities the kids are counting on. Wait until the last possible moment to pay your half so your kids have knots in their stomachs worrying about whether or not they'll be able to go to the camp with all their friends. Or refuse to respond to the text or email where the other parent asks for you to agree your kid can participate in the activity. Better yet, force the other parent to advance the cost so as not to disappoint the kid, then refuse to reimburse them because they "acted unilaterally" and didn't get your advance consent.
- Respond to a report that Olivia is cutting herself by telling your ex it is her fault, and there wouldn't be a problem if Olivia lived with you.
- Use photos of your kids as date bait on online dating sites. This is especially effective if you don't actually have custody.
- Tell your kids they don't have to go with the other parent if they don't want to and then suggest some fun alternative they could do with their friends.

CHAPTER 33

Pots and Pans

FIGHTS ABOUT POTS and pans *never* are. Instead, they're about power and control, hurt and rejection, unfulfilled expectations and sometimes, guilt.

Elsewhere I have offered suggestions for practical ways to divide furniture. Here, I want to talk about the dynamic that makes the division of personal possessions one of the most volatile issues in any divorce.

I have seen this reach epic proportions when the parties (who could easily afford their $30,000 *per month* mortgage payment) went to the mat over a single chair that could have been replaced for a few hundred dollars in any furniture showroom. I have seen multimillionaires fight over $500 worth of everyday china and kitchen utensils. Why?

Usually it's power. "I don't really want the glass-topped table, but I know that you do and so by insisting on having it, I win the power game." Or, perhaps, "If I force you to make the last concession, then that means I won." I have seen people fight for months and spend thousands of dollars in legal fees to obtain furniture they donated to Goodwill as soon as it was delivered. Anyone looking for monetary logic will be hard pressed to find it; psychological logic, now there's a different story.

I remember once settling a case in which we had resolved every issue, including disposition of the house, the cars, the pension, various investment accounts and all of the furniture with the exception of a single vacuum cleaner. *Vacuum cleaner?* Excuse me, but where is the logic in this? It is not as though Hoover has gone out of business. It ultimately became quite clear to the other attorney and myself that neither of our clients was going to make the last concession. In order to get the case settled, the other attorney (a long time veteran of the family law wars) suggested that he and I each agree to pay for half the cost of a new vacuum cleaner so that they would each have one and we could all go home. Of course, they then wanted to fight over who got the new one and who got stuck with the old one . . .

Pots and pans, lamps and sofas are almost always symbolic of something else.

It is interesting how often the very item that caused the most marital strife becomes the single thing that both parties absolutely *have* to have. Suppose that on a trip to an antique dealer, a couple found a particularly colorful and expensive Persian carpet. She insisted she absolutely had to have it. He hated the very sight of it, felt they were being gouged on the price, and only reluctantly agreed to buy it because she badgered him into it. For years thereafter, every time they got into an argument, he reminded her that she was the one who had insisted on buying that hideous rug, thereby subjecting him to the sight of it as a daily reminder of how he *always* gave in to her and she *always* got her way. Why should we be surprised that when we get the list of the furniture he wants out of the house, that very rug is at the top?

Dining room tables are another interesting psychological study. I was surprised to find the dining room set to be much more emotionally charged than the bedroom set, particularly in very long term marriages. It took me years to figure out why. Older couples who were married in modest circumstances and had long term marriages often had to wait years for their first starter house. In the 50's and 60's, most houses were not built with formal dining rooms. Therefore, acquiring the house with the formal dining room and the furniture to go in it were symbols of success, of finally having "arrived." The dining room was probably the last major item of furniture they purchased together.

This hit me when I was trying to talk a client out of paying her husband at least three times the value of the dining room set just to keep it from falling into his hands. He was gleefully extorting the cash from her because he knew she would never give it up. I insisted that she explain to me why she was making such an obviously unbusinesslike decision. She could easily replace the damn table with something much better for much less than she was paying her husband for it. That's when she said, "*That woman* will *never* sit at *my* table." In her mind, she had worked, struggled and sacrificed through many lean years to finally achieve this symbol of success. The new woman was never going to play hostess at that table, and she didn't care what it cost her.

All of us have items of personal property in which we are particularly invested. Hopefully, you and your spouse will have very few pieces to which you are equally attached. There are, in fact, unique, one-of-a-kind pieces that can never be replicated. If you and your spouse are not fortunate enough to have two such unique pieces of approximately equal value, you may have a real dilemma. However, if it isn't a unique piece and you find yourself getting hung up on pots and pans, take a deep breath, step back and try to get a perspective on what it is you are really fighting about. I suggest you adopt one of the methods outlined in Chapter 39, "Reasonable Solutions to Problems that Come Up in Every Divorce," for reaching an equitable division without consuming the cost of replacement in attorneys' fees.

A note about valuation here: Sometimes it will be necessary to actually have someone come in and appraise the contents of your house. I'd like to offer a few words of caution.

In the first place, 10 to 20 year old furniture is going to have substantially depreciated in value unless it consists of antiques, oriental carpets, original artwork and the like. This is particularly true if children and the dogs have been playing over, under, and around it for years. If you're the one moving out of the house, please recognize that fact. Don't wrap yourself in an air of sanctimonious generosity and say, "I would *never* deprive you and the children of the furniture," and then turn around and claim it is worth $50,000 and your spouse owes you $25,000 for the value of your half. It's probably worth a fraction of that. Check with your attorney for the rules pertaining in your state. In most cases, the court will look neither to the original cost of the item nor to the replacement value. Instead, they will consider what the furniture would bring today, *as is*, on the used furniture market. Imagine what you would get for the contents of your house if you were to put an ad in the local newspaper and have a garage sale next Sunday. You are probably better off dividing the used furniture between you. Since it is so expensive to replace an entire household, each of you would have some of the necessities, and neither one would have to start completely from scratch.

And please, *please* don't inventory the light bulbs, the kid's toys or the value of the meat in the freezer. I've seen all of these done. A colleague of mine had a good example of this. She once represented a woman who owned a horse jointly with her husband. The wife remained on the property after separation, and took care of the horse. At trial the following year, the husband demanded that the wife be charged with the value of the hay which had been stored in the barn when he moved out. With great glee, my colleague pointed out to the judge that the community property horse had consumed the community property hay, and the husband was entitled to half of the community property by-product. When would he like to pick it up?

Take a long, hard look before you go to war over who gets the family room sofa.

CHAPTER 34

—— ⌒ ——

The Paranoia Factor

YOU'RE SCARED. TERRIFIED. The person who is about to sit across a courtroom from you knows you better than anyone in the world. You have shared a bed with her for 14 years and told her every intimate secret of your heart. She knows where the old wounds are, the ones that have never healed. He knows the one thing that you fear most in the world and could use it against you if he chose.

Is that paranoia? I would call it legitimate fear. The problem arises when fear drives your judgment.

Anyone would feel vulnerable when an intimate relationship turns adversarial. That's the whole point of intimacy: If you weren't vulnerable, it wasn't very intimate.

So, what do you do? In this situation, fear is legitimate. The problem is that fear creates more unnecessarily nasty divorces than anything else, including money and infidelity.

Here is the scenario. You and your spouse, reasonably intelligent, conscientious and well-meaning people, have agreed that you simply cannot live together anymore. You must separate. One night after the kids go to bed, you sit at the kitchen table and have the hard discussion: Who is going to move where, how are the bills going to get paid, how are you going to tell the kids, and the like. There is nothing more gut-wrenching.

You both agree that for the sake of the kids, each other, and the years you had together, you want the split to be fair and amicable. You want to remain friends. Maybe you even agree to use the same attorney until you find out that simply isn't practical. Perhaps you both cry. Certainly in that moment, you both mean everything you say.

Everything goes along fine for a while, and then in a few weeks, one of you cancels the credit cards. The other one cleans out a bank account or diverts mail to the office. Whoever took the initial step undoubtedly viewed it as defensive, probably egged on by previously divorced friends or perhaps on advice of counsel. The other party is then made to feel like a chump for having trusted that moment of sincerity over the kitchen table, and battle is joined. Believe me, once battle is engaged, it will take six months, minimum, to get this process back where it should have been, if it can be done at all.

If you and your spouse have had, or are capable of having that conversation around the kitchen table, what can you do to ensure that the situation doesn't deteriorate?

First, make a vow to each other and to yourselves that you will do nothing, repeat *nothing*, to polarize the situation. Whichever of you is in the house and receiving mail will open it and make duplicates of every item, no matter how minor, and promptly forward them to the other. Trust me. The cost of scanning is cheap in comparison with the cost of attorneys' fees.

You agree to meet, on neutral turf if necessary and not at the house when the kids are present, to talk about the day to day problems: How can we get the bills paid in the interim? How do we pay down the credit cards? Who is going to use which cards and for what purposes? How are those bills going to be allocated between us? Which of the kids' expenses are we going to share? Where are we going to cut expenses?

The first one who violates the rules commits an act of war.

I am not saying that you should go blithely along, leaving your financial future in the hands of the person who is divorcing you. By no means. The rules need to be clear at the outset. You will share every, absolutely every, bit of financial data with one another. The first one of you who is caught withholding is responsible for the fight. Make that clear. I don't think it would hurt to even write up a contract between the two of you detailing how you will behave with each other in the interim. If you are capable of trusting one another enough to do what I am suggesting, you can put it on paper and you can each take a copy of it. The rules would go something like this:

- I promise that I will share with you every bit of financial data available to me, including incoming mail as it arrives.
- I promise that we will jointly discuss how best to approach our children, and we will tell them about the divorce together. To the extent that it is possible, we will present a united front with the common goal of reassuring our children that we both love them and we are divorcing not them but one another, and the divorce is *not their fault.*
- We will work in good faith with one another to try to allocate our present debt and limit the amount of new debt that we may be creating during this transitional period.
- Our goal is to come through this in such a way that we can dance together at our daughter's wedding (see Part VII, "Post Mortem"), and we will each give our respective counsel and advisors instructions designed to accomplish that goal.
- We will put our children's best interests ahead of our own and make certain, to the extent that it is possible, that they do not suffer from the course that we are taking.

If you can do this, you get a gold star. Moreover, your children will bless you.

You *will* feel fear. There will be times when you realize how much this person knows about you and how devastating it would be if he chose to use it against you. You are indeed vulnerable. So is your spouse.

Ugly divorces result from a violation of these rules. Somebody did something which they perceived as defensive and the other perceived as aggressive. Recognize that your spouse is feeling as vulnerable as you are. What may seem perfectly logical and reasonable to you may play as an indefensible act of war on the other side. It may make perfect sense to cancel the credit cards since neither of you can afford to incur additional credit. Perhaps you have already agreed that you need to put a curb on future bills. I guarantee you that if you cancel the credit cards without notice, however, you will be in for war.

Sometimes it happens completely innocently. You walk into the former family home without knocking, and your spouse, who now has exclusive occupancy, feels her privacy has been violated. You're the one who left, and you're treating "her" home as if it were still yours.

Recognize, too, that when your friends are all telling you what you "should" do in order to "protect yourself," their advice may be perfectly valid. Or not. All I'm suggesting is that you and your spouse make a vow that neither one of you will make the first hostile move. If one of you violates it, so be it. If neither of you does, what a great thing that would be. It seems to me that it is at least worth a try.

Then be vigilant. Don't be stupid, but keep your eyes open for a violation of the rules.

I will even go one step further. If you catch your spouse in what you believe to be a violation of the rules, this is a time to confront. Ask why it happened. Your spouse may in fact be quite chagrined to hear that what she thought was simply a "housekeeping" move is perceived by you as a hostile act. Decide your subsequent course accordingly.

Don't ascribe the worst possible motives and don't be foolish enough to assume that your spouse is going to be looking out for your best interests. Keep your eyes as well as your options open, and you will be less likely to suffer through the Divorce from Hell.

What if it isn't paranoia?

Maybe you have reason to be on the watch for nefarious dealings. I have seen cases where, before leaving the home, a spouse tampers with the computer to ensure that all emails are copied to another address without the sender's knowledge. They can install a program on your computer that tracks your keystrokes, so they know every email you send to your attorney, a friend, or new lover, every chat you enter into and every time you check out a porn site. Don't wait until your confidential communications with your lawyer appear in pleadings filed in court by your spouse to check to see if your computer has been tampered with. There are apps which can be downloaded to your phone which will do the same with text messages. If you aren't tech savvy, and have reason to expect tampering, find someone who is (*not* your kid) to check out your equipment.

I've discussed parental alignment and alienation elsewhere, but it bears mentioning here. Parents often overly involve their children in the divorce. Children may feel they "owe" it to the other parent to check out what you are doing when visiting at your house. Don't leave any compromising or otherwise private information where it can be casually or readily found.

Social Media

You've been warned to be careful who to "friend" on Facebook. This goes far beyond having compromising party photos posted which can come back to haunt you in a custody fight. Don't post false information about your relationship status, don't add a GPS tracking app so everyone can monitor where you go and when, and don't brag about how you are whupping your spouse in the divorce. It's unwise to get snarky about your ex, and could be downright actionable to go even further. You might get sued for libel or slander. Don't describe your recent trip to Cabo if you're being chased for past due child support. Most importantly, don't assume your ex can't get to the information on your social media. You may not have "friended" her, but someone you did "friend" has and it will get back. Everyone has a camera these days, and the information that knocks your strategy sideways or costs you custody may be posted by someone else on *their* social media. I suggest a complete moratorium on social media for the duration of your divorce, and cautious and limited use thereafter.

Dating Sites

It goes without saying, but what you post on dating sites is available. Don't misstate your marital status. Don't use photos of your adorable children as "bait" for future dating possibilities. Don't say you have custody when you don't. Don't use it as a platform to rail against your ex: believe me, that won't be attractive to a potential new love interest. They'll just wonder what you'll say about *them* if they date you and it doesn't work out.

Google

Google your ex. For a real shock, Google yourself. Remember, anybody can and does post anything on the web. Once it's out there, it is forever, whether it is true or not (remember the lawyer review on Yelp?)

Finally, remember that not only does everyone have a camera at all times now; anyone (including your ex) can record your conversations without your knowledge. Don't do or say anything that can be used against you, in or out of context.

CHAPTER 35

The Dreaded Prenuptial Agreement

"There must be a loophole — there's always a loophole."

"Peanuts" Lucy Van Pelt

MANY OF YOU signed a prenuptial agreement before getting married. These are typically negotiated before a second marriage when one of the parties has already been burned by one divorce and wants to make sure that the assets acquired in divorce No.1 are preserved for the children of marriage No.1 and are not then redivided in divorce No. 2. Philosophically, this is quite understandable.

The problem arises when the prenuptial agreement goes beyond that, i.e., not only does it say that the assets brought into the marriage will remain separate until our galaxy becomes a black hole, but also provides that no way, nowhere, no how can there be any future joint property of the new marriage.

I have drafted countless prenuptial and postnuptial agreements, including many of the "no way, no how" variety. My personal opinion is that (except in true cases of duress, as I will discuss later) anyone who signs the latter deserves what they get.

Now, I realize that many of you were presented with such agreements after the wedding invitations had been mailed or even on the church steps right before the wedding. Sometimes the agreement was accompanied with the threat that, "If you don't sign it, we don't get married." I understand that if the wedding has been planned and the invitations are out, the threat (overt or implied) of "no agreement, no wedding" carries inherent duress. No one wants to be humiliated in front of family and friends, particularly when the very person who is insisting that they sign the agreement is also saying, "Don't worry, dear; I love you and I'll take care of you." *Of course* you want to believe it. After all, you are about to marry him. I have seen prenuptial agreements which were presented literally in the car outside the courthouse at Reno as the couple was about to get the marriage license. I contend that by definition, such agreements are obtained by duress, as there is no possibility of meaningful legal advice. I also believe that most courts will recognize duress in that situation. Mind you, I say most courts. If your agreement was obtained in that way, a judge may agree that the circumstances were unfair and refuse to enforce it. However you cannot, repeat *CANNOT*, assume that is going to happen automatically or at all.

Good lawyers will carefully draft prenuptial agreements to cover several bases. First, they will make sure that the agreement is signed far enough in advance of the planned nuptials that there is no obvious presumption of duress. Moreover, they will insist that the other side has the agreement reviewed by independent counsel. More and more frequently, the attorney for each side is required to sign a certification which verifies that the attorney has explained all of the terms to his or her client and believes that the client understands not only the practical, but the legal consequences of the agreement. I frequently served as the reviewing attorney, advising the client of the legal and practical impact of an agreement which had been drafted by an attorney representing the other side. Until relatively recently, the party asking for the agreement was usually the prospective groom, but it is more accurate to say that the party with the greater risk in terms of income and property, or with children from a prior marriage they want to protect, is going to be more invested in obtaining such an agreement.

In most jurisdictions, prenuptial agreements are perfectly valid as long as they are properly done. I like to see them signed well in advance of the wedding, preferably before the date is set. I like to have two attorneys involved in the negotiation throughout the various drafts of the agreement and not just at the final review, and I want an attorney certification so that I know someone has explained the legal consequences of signing to the other side.

All that being said, the person signing the agreement has the ultimate responsibility for its content. I have reviewed hundreds of these things. I cannot count the number of times I have explained in thorough and very practical detail all of the reasons why my client should *not* sign the obviously unfair and one-sided agreement which has been presented to me for review. More often than not, I am met with a wide-eyed stare and the protest, "But I *love* him!" That, of course, is patently true. However, that doesn't mean you should sign the damn agreement.

Equally as frequently, someone will consult me about a prospective divorce. Somewhat sheepishly, midway through the initial interview, and after I have explained her property rights, she will venture, "Well, there is a slight complication; there is this agreement . . . " It turns out that I have just spent 45 minutes explaining all of the property rights which were waived by the agreement which the client has only now revealed to me.

Guess what . . . unless this is one of those gems which was signed on the courthouse steps or in the limo outside the church while the family and friends are all waiting for the first notes of Lohengrin, you're out of luck.

I invariably ask such a client whether she saw counsel before signing the agreement. More often than not, the answer is yes, she did. When I ask her what her attorney told her, she'll say, "Oh, he told me not to sign it." I'm sorry. He *told* you not to sign it. You signed it anyway. Whose fault is that, and what do you expect *me* to do about it?

More of the bad news is that these agreements are very difficult to set aside if done properly. If your agreement is a post-marital agreement (that is, signed after you were married rather than before), it may be even harder to set aside, unless it violates fiduciary duties between spouses. In that case, you won't even have the implied duress of, "If you don't sign, we don't get married." You are already married, and you signed it anyway.

Believe me, I know that it is uncomfortable to feel you need to get legal advice to protect yourself against the person you are either contemplating marrying or already married to. It is awkward, embarrassing, all of those dreadful things. It is also necessary. If you signed an agreement either without legal advice (because you didn't want to make waves) or ignoring the legal advice you got ("You're crazy if you sign it"), you have a problem, and it is entirely of your own making.

When asked why they signed it, people often respond, "I didn't think it would hold up." If they really didn't think it was important and didn't think it would hold up in court, why on earth was the other party so insistent that they sign it before walking down the aisle? I know, I know, love is blind. It is also sometimes deaf and dumb. Nevertheless, I am astounded at the number of people who seven or eight or 10 or 15 years later will wander into my office and be shocked to find out that the agreement they signed does in fact mean precisely what it says.

I also know that after you are married, when your spouse brings you a quitclaim deed to sign because, "It's just a formality," or, "the bank needs it," you want to believe that is true. I too would want to believe that is true. I might even sign it. I would also know who to blame if it came back to bite me later: Myself.

We are now seeing more and more of these agreements. It used to be that they were limited to the traditional fact pattern of a previously divorced husband who was marrying wife No. 2 and wanted to prevent his assets from being divided again. However, in recent years it is increasingly common for both parties to have been divorced, and as often as not, Wife No. 2 ("W-2") is a highly paid executive who wants to preserve her assets as well, sometimes with respect to a significantly less financially secure prospective husband. My advice to anyone who is faced with such an agreement is to assume that it is in fact enforceable and means precisely what it says. Read it. It doesn't take someone well versed in legalese to understand that the words "All right, title and interest to 123

Elm Street, together with the rents, profits and dividends, now and in the future, shall remain separate," mean you don't get any of it, now or later. This is not rocket science.

And, if you are the one who is presented with such a contract or with quitclaim deeds or other documents relinquishing title after the marriage and you agree to sign them, you made a choice. I realize that refusing to sign these documents could have caused a terrible family rift, great conflict, trauma, potentially even a divorce. I understand that you may have chosen to sign the document rather than risk any one of those things. Nevertheless, there was a choice, you made it, and you're going to have to live with the consequences.

In closing, I am reminded of a story told by a colleague. She was a highly skilled family lawyer who once found herself in the position of trying to set aside not only a premarital agreement but two post-marital agreements. Her unfortunate client had not only signed an agreement well in advance of the wedding, but within two or three years thereafter had signed a second and some years thereafter signed a third, all of which not only relinquished any interest in the husband's assets at the time of the marriage, but assets he acquired thereafter, including commercial buildings, businesses, etc. My colleague is a highly effective and articulate attorney and was passionately arguing her client's position before a crusty old judge. At one point during her argument, the judge stopped her, leaned forward over the bench, looked at her over the top of his half glasses and said, "Counsel, can't your client *read*?"

Take it from me: Lucy Van Pelt was wrong.

CHAPTER 36

New Mates: The Ghost
of Marriage Past

BY THE TIME you read this book, some of you will have embarked on a new relationship and will simply be waiting to get the judgment filed in the old one so you can tie the knot with someone new. Or you may in fact be the new mate, reading this book to try to find out what on earth you can do to help your loved one get through it.

I caution people against running into a new relationship too fast. It's hard to make good judgments about a new relationship when you are still trying to sort out what went wrong with the old one. Sometimes the urgency for a new relationship has little or nothing to do with the new partner, and is driven by an inability to be alone. Sometimes the loneliness is so bad that you rush to fill it with someone, anyone. Sometimes it's even worse. If the motivation to embark on the new relationship is to demonstrate to your spouse, "see, you may not want me but *somebody* does," that's really not fair to your new partner. Also, while it might be comforting to have a partner to give you emotional support through the divorce, it may ultimately be at the expense of the new relationship.

There's another reason not to rush in too quickly. There's something magical about the glow of a brand new relationship. If that glow is contaminated by the divorce, the memories will always be intertwined. You can never get it back, or get a do over on the new relationship without the overlay of the last one.

How to Avoid the Divorce from Hell

If you are already in a new relationship, there are very specialized problems which will be faced by the new mate.

First and foremost is the temptation to get utterly invested in your partner's fight. This may be from a need (yours or hers) to prove that you are "there for her." It may be your own sexual jealousy directed toward the person who shared such a major part of her life. Whatever the cause, recognize certain facts:

- You are *not*, repeat *NOT*, objective.

Of course you can't be. You love her. How could you be objective? You are watching someone you love go through terrible pain, possibly feeling attacked and betrayed by someone she trusted for many years. Recognize your feelings and temper your actions accordingly.

- Do not offer legal advice.

Your job is to be lover and supporter. You are not the lawyer, you are not the therapist, and you cannot be either in this case. Even if you are a lawyer or therapist by profession, you will be unable to function in those roles in your own relationship. Take off your lawyer or your therapist hat and put on your lover hat, and be loving, supportive and nonjudgmental. If you can do all of these things, listen sympathetically, and offer no advice, give yourself a gold star.

If you find yourself getting sucked into the controversy, recognize your lack of objectivity and back off. Don't go with your lover to see her attorney. It's her divorce, not yours, and your mere presence will alter the level and content of communication between your lover and her lawyer. It may also result in an automatic waiver of attorney/client privilege, and enable the ex to discover what she and her lawyer discussed.

There is another pitfall into which many new mates stumble. It is extremely difficult to build a new relationship when your lover is preoccupied with the one just ending. Accept certain facts as true: If your lover is going through a divorce, he *is going to be* obsessed with the process. That is a fact of life. The divorce is probably the most traumatic, most significant thing that has happened in your lover's life for many, many years. You will hear about it constantly, and there is going to be endless venting. Frankly, it can be difficult to build a new relationship while the specter of the old one constantly hangs over your dinner table (not to mention your bed). Your lover is not going to be able to give you 100 percent when about 110 percent is being given either to the fight with the ex-spouse, or simply the struggle to stay alive and marginally *compos mentis* through the process. Many people characterize divorce as a period of diminished mental capacity, and it frequently is.

Couples often find that the divorce itself becomes a primary focus and glue in their new relationship, i.e., what keeps them together is their united front against a common enemy (W-1). All of the faults and misconduct of W-1 consume their conversation. "The Divorce" is the major event in their lives and in their relationship.

Many years ago, my county had court reporting by videotape. As we left court, we could pick up a tape of the entire proceeding which we could then pop in our VCRs. This was a wonderful tool to help a client see where they screwed up their testimony and how they might be a more effective witness the next time around. It is not entertainment, however. I was once stunned to learn that my client and his new girlfriend had watched the tape of a two hour hearing six, seven or eight times, minutely dissecting every nuance! Please . . . it *can't* be that exciting. If it is, the new relationship is in big trouble.

In such situations the couple's primary bond is its alliance against the enemy. When the rival is vanquished (i.e., divorced), the new relationship falls apart, having never built any foundation of its own. As new mate, you need to be very careful of this. It is important to be supportive, loving and understanding. It is also important to recognize that if you and your new mate are to have a future, you must build a life together independent of the ghost of marriage past.

CHAPTER 37

Mind Games and Button-Pushing

EACH OF US has an Evil Twin. No matter how lofty our ideals or sincere our motivation as we embark upon the perfect Amicable Divorce, the Evil Twin will try to take over at some point. You know every sore spot, every vulnerable point and every low blow that will get an explosive response from your spouse. She knows the same about you. Times will come when the temptation to use that information will become almost irresistible. The operative word here is *almost*. Don't. And if you do, forgive yourself and promise not to do it again. Nothing, but nothing, will cause a divorce to deteriorate from amicable to abysmal in less time than pulling out the heavy artillery, betraying a confidence or airing the dirty laundry. The price is paid in thousands of dollars of attorneys' fees and in sleepless nights anticipating the next court appearance. It also gives the other side a get out of jail free card to do the same to you in retaliation.

I have seen it all too many times. You are getting ready for a four-way settlement meeting with your spouse and both attorneys at one of the attorney's offices. A hearing or a settlement conference is scheduled for a week or two thereafter, and what you really want is to reach an agreement so that you don't have to go to court. You don't want to have to pay your attorney to prepare for the hearing and you certainly don't want to sit across the courtroom from your spouse or suffer the anxiety which will precede that "day in court." Equally important, you do not want that court day to be postponed for another three or four months because the judge ran out of time.

So you all assemble in the lawyer's office on the appointed day. Everything goes smoothly until one of you mentions a hot button. It doesn't matter what it is. It could be the suggestion that you don't really need the money you are asking for and we don't need to discuss the issue of who's going to pay for your attorney's fees or help you with the house payment if money runs short, because you always were a Daddy's girl and Daddy will bail you out of this one too. It could instead be the implication that he's a lousy parent who doesn't really care about the kids or she's always been an irresponsible spendthrift. Whatever it is, the result is quite predictable. The situation will escalate until one or the other of you storms out of the room and all settlement discussions end.

If you are the instigator, you may have obtained momentary gratification. But what did you really accomplish? Well, you probably got hundreds, if not thousands, of dollars in additional attorneys' fees, another delay, lots of uncertainty about the ultimate result, hard feelings which might contaminate your relations with your ex for years to come, and very little else.

I promise you that the opportunity to push your spouse's buttons will arise. There is not one of us who is above that image flashing on the mental screen. There is not one of us who is above relishing the delicious sense of visualizing our spouse's response. All I am saying is *do not act on it.* You will pay a price. Remember also, that your spouse knows where all of your buttons are, too.

Instead, to the extent you can, try to take the high road. I fail to understand the psychology of someone who thinks they will benefit by destroying their opponent's dignity. All it does is force the other side to fight harder to try to recover it, usually by trying to take away your dignity in retaliation.

As a friend of mine is fond of saying, "He who engages in a pissing contest always ends up with wet shoes."

Two other truths to consider:

- The person you are divorcing is not the person you were married to.
- The person you are divorcing is precisely the person you were married to.

How to Avoid the Divorce from Hell

Both of those statements are absolutely true. If your spouse was always weak and indecisive or an arrogant control freak, he is not going to change his stripes simply because you are no longer together. A lousy parent is not likely to turn into a model one. An indifferent mother who would rather play tennis and work out at the gym than help the kids with their homework is not going to suddenly become Mom of the Year. Don't complain to me because your spouse is unreliable and always late for visitation when he was never on time for *anything* during your fifteen-year marriage. If *you* couldn't make him be punctual at a time when he had an incentive to please you, the judge and I are not going to succeed either.

On the other hand, you cannot simply assume that the way your spouse would have responded to a situation during the marriage is the way he will during the divorce. For one thing, during the marriage your interests were aligned. They are most definitely not now. So, even if he always deferred to you in child rearing matters before, he may not now. And if you could always charm him into doing what you wanted in the past, you may find someone else is doing a better job of blowing in his ear these days . . .

CHAPTER 38

Unfinished Business: The Endless Post-Judgment Minuet

By NOW, YOU should have realized that I believe divorce should be done by the book, as cleanly and conscientiously as possible. I can assure you that if you don't get it right the first time, you'll be given ample opportunity to try it again, either in the next divorce or more likely, the post-divorce modifications of custody and support.

Here's how it goes. A new client comes into my office. The divorce was final six years ago and the parties still can't speak to each other. They've been involved in a series of bitter conflicts over visitation, support, or the family dog. One of them doesn't pay support on time, and the other withholds the kids. Perhaps the client has had two or three attorneys in the intervening years, each of whom was worse than the one before. Now he wants not only to resolve the current conflict, but to be compensated for all of the perceived "losses" of the last six years.

I don't take this case. The parties clearly have unfinished business, and neither is willing to let go of the conflict and get on with life. I don't want to be a part of that dance. I won't be able to solve the problem and he'll never be satisfied.

In this kind of case, the stated reason for the conflict is never the real reason. No, I'm not saying that the motion to enforce support, or whatever triggers the next round in court isn't real; it's just that it is symptomatic of something deeper. The most common are payback for a perceived betrayal, humiliation, control, or revenge.

How to Avoid the Divorce from Hell

It is, of course, axiomatic that two people who are committed to fight with one another will find something to fight about, especially if they have children together. Of course, kids are the worst battleground imaginable.

Whether the current conflict is children, money, medical coverage, or an IRS audit of an old tax return, the result is the same. Until you've resolved your unfinished business, the divorce isn't over. It will consume your life for years to come, whether or not you've remarried or moved. As I write this, I think of a client who appeared in my office wanting me to represent her on a post-divorce matter. She cried as she told me how differently she would have handled the initial divorce if she had known at the time that it would go on for years. Now, six years later, she was still responding to his demands for her financial data and he was trying to dictate which school the kid attended. Had she known she would still be dealing with him years later, she would have approached him very differently at the beginning, to build a better basis for future dealings. Well, you're now on notice. It *can* go on for years.

Another manifestation of this dynamic is the couple who keep fighting even though they really have nothing to fight about. On examination, it turns out that to them any relationship, even a hostile one, is better than none. If you find yourself locked in this type of dance, consider what *you* are getting out of maintaining the connection. This is a good topic for your therapist.

This dynamic most commonly occurs when there are constant post-divorce battles over visitation, custody and support. Frequently the new mates get drawn into the conflict as well, each feeling the need to protect or stand by his mate, and the situation becomes even more polarized than it was in the beginning.

A couple engaged in constant post-divorce fighting has never really divorced. This was brought home to me once by a very wise man. I represented his current wife who, years after the divorce, was still locked in a bitter struggle with her ex-husband. Nothing was too small to trigger a major explosion, although each of them was now remarried. On one occasion my client brought her new husband into my office for moral support as we discussed the various options available to her in the latest round (Round 27, I think it was). My client's new husband (H-2) listened intently as I described the parameters of the current fight and the options available, as well as what I felt to be reasonable settlement possibilities. His wife bristled at the suggestion that she should make any concession whatsoever.

A couple of days later the new husband called me and told me that his conclusion from what he had watched was that his wife had unfinished business with her ex-husband. He felt that her constant conflict with her ex was having an adverse impact on their marriage, and until such time as his wife and her ex-husband resolved their own issues, the old marriage would continue to intrude on the new. He wanted to know what I thought about his suggesting that the long-divorced couple go into "post-divorce counseling" together. He felt that both of them would be resistant to it unless it was couched in terms of dealing with issues regarding the children. Before suggesting it, he wanted to know whether I would support the idea. I did, and gave him the names of a couple of outstanding therapists in the area.

The results were better than I had hoped. The new husband (H-2) was able to convince his wife (W-1) that her former husband (H-1) would never straighten out unless a therapist pointed out to him the error of his ways. He told her that H-1 was such an arrogant control freak that no solution imposed upon him by the court would be nearly as successful as one which a therapist could finesse. Meanwhile, he enlisted the support of the ex husband's new wife (W-2) with the promise that this strategy, at least, had some hope of resolving endless conflict. Frankly, both new mates were sick and tired of living the wars of marriage past.

Although it was rocky at the start, it did work. H-1 and W-1 were finally able to disengage, at least enough to stay out of court with one another. H-2 and W-2 got what they wanted, which was to be able to live their own lives without the specter of a former marriage constantly intervening in terms of summonses and court appearances, etc.

I have every reason to believe that the solution was successful in the long term. I am sure they preferred spending their money on vacations rather than legal fees.

If you are engaged in one of these dreadful post-dissolution conflicts, your life will never be your own. Certainly, any new relationship on which you choose to embark will forever be tainted by the specter of the former spouse raising his or her ugly head summoning you back to court. Not only does this create tremendous stress within the family, it is a significant financial burden as well. I am certain you and your new mate would much rather spend your money on that long-awaited trip to Hawaii than on one more visitation modification hearing.

The best way I know to make sure that you avoid this problem is to make sure that you finish your business through the process of the divorce itself. Do it once, and do it right.

PART VI

Solutions

CHAPTER 39

Reasonable Solutions to Problems That Come Up In Every Divorce

How to divide the furniture fairly and equitably

FURNISHING A HOUSEHOLD is an expensive business. It's a rare family that has enough of everything to comfortably supply two households. Moreover, at a time when your entire life is disrupted, no one should have to go home to a bare apartment, sit on a folding chair and eat off a card table. It simply isn't right. So here are some very practical suggestions about ways you can solve this problem:

- Inventory the house jointly with your spouse.

Each household consists of a mixture of practical necessities (washer, refrigerator, etc.), sentimental items, and valuable pieces (entertainment center and antiques). For this method, inventory the house with your spouse. (I don't mean that you each have to march from room to room with a clipboard in your hands. One of you should inventory the house and the other should have an opportunity to check the inventory to make sure it is complete and accurate.) Then flip a coin to determine which one of you is going to divide the single list into two lists of approximately equal value. It really doesn't matter who prepares the list. Call one "List A" and the other "List B." Then the other party gets to choose which list he wants. This is an excellent method for ensuring that the practical, sentimental and valuable items will be fairly equally sprinkled between the two lists. It avoids the necessity of having to hire appraisers and generally works quite well. The person making the lists usually "loads" one to be more attractive to the other side. However, he can't afford to load it too much or he'll end up with the short straw. In my experience, once a selection of "A" or "B" is made, there is some horse-trading back and forth and everyone goes away relatively satisfied that it was fair.

- If you can afford it, duplicate the necessities *at joint expense.*

Purchase another refrigerator, another washer/dryer, another set of dishes, towels, etc. You then trade off; one of you gets the new toaster, one of you gets the old one. You reverse it for the blenders. This way, each party has the dignity of a fully furnished household (or relatively so) and you avoid the nasty tug of war that frequently ensues in furniture divisions.

- For God's sake, the kids' furniture goes with the kids.

It is not valued or divided. In fact, it is my belief that for the sake of the children, you should purchase kid's furniture for use at each parent's home with joint funds. See that each home has some of the old familiar furniture, and involve your child in shopping for some new things to fill out and fix up the "new" room at each house. This is not done as a favor to your ex-spouse. It is done to ensure that your children have a safe, comfortable and nurturing *home* at both residences. Children should not have to sleep on cots or the couch when visiting their parents. Divorce is stressful enough for them without uncomfortable or unsafe physical surroundings. And don't do what I saw one parent do, and try to determine the value of the toys and games that stayed in the house with the kids and demand that the other parent pay him for half the value. Yes, the toys were purchased with joint funds. The kids don't have money of their own. That's not the point. The point is that the toys belong to the kids.

Pets

Pets should go with the party to whom they are emotionally connected, regardless of whether the puppy or kitten was originally a gift to the other party. And if both of you have a connection to the animal, share. It isn't that hard to allow play time or let your spouse take the dog for a run at the dog park. Animals don't understand why they are abandoned, and can provide a great deal of emotional support at a trying time. If the kids are particularly attached to the dog, send him back and forth between houses as the kids transition.

Family Photos and Videos

This used to be one of the most difficult and emotional parts of a divorce. I have presided over countless tear-stained meetings where beloved family photos are identified and divided. Fortunately, technology has now made it easy and cost effective. These should be divided equally between the parties without fail. Scan them so that each party has a complete set. Ditto address books. It isn't hard or costly to scan them, and there's no excuse for holding them hostage.

Financial Records and Tax Returns

By now you've figured out that I think all cards should be on the table and both parties should have all the tools and information necessary to negotiate a reasonable property division with full knowledge of all relevant facts. There is also lots of joint financial information that both of you will need in future years. Here's how to do it right.

If you don't have a good all-in-one printer/ scanner, buy one. They're cheap and reliable. Scan the following documents to a CD or thumb drive:

- All federal and state tax returns during the marriage, including schedules and worksheets, if available.

- Deeds, promissory notes and deeds of trust regarding all real property owned by either of you, even if you claim it is separate or mixed (part separate and part joint).
- All date of separation bills.
- Statements for all credit cards, even if they have a zero balance.
- If you claim inherited property, copies of the probate or other documents which prove you got it by inheritance and not by purchase with joint funds.
- At least three most recent statements (and preferably a year) for all bank accounts, retirement accounts, 401(k), IRA, Roth IRA, brokerage or other investment accounts.
- Check registers for at least a couple of years. If you use Quicken, download the whole file so you each have a complete copy.
- Three most recent paystubs plus last year's year end paystub.
- Employment agreements, if they exist. Ditto employee benefit booklets from each of your employers.
- All insurance policies
- Current wills of both of you.
- Any other joint financial documents that you know will become relevant to negotiating a resolution.

Each party should make copies of any such documents in their possession. Usually, but not always, this falls to the person who initially stays in the house. A rule of thumb is that, if in doubt, copy it. Make three identical thumb drives. Give one to your spouse, one to your attorney, and keep one as an archive.

Each of you should have your own original passport and a copy of your spouse's. If your children have passports, you'll have to decide who will be custodian. Note that there are restrictions on the handling of children's passports. The State Department posts these rules on its website at state.gov.

Canceling Credit Cards

The average family is going to have several credit cards, most with outstanding balances that they cannot afford to pay in full at the moment of separation. Make sure that you and your spouse each have complete knowledge of the current balances on all of your existing credit cards. Also, make sure that you know if there are old open credit accounts which you may have paid off but never closed.

A good way to accomplish this is to get a copy of your own credit report, which is easy to do online. Although not a perfect solution, this will give you a place to start identifying not only the extent of your debt, but the existence of any old credit cards or credit lines. Most of us have old credit accounts which we have not used in years and about which we may have forgotten. These must be canceled. Don't wait until you find out that your ex has borrowed $20,000 on an old credit line that you forgot you had signed for ten years ago. You may still be liable to the bank even if the divorce court ultimately orders your spouse to pay the debt.

As I've stated throughout this book, I am not an advocate of canceling credit without notice. Assuming that you and your spouse are still communicating, you should discuss it and determine which one of you is going to use which card(s), who is going to make the minimum payments on which obligations and how are you going to account for those payments between the two of you.

This way, nobody has any nasty surprises when they try to use a credit card and have it rejected, nor does either party have the ability to borrow against a forgotten joint credit line without notice to the other.

Sometimes people are reluctant to make the minimum credit card payments after separation because they aren't sure they will be reimbursed for half by the other side. If a credit card is a joint one, I think it is a good idea to decide who will make the minimum payments until they are paid off. Then equalize the payments so that you have each effectively paid half. This is preferable to debts going into collection or damaging your credit rating because you were afraid you wouldn't get reimbursed if you did the right thing and kept the payments current. If this reimbursement isn't the law in your state, try to work out an agreement with your spouse.

Children's' Unreimbursed Medical Expenses

One of the more common post-dissolution tugs of war involves the handling of medical, dental and orthodontia expenses, insurance premiums, co-pays and reimbursements for the kids. Typically, there is an order requiring either or both parents to cover the children on health insurance available through employment. One parent takes the kid to the doctor (and advances the cost), and the other has to process the claim (and perhaps pockets the reimbursement check). Sometimes this is done with the intent of playing games; sometimes it is just out of reluctance to deal directly with the ex to resolve the accounting. The amounts are rarely high enough to justify getting the lawyers involved, but large enough to create an ongoing irritant and source of conflict.

Instead, I suggest opening a dedicated joint bank account for the sole purpose of covering these expenses. Each parent deposits an agreed amount at the beginning, and each is authorized to sign checks. There should be an order, or at least a written agreement detailing the rules. All agreed expenses are paid from the account, including that initial visit to the doctor. All insurance reimbursement checks are redeposited into the account. When the statement comes in, the party receiving it scans it and emails it to the other including notations explaining the payments if they are not self evident. When the balance drops below a designated amount, each party replenishes it. Here are some suggested terms:

- Each parent deposits $500 (or some other agreed amount) when the account is opened. In the alternative, the deposits may be apportioned to the parties' respective incomes after adjusting for support.

- The parent who is most likely to take the kids to the doctor has primary control of the checkbook, subject to accounting.
- Agree on what expenses will be covered.

Sometimes there is a dollar limit, i.e., advance approval is required for non-emergency treatment of over $300. Sometimes orthodontia is treated separately. The payments can be limited to routine medical and dental care. However, with all the activities kids are involved in these days, the list can be readily expanded. For example, if you don't want to get into a battle over whether the child support is supposed to cover soccer camp or music lessons, you might want to include some or all of the following:

Music, tennis, dance and other lessons
Sports camps
Tutors
School fees
Ski or other sporting equipment
Yearbook and other non-recurring school fees
Other "extras" you both agree on

- Decide on the timing and method of replenishment.

I have found this to work well if the parents stick to the rules. Certainly the kids love it because they don't miss the soccer camp registration deadline because Mom and Dad are jockeying for position about who should advance the fee and take the risk of not being reimbursed.

Wills and Estate Planning

If you are contemplating divorce, you may not want your soon-to-be-ex spouse to be the heir to your estate. You and your spouse probably signed reciprocal wills at some time in the past and you should review these to see if you want to make a change. I have had some clients who chose to name their spouses as heirs after the divorce. Most don't, and wish to change their wills to make their children or other family members their beneficiaries.

At the early stages of the divorce, you won't know what property you are going to receive in the ultimate division. Therefore, it is impossible for you to do a comprehensive estate plan. However, you can do an interim will and revoke the prior will. Then, when the property division is completed, you can make an estate plan which reflects your post-divorce financial situation.

Note as you are doing this that many states have rules preventing you from changing the beneficiaries on insurance policies, IRAs, 401(k)s, pensions and other deferred income accounts, until after the court has made an order allocating and dividing them. Ask your attorney before changing beneficiaries on anything except your will, and you won't find yourself in the unhappy position of having inadvertently violated a court order or potential fiduciary duties to your spouse.

CHAPTER 40

Taking Responsibility for Your Own Lawyer's Conduct

WHAT HAPPENS WHEN you are part way through the divorce and find you are not comfortable with the strategies or tactics employed by your attorney? You thought you were going to proceed to a negotiated settlement and instead you are facing a seemingly endless series of court appearances.

We've already talked about how to select a lawyer, and hopefully you've made a wise choice. However, there are times when you find it simply is not going the way you thought it would.

The first rule is that it is *your* divorce. You will be living with the consequences of the strategies adopted and the decisions that you and your attorney make for the rest of your natural life. Your attorney will not. Therefore, the ultimate decision-making authority and the ultimate responsibility are yours.

We've already assumed that you want the divorce to be as smooth and amicable as possible and that you are going to insist on good communication with your attorney. If you find that the conduct of your case is making you uncomfortable, discuss it with your attorney, *not* her legal assistant. Get a second opinion. If after doing so you are still not satisfied, change attorneys. Some lawyers confuse belligerence with advocacy, not realizing that it is quite possible to be professional, cooperative and effective at the same time. It is your responsibility to tell your attorney if you believe her conduct is too confrontational, if you believe that unnecessary discovery is being done or you want a different strategy adopted. Your attorney may want your instructions in writing. That is perfectly fair. Recognize that you are not a lawyer and are not objective. If after seriously considering your goals, the strategy adopted so far, and your attorney's recommendations, you still believe a different strategy is required, you should not hesitate to give those instructions in writing to your attorney. If they are not followed, make a change.

I have already said that selecting your attorney is probably the single most important determining factor in charting the course of your divorce. Even among equally competent attorneys, there will be wide variations in style, tactics and strategy. After getting into the case, you may find that the style you originally thought was going to work best is counterproductive or is one with which you are simply not comfortable.

I am not talking about firing your lawyer the first time you disagree on a strategy. I am talking about taking responsibility.

I have always been of the opinion that anyone can make one mistake in the selection of an attorney. I have never hesitated to give a second opinion to a client and will generally agree to substitute in as the second attorney in a case if I think I can help. However, I would never be attorney number three, four or five. When a prospective client comes in with a litany of complaints about the four or five attorneys who have previously represented him, each one worse than the last, my antennae go up. If someone has been through that many lawyers, it tells me that either he is the worst judge of character in recorded history or he is more interested in finding someone who will tell him what he wants to hear than in hearing the truth. He will continue to look for someone else to blame rather than take responsibility for his own role in the divorce. Also, don't be surprised if your prospective new attorney asks if you have paid the last one. If you haven't, they may assume you won't pay *them* either when you decide the bill has gotten too big.

So, if you've started the divorce and you're feeling uncomfortable about the way the case is being handled, get a second opinion or even a third, remembering, of course, to do the research I've suggested for selecting an attorney in the first place. You want to be sure the second opinion is a qualified one. If, after doing so, you are still unhappy with the course your attorney has adopted, that is the time to make a change, and the sooner the better. Don't wait until a counterproductive strategy has been put in place and then go to a new attorney to try to undo all the harm that has already been done. Make the decision and act on it.

Finally, be sure your next choice is an improvement. The more times you've changed attorneys, the fewer really competent attorneys will be willing to talk to you, much less take over the case.

CHAPTER 41

Keeping a Rein on Fees and Costs

"Yes, Virginia, you will have to pay for it."

ONE OF THE most important things that you can do to maintain a realistic attitude toward your divorce from the beginning is to assume that you are in fact going to have to pay your own attorney's fees. I have had this conversation with hundreds of clients. The old days when the husband paid all the fees because he was the sole wage earner are long gone. Many courts have now adopted the philosophy that the fees on *both* sides should be paid from the marital estate. The theory, of course, is that it took two of you to make the marriage and it takes two to make the divorce. Although this sometimes favors the party who runs up more fees, in general I find the philosophy a sound one. People also tend to be more reasonable and realistic about the positions they take and the concessions they are willing to make if both sides have skin in the game.

Do yourself a favor: Assume at the beginning that you are likely to pay all of your own fees and, more important, since divorce attorney fees are tax deductible only in very limited circumstances, you will pay them with after-tax dollars. This means that in order to pay $1,000 worth of attorneys' fees in your divorce, you will have to earn $1,300 to $1,500, or some other amount, depending on your income tax bracket. Unless you happen to be sitting on a pot of gold, it's going to hurt. And if you are sitting on a pot of gold, chances are that you are in a high tax bracket, so that $1,000 of legal fees may well cost you close to twice that much in real dollars.

Keeping a Rein on Fees and Costs

Before the fees run into the tens of thousands and you suddenly realize that there is insufficient money to pay them, become involved. You are not powerless. Here are some things which you can do from the outset to help you keep fees and costs under control:

- Provide every bit of information and financial data that you can to your attorney without the necessity of subpoenas.

Subpoenas are costly and time-consuming. If you have family financial records in the file cabinet at home, take a weekend and go through them. If you can access your financial data online, do so. Scan it to a CD or thumb drive for your attorney. If your spouse wants a set as well, make a copy available. The cost of an extra thumb drive is cheap at the price. This means that neither side will be required to send out subpoenas for documents that are readily available. I cannot begin to tell you how many times I have received a subpoena from opposing counsel for records which were readily available from his own client or in the file cabinet at his client's house. And here's a hint: If your own attorney sends out a demand for documents you've already given her, call her on it. You should not be paying her to ask for something she already has.

- Give your attorney financial information that is as complete as possible, even if it isn't perfect.

If you haven't historically been active in managing the family finances and have a secretive spouse you may in fact not have access to much information. However, if you know that there is (or at least was) an account at ABC Bank, even if you don't know which branch or the account number, tell your attorney. This at least gives him a lead on where to go looking for the money. It is financially prohibitive to subpoena all of the possible asset repositories where your spouse may have stashed the cash. Private investigation services are expensive and, TV mythology notwithstanding, in my experience the results can most kindly be described as spotty. For starters, pull a copy of your own credit report. Anything you can do to narrow the field of inquiry and investigation will help keep your fees and costs to a manageable level. Do as much research as you can on the internet. You will be amazed (and perhaps dismayed) at what you can find out by simply Googling your spouse or yourself.

- If you don't have the records but know where to get them, do so.

For example, banks frequently charge a great deal for subpoenas of their records, particularly if they are voluminous. However, if you, as a signatory on the account, go to the bank to get the records, the charge may well be significantly less. If you bank online, you may be able to print them for free. Additionally, if you know that there are specific checks you need, you don't need to order and pay for all of the checks. Get copies of the ones that you know you need. You can always go back and get others later if you have to.

- If your attorney doesn't ask you what financial records you have or have access to, ask *him* what you can do to help prepare your case.

Get a list of the information your attorney is going to want and start doing your own leg work. You have a greater ability to get information informally than your attorney does. Anything that you can do to accomplish this may well mean one less subpoena or deposition and can save you hundreds if not thousands of dollars.

- When your attorney receives records from the other side, go through them yourself.

This is very important. Your attorney cannot know everything about you or your life. There may be a notation in a check register which would mean absolutely nothing to your attorney or her paralegal. However, you know that it is your spouse's best buddy from college with whom he always had financial deals going on the side. Only you will know that the appearance of this name in your spouse's financial records is a red flag to possible diversion of funds. Your attorney will have no way of knowing this unless you become involved in the process yourself.

- At every stage in the proceeding, do a cost/benefit analysis.

For many of you, this will be the first time you have had to do such a formal analysis. If so, it's time to learn how. Suppose that your spouse has filed a document with the court which contains a lie, a boldfaced, absolutely provable lie. However, if the lie is about a $600 item and it is going to cost you $500 to subpoena the records necessary to prove the lie, or double that to take the deposition, what is the point? Discuss the discovery plan with your attorney. Find out what subpoenas she thinks are important and what depositions should be taken. Find out the approximate cost of each of these and the approximate benefit *in financial* terms if the discovery turns up the evidence you expect. Consider also the risk of the specific discovery not being fruitful.

If you happen to live in one of those jurisdictions where the courts charge these fees to the person who is caught in the lie, so be it. However, don't count on it. Attorneys' fees are almost always the last issue settled, and even a relatively good claim for fees frequently gets swept under the rug as part of an overall global settlement of all issues.

Accordingly, at each stage of discovery, you should know the likely benefits of the discovery and the attendant cost. The same goes for the cost of a court hearing.

Sometimes your attorney will want to send out a subpoena which you do not think is worth the cost. I have set forth in much greater detail in the previous chapter ("Taking Responsibility for Your Own Lawyer's Conduct") my theories about who is ultimately responsible for the conduct of the case. It is *your* case. If you really believe, despite your attorney's advice, that the proposed discovery is not justified, instruct your attorney not to pursue it. If she asks you to put those instructions in writing to protect her from a later malpractice claim, comply. It isn't fair to tell your attorney not to take steps to protect you and then, when the result turns out to be something other than you had hoped, use the fact that there is no written record of your instructions to sue her. If you are going to take responsibility, take it. If, on the other hand, you don't want to take the responsibility, you will pay for it. Remember, your attorney's ethical duty is to perform what is called "due diligence" to protect you. He can't afford to guess or gamble with your future. You, however, can take calculated risks, but only if you involve yourself in the process. People often complain that lawyers spend too much time and money on discovery. Interestingly, more attorneys get sued by former clients for not doing enough discovery than for doing too much. Go figure.

Don't passively stand on the sidelines as the fees creep up to $10,000 and $20,000 and then suddenly decide that it wasn't worth it and you can't afford to pay for it. Too many people then settle for less than they are entitled to out of panic instead of taking a reasoned approach from the beginning.

- Don't use your lawyer as a therapist.

One of the prime causes for fees which go literally through the roof is that you are constantly in your lawyer's office for moral support. This is a lousy use of your lawyer's time and your money. You can probably hire a first-rate therapist for a lower hourly rate than you are paying your attorney. This goes for the attorney's staff as well. They are genuinely interested in helping people, or they wouldn't have chosen to work in such an emotionally demanding career. That doesn't mean they are qualified or wish to serve as your shrink.

- If you are pursuing a fight to score emotional points against your spouse, I guarantee you that your legal fees will be out of proportion to the satisfaction ultimately attained.

Keeping a Rein on Fees and Costs

If you insist on litigating the minutia just to prove that your spouse has lied in court documents, or prove to the judge what a scum your ex is, you will incur a fee bill all out of proportion to the value received. Your spouse may be a walking oil slick. Chances are that the judge has figured that out for himself. If you insist on paying your lawyer to marshal all of the "evidence" of the lies that he told you for the last 20 years, you will be faced with a fee bill you will not want to pay. Rather than get into a fight over fees with your lawyer, why not be realistic about it from the beginning? And don't wait until the legal fees equal the equity in your house before taking control.

- If the fees are getting beyond what you can comfortably pay, consider limiting the scope of your lawyer's involvement, and represent yourself on the easier tasks and issues.

Another recent development which is helping people keep their divorce costs manageable is called "unbundling," or limited scope representation. In limited scope, you do part of the case with your lawyer's assistance and coaching, while your lawyer handles the more complex tasks or issues. Perhaps your lawyer will draft documents and script questions for you, but coach you how to go to court on your own. In other cases, your lawyer will assist you with the custody, pension, stock options, or other complex issues in the case, while you represent yourself on the simpler issues. You pay your lawyer only for the work that he does, and save the money which you would spend to have "full service" representation, that is, if the attorney handled the entire case. It can be very satisfying to find out that you can do part of the case yourself, and it can save you a huge amount in attorney fees.

It is beyond the scope of this book to go into the myriad ways in which you and a creative lawyer can tailor a limited representation agreement to your needs and the law and facts of your case. Fortunately, I've written another book which goes into great detail on how you can do this effectively, as well as warning you about the situations where you probably shouldn't try it. That book is *Unbundling Your Divorce: How to Find a Lawyer to Help You Help Yourself,* (2006) Nexus Publishing Company. You can find it at amazon.com or at nexusbooks.com.

CHAPTER 42

What About the House?

By now you have had some opportunity to think about what is important to you.

Recognizing that at the end of the process you are only going to have about half of what you thought you owned at the beginning (since as couples we all think we own all of it collectively), you should have spent some time thinking about which half you would prefer. And lose 10 points if you still think you can guilt-trip your spouse into letting you have it all. That one is a recipe for disaster.

I have already cautioned you not to make irrevocable decisions in the early months after separation because your goals will change as you get more perspective. But assuming you have already come through that part of the process, you should be in a position to make some decisions. Since you are not going to get it all, what part is most important to you?

For many of you, goal setting will be second nature. Either you do it daily in your business or it is simply a knack which you have. For others, it will be a struggle to simply learn the mechanics of how to make a decision and set priorities. It may be as simple as taking a sheet of paper and writing down the pros and cons in parallel columns. Some of you may let options roll around in the back of your heads until the correct one pops out, as if by magic. Others will be able to weigh the probable consequences of their decision at lightning speed. Whatever method works will be the right method for you. Here are some suggestions of things you might consider.

How to Avoid the Divorce from Hell

One of the issues which generate the most angst is whether to keep or sell the house. For some of you this will not be a decision at all; keeping it will not be an option because neither of you can afford to keep it without contribution from the other. On the other hand, selling it may not be an option right now if it is under water.

Suppose the mortgage is $200 per month because you and your spouse have been living there since dirt was invented. However, you may be thinking, "The house is too big for me," or "It's too much upkeep," etc. It may be a financial disaster to sell the house. You may be motivated by emotional considerations ("There are too many memories here"). I have asked many a client to consider whether it is better to live in a house with a $200 per month mortgage payment and lots of memories or a condo on which your payment is $1,400 and you live on spaghetti for the rest of your natural life. This is a *financial* decision. You have to weigh the cost of the existing residence against that of a replacement. If you sell it, will you be able to buy another house in the same neighborhood or will you have to move to a cheaper one? Also, weigh the capital gain consequences. If you keep the house, you will be solely responsible for all (not half) of the capital gain and all (not half) of the costs of sale when it is ultimately sold. You can't make a good decision until you know the financial consequences of each option. Now, if you make the decision for emotional reasons, you may determine that it is worth the additional $1,200 a month to you not to be surrounded by familial memories. It is clearly your right and your decision. However, recognize that you are making an emotional decision rather than a financial one and be certain that you are willing to live with the consequences before the "for sale" sign goes up. And you can erase a lot of memories by some creative redecorating. One of the most satisfying things you may do is redo the house to make it truly yours. I have a friend who struggled mightily with this one. He ultimately decided to keep the house and completely redecorate it. When he did, he realized that it was the first time in his life that he lived in a place which reflected only his personal taste without anyone else's fingerprints on it. It felt so good to have a nest that was totally his that he gave a huge party to celebrate.

If the house really is too big for you, this may be the time to sell it and share the capital gain liability and costs of fix up and sale with your spouse. All these factors need to be included in your decision. This is where your attorney, accountant or financial planner can be of great assistance.

Perhaps you are in the reverse situation. You assume that you "have to" keep the house because you've got the kids. Many kids are quite adaptable and yours may be among them. Make the decision based upon the facts as they exist in *your* case. Be willing to consider other options and don't assume that just because it has always been this way, it has to be in the future. And if the current house is a drafty old money pit with lots of deferred maintenance you don't want to be responsible for, you and the kids could have a wonderful time shopping for and fixing up your new home together.

I have had clients tell me that they simply can't stand to spend one more month in the family homestead because of all of the baggage and memories that it carries; others believed they would utterly fall apart if required to leave their sanctuaries. Only you know what is most important to you. The important thing is that you understand the emotional and financial price of either course of action, including potential tax consequences, quantify them, and make the best decision you can under the circumstances.

Once you have made the decision, *LET IT GO*. We could all spend the rest of our lives second guessing ourselves with what-ifs. Make a deal with yourself that if you have made the best decision you could under the facts and circumstances then known to you, you will not beat yourself about the head and shoulders over it for years to come. Decide and move on.

CHAPTER 43

How to Evaluate a Settlement Offer

SOONER OR LATER during the course of your divorce, you are going to be called upon to either make or respond to a settlement proposal, perhaps several. If you are not accustomed to negotiation, it is going to be important to educate yourself so that you don't lose an opportunity to resolve your case satisfactorily outside of court.

I'm a broken record on the point that court is a last resort. The only reason you and your soon-to-be ex would be sitting across a courtroom from one another is because one or both of you has failed to realistically assess your case and negotiate a reasonable settlement.

Sometimes a total settlement simply cannot be pulled off and part of the case must be tried before a judge. However, I have never seen a case between two sane people in which at least some of the issues cannot be agreed upon. Perhaps you are at a complete impasse on the value of the family business but at least can agree on where your kids should live. Perhaps you can agree on who is going to be in the house and what it is worth, but can't seem to get over the issue of support. At least agree on the things you can. This will mean that the judge will have more time to devote to those areas where you really are stuck. It also assures that, at least as to the issues you've settled, you (and not a stranger) will be deciding where you make concessions.

The toughest situations are where you both want the same thing. You may both be invested in having the house and no other house will do. However, if you find yourself in that position and are about to walk into a courtroom to have the judge decide, at least make sure that you have made every effort to resolve the issue on reasonable terms.

How to Evaluate a Settlement Offer

Before describing what to do in this situation, I'd like to spend a little time on what not to do.

Many clients have assured me throughout the course of a bitter, hard-fought divorce that *all* they want is to settle. I have learned that phrase can mean very different things to different people. If the only "settlement offer" you will consider consists of the sum total of your best case result on every issue, you are *not* negotiating. Unless your spouse and his attorney are both idiots, you are wasting your time and money. If you make a ridiculously overreaching demand, the other side may well decide you aren't negotiating in good faith and refuse to counter. What good did that strategy accomplish? It certainly didn't get you closer to the stated goal of settlement out of court. You want to give them an incentive to accept your offer, not an incentive to go to trial.

You will be equally unsuccessful at settling your case if you define every concession as a loss. Divorce, as with marriage and life itself, is a series of compromises and if you start out with the mind-set that the other side "wins" every time you concede a point, there will be precious few concessions and no real chance for settlement.

So what *should* you do?

Know your best-case and worst-case positions. Thoroughly and objectively analyze your case with your attorney and understand precisely what the most likely winning and losing issues are. Ask your attorney, issue by issue, what she thinks the judge will do. She will be unlikely to give you a firm commitment in all areas because so many of these things are within the discretion of the judge. However, she should be able to tell you within some reasonable percentage or range of results. This exercise is very helpful for both of you, as it forces you to step back and quite critically and dispassionately look at the weaknesses of your own case. One of the hallmarks of a good attorney is that she knows the weaknesses of her case, knows how to try to parlay them into a good settlement, and when to cut to the chase and concede a loser in exchange for something else.

How to Avoid the Divorce from Hell

In evaluating your best and worst case scenarios, you must assume that neither you nor your ex is going to get everything you want. Family law judges loathe sending people out of their courtrooms empty-handed. Therefore, chances are very good that even if the judge has to stretch a little bit, she's going to find a way to make sure that everyone goes away with something. This means that for starters, you'd better be willing to decide before you go into court which issues you would rather concede if you have to.

Analyze the other side's case using the same process. You may figure wrong, but after all, the opposing party is the person you know best in the world. If you think he is utterly committed to ending up with the house and in your secret heart of hearts something else is more important to you, file that information away. I smell a settlement somewhere. Is there some way you can trade things you don't really want (but the other side does) for things you do want? The corollary of this is, of course, that even if you don't particularly want it right now, don't give it away until you're sure you can't trade it for something you *do* want.

Package your proposal in such a way that the other side wins something, too. Preferably, package it so that that it looks like the other side is winning a whole lot more than he is. Don't get ridiculous about this, but after all, the goal is to have him accept the offer. If there's nothing in it for him and he has nothing to lose by going to trial, why on earth shouldn't he roll the dice and see what happens in court?

Strategize the settlement negotiations with your attorney. Find out your attorney's style of negotiating and what strategy she thinks would be most likely to work, given the facts of your case and the personalities of your spouse and the other attorney.

In my negotiations, I frequently opposed attorneys with whom I have had other cases and other settlement negotiations. I had formed an opinion of their negotiating styles and of course, they had formed one of mine.

At this stage in the proceedings, I always hope there's a competent attorney on the other side. Two skilled attorneys will each know an approximate range within which the case should resolve, given all of the facts, the law, the risks, and the judge's personality, as well as the personalities of the litigants. They will be able to come up with creative solutions that would only baffle stupid attorneys. They're not always right, but more often than not, there's a range. I know I'm going to get to that range sooner or later and so does the other attorney, if he has any idea what he's doing. It is a waste of my time and my client's money to make a settlement proposal that is way outside the range. Accordingly, when I commenced negotiations with an attorney I'd never dealt with before, I always made a point of telling him that my offer is designed to be a very serious, middle ground compromise and not simply an invitation to negotiate. Therefore, I would thoroughly and carefully evaluate the risks of my case before the first settlement offer was made, and then I would probably not move a great deal, certainly not outside the range I'd already established for myself. This means we got to the bottom line much faster with much less money spent in attorney fees, and I think everyone ended up happier in the long run.

I don't respect attorneys who make either a ridiculously high or ridiculously low offer, or set unreasonably short time deadlines to analyze a comprehensive offer. They will send a seven page settlement proposal letter which ends with a statement that the offer expires at 5:00 p.m. tomorrow. If I'm in court, I may not even see the offer before the deadline, much less be able to analyze it thoroughly, review it with my client, and give him a chance to digest it before we respond. These tactics may work in other areas of the law, but I find them counterproductive and insulting in family law. They may even draw a sanction from some judges.

The worst thing about trying to negotiate with an incompetent attorney is that although you might assume she would give away the store because she doesn't know what she's doing, the opposite is actually true. Because she doesn't know how to evaluate the risks of her own case, she tends to dig in and refuse to concede even the obvious losers. One of the worst lawyers I ever knew prided herself on being such a tough negotiator that everything went to court. When bragging about the lineup of trials she had on calendar, she would titter proudly "I'm such a bitch!" As if that made her a good lawyer. (See Chapter 8, "Why You Want Your Spouse to Have a Good Lawyer, Too.") This runs up legal fees and requires unnecessary trials. It may be easy to beat up on the stupid attorney at trial, but I always find it frustrating and so do the litigants. It isn't fair to the client who's being well represented because she has to go through a trial she neither needs nor wants simply to get to a reasonable solution. It is equally unfair for the client who is being badly represented because he is being given false expectations that he is going to win the unwinnable, all because his lawyer doesn't know better and wants to prove how tough she is.

Always, always, always factor the cost of the fight into any evaluation of a settlement proposal. If you've done as I suggested, you already have a relatively clear understanding of your best and worst case scenarios. You should not only be advised where the range of settlement might be, but which are your weakest issues. Add to this entire soup the cost of trial. By that I do not mean just the attorney and accountant or other expert witness fees that a trial will entail. These can be substantial and run to the tens of thousands of dollars for even a relatively short trial. There is also the cost of preparing for trial only to find that the court's calendar is too busy and there is no other judge available that day to hear your case. This means that you come back two or three months later. You'd think that you wouldn't have to prepare for trial all over again because, of course, all the work was done . . . right? I'm afraid not. Property values and bank balances may have changed, requiring updates. Trial notes have gotten cold and you are going to pay your attorney to prepare again so that he is on top of all of the evidence, the witnesses and the testimony when the case is called. When trials are continued more than once, the costs become horrendous. And of course, each time you show up for trial, you have to take off work and lose income you really need.

Finally, consider the emotional wear and tear that you, your spouse and your children will suffer if you go to trial.

How to Evaluate a Settlement Offer

I don't mean that you should roll over and play dead at the thought of going to court, but you should quantify the cost. Educate yourself about the risks and benefits and recognize that nothing is utterly predictable. Let me give you two examples:

- You say to your attorney, "I realize he's insisting on a value of the house that's thousands of dollars higher than market. However, this has been dragging on for two years and I simply can't stand it anymore. I'll do *anything* to get this over with. Just accept the offer and be done with it."

Six months or a year from now when you're comfortably ensconced in what is now *your* house, the emotional pressure that caused you to simply throw up your hands and give in is a remote memory. You are going to start thinking of all the uses you might have had for that $30,000 (or $10,000 or $5,000) you walked away from, and human nature being what it is, you will probably conclude it wasn't worth it.

- Or you say to your attorney, "You and I both know that they're being outrageous in insisting on such a high value for my business. Not only is our appraisal lower, even their appraisal is lower. This is just extortion."

You may be right; it is. I hate giving in to extortion as much as the next guy, except that sometimes it is cost-effective. If the other side is insisting on an unreasonable position but the cost to you of giving in is less than the cost of actually trying the case, you may want to seriously consider compromising that issue. This is particularly true if there's a chance that you will have to pay the other party's attorney's fees as well as your own. I know, this isn't fair. But who said anything about fairness?

Vindication carries a big price tag. I realize that some states now allow an order for attorney's fees in the form of sanctions, so that an unreasonable party (or an attorney, for that matter) can be ordered to pay your attorney's fees for fighting stupid issues. These orders can be extremely difficult to obtain and are used only reluctantly by most judges. Accordingly, in evaluating a settlement proposal, assume that you're going to be paying your own fees and factor that cost into your analysis.

Quantify, quantify, quantify. When evaluating an offer, you have to be able to estimate with some degree of confidence the probable cost of going to court versus the probable cost of conceding whatever issue you're being asked to yield. Only you can quantify the emotional cost. Your attorney can help you with the financial part. However, this is another place to remember that no matter how predictable we think a particular fact pattern will be with a particular judge, anything can, and does, happen at trial.

Sooner or later, almost everyone comes to an issue about which they say, "It's not the money. It's the *principle*." Those words are red flags. If you find yourself saying anything like that, quantify the principle. "Is this principle worth $300 to you? $3,000? $30,000?" At some point on this continuum, you are going to find an amount you are not willing to pay for the principle. Once you have done that, take one more hard look at yourself to determine whether you really are willing to pay the price of vindication. Remember, also, that the good feelings that go with vindication are momentary at best. After you do this analysis, if the answer is still yes, then pull out your checkbook and write the check.

This is a prime area for "sellers' remorse." Just as the party who concedes too much to just get it over with finds six months later that it probably wasn't worth it, the individual who insists on fighting "for the principle" invariably reaches the same conclusion. Once you've been proven "right" and wrapped yourself in righteousness and the American flag, couldn't you think of a better use for that $5,000? I can. Taking a trip to Europe or maybe even paying for your kids' braces come to mind. Think about it.

Remember, whatever the ultimate settlement, you're probably going to be unhappy with it. This is simple human nature. Before you and your spouse split, you jointly owned everything. Now you find you own only half of it, and "it" may have been substantially depleted by the twin costs of litigation and supporting two households. Anyone who's ever negotiated a business deal knows there is give and take. There are things you wish you could have kept that you had to give up, and in exchange you got something else. People who are not familiar with negotiation frequently find this the most baffling part of the entire process. Their usual reaction is to simply dig in their heels and refuse to settle for fear of making the "wrong" decision. These are the cases that go to trial and shouldn't.

So if you find yourself contemplating divorce and you're not comfortable negotiating business transactions, educate yourself. There are many good books out there on negotiation skills and techniques. Buy them, read them and, most important, to the extent that it is possible, take as objective and rational a view of your own divorce as you can. I always tell clients to pretend it's a business deal. We know it isn't, but if we can pretend so, at least for purposes of the negotiation process, we will do a lot better.

And if you are the hotshot negotiator of the Western World, recognize that you are personally invested in this particular negotiation, and your lack of objectivity will make you much less effective than when you negotiate an arm's length business deal.

There is no "perfect" solution. Make the best decision you can under the circumstances and move on.

CHAPTER 44

Disengaging

*"Evil will simply disappear when given
nothing to push against."*

TAO TE CHING

IT TAKES TWO to make a war. Even if you are divorcing a total jerk, you *can* disengage to some extent. You won't be able to do it, however, unless and until you understand that the conflict of the divorce has its roots in the conflict of the marriage. That's another way of saying that you both have responsibility for the degree of negativity in the process.

This is not a book about psychology. It is a book about the process of divorce. However, there is a huge amount of psychology which goes into a simple, common-sense approach.

If you are involved in a war that you don't want, take a hard look at what you are doing to feed the conflict and, more important, what you can do to disengage. There are ways to disengage without sacrificing important legal and financial goals. You will never achieve it, however, if you are still trying to:

- Get even for past bad treatment or marital wrongdoing.
- Catch up or recoup what you gave away in the past which you now feel was overly generous.
- Engage in any kind of payback or one-upmanship.
- Prove that you are "right."

Disengaging

- Prove that it's your spouse's fault.
- Prove that your spouse is a bad parent.
- All of the above and more.

These are all issues which you should examine with the assistance of your therapist. If you can't afford a therapist, take a good hard look at yourself in the mirror.

I have found that it is simply impossible to look yourself in the eye in the mirror and lie. If you are at this stage and having to figure it out for yourself, pull a chair up in front of a large mirror. It might be helpful to have a box of Kleenex handy as well. Choose a time when you know you will be uninterrupted for at least an hour. Promise yourself that you will be absolutely honest.

When you have done all of the above, ask yourself the hard questions. What are *you* still getting out of the fight? What are *you* doing to promote it? In what ways are *you* continuing to feed the conflict? Why? Ask all of these questions while holding a fixed gaze into your own eyes in the mirror. If you find that you look away when you try to answer any of these questions, you are lying to yourself. If you find your mind wandering to whether you should try a new hairstyle, get your teeth fixed, or whether there's more gray hair than there used to be, you're lying to yourself. As soon as you find you can't look yourself in the eye in the mirror and answer your question, you have hit pay dirt. That's the issue you need to work on. Until you have resolved it, you will remain engaged in the conflict yourself and you will not be able to move beyond it.

If you want to end the war, you have to be willing to let go. You will never be out of the relationship until you let go of the war. Even if you are giving away the store out of martyrdom or guilt, you are continuing the conflict, albeit in a passive/aggressive way.

I have seen divorce wars go on for years after the final judgment. People who are truly committed to war can fight about everything from how the kids' hair is cut to who takes Jason to baseball practice or anything else that requires them to interact with each other. I remember

How to Avoid the Divorce from Hell

talking to a client whose divorce had deteriorated into monumental conflicts over minute post-judgment issues. The other party was, if anything, more bitter and vindictive than on the day the marriage ended. As my client was expressing his frustration at the waste of time, money and energy being spent on minutia, I suggested that he simply disengage. He looked at me in horror. "But then *she'd* win!" Yes, this time she would win and maybe the next time and maybe the next time. But really . . . the issues at stake were whether the visit ended at 6:30 or 7:30, and the like. They were hardly life-threatening. I thought there was a reasonably good chance that after a while, things would calm down when the ex found there was nothing to push against. One always can (and should) hold firm on an important issue which involves children's welfare and the like. However, it takes two to fight about how Jessica's hair is cut.

If you want a graphic illustration of what negativity can do to a couple, I strongly suggest that you see the movie *War of the Roses* with Kathleen Turner and Michael Douglas which was released some years ago. I found it to be a brilliant (and quite accurate) demonstration of what can happen when two people allow divorce conflict to consume them.

Interestingly, the movie didn't do particularly well at the box office. I understood why when I was sitting in the movie theater and realized I was the only one laughing out loud. Of course, I had seen every one of the stunts these people pulled on one another in real life (except for peeing on the fish – I hadn't seen that one before) so it was old hat to me. I was able to appreciate the satire while recognizing the reality.

Leaving the movie theater, many of the couples were not making eye contact with one another. The dark humor of the movie simply cut too close to the bone. That's precisely what made the satire so delicious but disturbing. Several couples were obviously uncomfortable. The next morning I called opposing counsel on a particularly nasty divorce and offered to make a deal with her. I told her I would make my client go see the movie if she would do the same with hers. Ultimately, both of our clients were so invested in their conflict that I don't believe either of them ever saw the movie. Certainly neither of them stopped living it and creating new variations of their own diabolical divorce games.

If you are seriously wrestling with this issue, be honest with yourself. Sit down and make a list of what is important to you in life. Revise the list periodically and choose carefully what is important enough to go to war over.

Two good communication techniques can help you keep from engaging with a hostile ex. When subjected to a diatribe from your ex, say, "I'm sorry you feel that way." This doesn't promote an argument, because you are not getting into whether it is "right" or "wrong" to feel that way.

Another is to say, "You are entitled to your opinion, but I choose not to engage with you." Then walk away. There are lots of good communication techniques in the book *Joint Custody With a Jerk*, described in the next chapter, "More Resources."

If all other motivations fail, imagine this one. Your spouse wants to fight for the next 20 years over everything from what time the sun will rise to what day of the week it is. If you simply disengage and get on with your own life, it will drive him nuts.

CHAPTER 45

More Resources

TWENTY YEARS AGO when the first edition of this book came out, there were a few dozen books on divorce and little else. Since then, resources on divorce have exploded exponentially.

Divorce on the Web

There is a wealth of information available online. It requires selectivity, however. A simple search for "divorce" will result in thousands of hits. These range from serious resources to lunatic fringe groups and individuals who post a single piece ranting about their own divorce experience, which may not have been shared by anyone else on the planet. You will find literally anything there. Expanding the search to include "parenting," "mediation" or "custody" will give you even more information, both useful and not. Keep looking. When even the Huffington Post has a section devoted to divorce, you know there's a lot of information out there.

There are sites dedicated to virtually every aspect of divorce. You will find mother's rights, father's rights, custody, property division, resources to help you raise (or lower) your support and lists of services, newsletters, therapists, attorneys, mediators and special interest groups.

Add to these the countless chat rooms, forums, and blogs and you can easily be overwhelmed by the volume of information.

Divorce blogs come in two general flavors. There are those done by professionals, lawyers, mediators, therapists and the like. Some of these are thoughtful and informative, others are merely disguised advertising tools for their own professional practice. Don't choose your lawyer just because he happens to have a blog. However, as you are doing your research, a blog will tell you a lot about the lawyer you are thinking about retaining.

The second flavor is blogs by people who want to chronicle their own divorce experience. Anyone can and does blog about their divorce experience. Some are useful, others downright nutty. As I write this I have just read a blog listing 5 things you should do in your divorce. The first bit of advice was "don't listen to your lawyer." Say what? Why even have a lawyer if you're going to ignore their advice? If you don't like your lawyer's advice, that's the time to get a second opinion. Why would any sane person deliberately ignore advice they are paying hundreds of dollars an hour for? That gem is followed by "don't talk to your ex" and equally unhelpful others. That blogger's recommendations are certainly not going to foster a long term goal of dancing at your daughter's wedding.

For purposes of the following discussion, I have focused on resources which promote non-adversarial resolution of divorce problems, and provide useful resources designed to help reduce conflict. I have ignored the ones which advocate scorched earth litigation, purport to tell you how to clean out your spouse, as well as sites where someone is clearly bearing a grudge or has a personal agenda.

I also encourage anyone contemplating divorce to visit a chat room or two (after carefully considering the warnings below). A conversation with someone else going through the same experience can be invaluable, if only to let you know that you are not alone.

As with every other suggestion in this book, use your own judgment. If it doesn't feel right to you, move on. There will always be something else you will find helpful.

Numerous sites have state-specific listings of attorneys, mediators, therapists, financial counselors, paralegals and the like. These range from hit and miss to downright unreliable, but if they list lawyers in your community, it may be a good place to start. Do be careful, however. You should never hire a professional just because they advertise on the web, any more than you would rely solely on the yellow pages. Many of them pay to be listed online, it's very cheap to post your own website touting your legal skills (real or imagined), and there is absolutely no quality control. Anyone can (and does) post *anything.* Even a site which includes a promise of a non-adversarial approach may be no more than false advertising. I actually saw the individual I used as the prototype for the "Lawyer from Hell" listed in an online mediation service promising to promote settlement (yeah, right). Don't forget that his clones might just be online, too, and think that this would be a great way to get new clients in the door, before convincing them that, although mediation may have been the starting point, for some reason *this* case is different and requires scorched earth.

When surfing the net for divorce services, watch out for people who clearly have an ax to grind. Just about everyone who goes to the effort to create a website or a blog involving divorce will have an agenda of some kind. All agendas aren't bad, but it is important to know what they are. What is the energy of the site? Is it constructive? Cautionary? Vengeful? If you get the feeling that someone is more interested in venting or teaching others to fight dirty, steer clear. There are plenty of constructive resources which will serve you better in the end. Remember, the long term goal.

Don't reject so-called "father's sites" if you are a mom, and vice versa. Sure, there's lots of anger and a sense of being victimized by the other gender on both sides of these issues. But even though the focus of the site may be from one specific viewpoint, some of them are actually balanced and helpful. Also, it can't hurt to have a better understanding of how the other side thinks, especially if you want to negotiate a settlement you both can live with.

Many divorce sites offer referrals to divorce attorneys and therapists. This may be a way to get a lead on an attorney, but it is NOT a substitute for the homework I've detailed for you in Chapter 7. Always go through the screening process I've described before hiring a lawyer.

A couple of final cautions about surfing the web: *NEVER* put your personal information out there. There are unscrupulous types who would love to take advantage. The beauty of the web is that you can reach countless helpful resources virtually instantly. The flip side, of course, is that you can reach the bad guys just as fast (and they can reach you).

Equally importantly, don't *ever* discuss your legal strategy or the details of your divorce in a chat room or with an individual you met online. You have no way of knowing who is using the handle "SingleAgain." What if it is your ex or someone who recognizes the facts of your case? I promise you, it has happened to someone I know, and the results weren't pretty.

And if you surf and find a gem I haven't mentioned, please e-mail me at sue@privatefamilylawjudge.com, and I'll post it on the updated Resources page there.

Online Resources

I've listed below some online resources I recommend, but they come with a caveat: I recommend them for their *content only*, as a source of information about divorce. Some of them offer referral services, do-it-yourself divorce kits or links to document preparation services. I do *not* recommend them for that purpose, but rather for the common sense resources they contain. There is no substitute for individually targeted advice from a competent divorce lawyer, even if you decide to represent yourself thereafter.

DIVORCEINFO.COM

This is my favorite and contains a wealth of information. It is balanced and reasonable, with a clearly stated purpose of demystifying divorce and reducing pain and conflict. There are pages on the emotional stages of divorce, on property division and custody, how to get through the process, lots of practical hints on common problems, and even humor.

The site itself is extremely deep. It is tantamount to a book in itself, and a thorough search of the table of contents could take days. However, it is so well organized and cross-linked that it is a snap to navigate. It's also quick to download if you're an impatient type.

Two of my favorite sections are called <u>Divorce Stinks</u> and <u>Cutting Through the Crud</u>. You can find suggestions on everything from "getting through the holidays" and "why is my spouse behaving this way?" to the mistakes people make most often (including how to avoid them) and how to take care of yourself in the process. Sections which are state-specific are nicely set off so you don't have to wade through irrelevant info to get what you want.

One of the things I like best about this site is the person behind it. My friend Lee Borden is a former mediator from Birmingham, Alabama. The site reflects his heart, his intellect, his commitment to non-adversarial resolution, and his considerable wisdom. He discloses his personal and professional background, even his politics, and includes a mission statement. You know you are dealing with a real person without hidden agendas. DivorceInfo is clearly a labor of love, and it shows in the quality of the product.

Put a bookmark on this one, as you'll come back to it again and again. I hit it frequently just to see what's new. I can't recommend it highly enough.

YourSocialWorker.com

This Canadian site, maintained by Gary Direnfeld, MSW, is a treasure house of useful information on parenting issues, and isn't just limited to parenting through and after divorce. Check out the video clips, and read the articles which are relevant to your situation. Parents in Canada face the same issues as parents in the US, and there is much valuable information here. Go to the Divorce Articles section, and read what is posted there. I particularly like the article entitled "Keeping a Child From the Other Parent Can Backfire."

COFAMILIES.COM

This is a great scheduling site for parents, kids, daycare providers, or anyone else who needs to keep track of kids' joint custody schedules. You log in to a secure calendar dedicated to your family, and the information is available on your smart phone or other ·device. There seriously is no longer any excuse for screwing up a joint custody schedule.

OURFAMILYWIZARD.COM

Before cofamilies.com came along, this was my go-to site for coordinating kids' schedules. Unlike cofamilies.com it isn't free, but it has gotten rave reviews from the families who have used it. You can set it up so the kids can access their own schedules, as well as preserve the access for the parents. It has lots of other resources, and is committed to making joint custody work for parents and children.

UPTOPARENTS.ORG

This site is funded by a non-profit organization, dedicated to helping parents reach agreements by keeping them focused on the long range best interests of the kids. I strongly recommend watching the video "Who do those judges think they are?"

UpToParents has developed an extremely useful tool for facilitating these agreements. It is based on the simple idea that if parents can agree on the answer to one question, "Who do I want my kids to be when they are 25?" and keep focused on the answer to *that* question, they can agree on just about *anything.* You and your spouse can access the site separately. You each fill out a confidential questionnaire about your kids and your goals for them. Your spouse can log in, also confidentially, and complete the same questionnaire. You don't see each other's answers. What the program does is look for areas where you agree, so you can build on them. It's a wonderful tool, and many custody mediators require that parents use this resource first, before coming to their first mediation session. It provides a basis for discovering common ground in goal setting for your children, and helps you start out on the right foot.

BonusFamilies.org

This site is maintained by Jann Blackstone-Ford and Sharyl Jupe, who are, respectively, the current and former wives of the same man. They lived through their own struggles in blending their families and learning to co-parent effectively. They worked it out, and then gave other blended families a wonderful gift by writing a book called *Ex-Etiquette for Parents* so that others can learn how to do it. Their advice is child-focused, reasonable, and practical. They don't simply gush about how wonderful it all is when everybody acts like a grown-up. They recognize it is hard because they've been there themselves. However, they have figured out what works, and developed clear and reasonable guidelines and suggestions which can help parents navigate these tricky waters.

Puttingkidsfirst.org

Putting kids first is a nationwide children's rights organization. They teach live and online parenting and co-parenting classes. It is based on the book of the same name, and I highly recommend it.

Parentsareforever.org

Anything Shirley Thomas does is bound to be helpful, and this is no exception.

Here are some other resources, organized by category. Some are better than others, and I encourage you to keep looking for the ones which speak to you. Don't be put off by the fact that some of the books may date back to the 1990's. The dynamics of divorce haven't changed, even as technology has made it possible for couples to invent endless new ways to torture each other. Among my favorites are the following:

Books

GENERAL DIVORCE

The Good Divorce: Keeping Your Family Together when Your Marriage Comes Apart by Constance Ahrons, Ph.D. (1994) Harper Collins

Yes, it can be done. Connie Ahrons followed the children of divorce for more than twenty years. By interviewing the parents and children at various stages, she has identified patterns which predict how well children of divorce will function in adult relationships and with their own children. Thorough research and clear writing made this an instant classic.

For Better or For Worse: Divorce Reconsidered by Mavis Hetherington and John Kelley (2010) Norton

Like Connie Ahrons, Mavis Heatherington followed a group of children of divorce for almost thirty years. She debunks the popular myths about divorce which are *not* supported by her considerable research. A hopeful, helpful and scholarly approach to the subject. I recommend it highly.

The Good Karma Divorce: Avoid Litigation, Turn Negative Emotions into Positive Actions, and Get On With the Rest of Your Life by Michele Lowrance. (2011) available on Amazon.

I just found this one, written by a lawyer and family court judge.

Getting Divorced Without Ruining Your Life by Sam Margulies, Ph.D., J.D. (2002) Fireside

This is a practical guide to the legal, emotional, and financial issues involved in divorce negotiations.

Between Love & Hate by Lois Gold, M.S.W. (1992) Plenum Press

Lois Gold has provided one of the best and most balanced divorce handbooks. It offers excellent insight into the psychology of divorce and realistic use of the legal process.

Conscious Divorce: Ending a Marriage with Integrity by Susan Allison (2001) Random House

How to Avoid the Divorce from Hell

The author takes readers through each step of divorce from a healing and spiritual perspective.

Crazy Time: Surviving Divorce and Building a New Life by Abigail Trafford (Third Edition 2014) Harper

One of the first, and recently updated. An excellent resource.

CHILDREN AND DIVORCE

The Truth about Children and Divorce: Dealing with the Emotions So You and Your Children can Thrive by Robert E. Emery, Ph.D. (2006) Penguin Books

Thoughtful and constructive, this book is well researched and written. Note particularly the Children's Bill of Rights on page 83, and Chapter 6 on why mediation is the best resolution option.

Putting Kids First: Walking Away from a Marriage Without Walking Over the Kids by Michael Oddenino (1995) Family Connections Publishing

The author is an attorney for the Children's Rights Council, and tells it like it is.

Good Parenting Through Your Divorce by Mary Ellen Hannibal (2008) Marlowe & Company

Kid's Turn is a popular counseling program in Northern California which has helped thousands of kids cope with their parents' divorce. This book is based on the Kid's Turn program. The author distinguishes different techniques based on the age and developmental level of the children. It is also filled with examples of good and not so good ways to handle co-parenting issues.

We're Still Family: What Grown Children Have to Say About Their Parents' Divorce by Constance Ahrons, Ph.D. (2005) Harper Collins

This is my current favorite. If you want to know how divorce impacts children, see how the children of divorce function twenty or thirty years later, in their own relationships and with their own children. The author followed a group of children of divorce for more than two decades. The results will surprise you. Read this book to find out which children of divorce function well as adults and which ones don't, and take a hard look at how their parents behaved in the divorce. Then copy the patterns of the parents whose kids did well as adults.

Based on a twenty-year landmark study, this book shines a spotlight on the disparity between what parents *think* their children think about divorce, and how they really experience it, in the words of the adult children of divorce.

Why Did You Have to Get a Divorce (and when can I get a hamster?) by Anthony E. Wolf, Ph.D. (1998) Farrar, Straus and Giroux

Common sense and practical, this is filled with explanatory examples of common situations.

12 Things your Kids Think About Your Divorce

Here's a link to a nifty little article about divorce from a kid's perspective: http://www.yourtango.com/experts/tara-kennedy-kline/-marriage-parenting-top-12-things-your-kids-think-about-your-divorce Anyone with kids should read this at the start of the divorce, and re-read it periodically thereafter.

CO-PARENTING AFTER DIVORCE

Parents Are Forever: a step-by-step guide to becoming successful co-parents after divorce by Shirley Thomas, Ph.D. (2011) Springboard Publications

This is the classic co-parenting book, still a great resource.

Two Happy Homes by Shirley Thomas, Ph.D. (2005) Springboard Publications

The sequel to **Parents are Forever**. Both are available at www.parentsareforever.org

My Kids Don't Live With Me Anymore by Doreen Virtue (1988) CompCare Publishers.

The author focuses on the custody process. She offers excellent insight into the emotional issues involved, and the book is filled with practical suggestions for coping. This is one of the best I've been able to find of its kind.

Families Apart: Ten Keys to Successful Co-Parenting by Melinda Blau (1995) G. P. Putnam's Sons.

This is full of sage advice for establishing a working co-parenting system and avoiding common pitfalls that will negatively impact the children.

Making Divorce Easier on Your Child: 50 Effective Ways to Help Children Adjust by Nicholas Long, Ph.D. and Rex Forehand, Ph.D. (2002) Contemporary Books

There really are 50 effective techniques. The list of resources is fantastic.

Ex-Etiquette for Parents: Good Behavior After a Divorce or Separation by Jann Blackstone Ford and Sharyl Jupe (2006) Chicago Review Press

The authors are the current and former wife of the same man. They've been there, and know what works and what doesn't. This book is full of practical advice for how to handle the inevitable issues blended families create. Find it at www/bonusfamilies.org

Joint Custody With a Jerk: Raising a Child with an Uncooperative Ex by Julie A. Ross and Judy Corcoran (2011) St. Martin's Griffin

This is filled with practical suggestions for successful co-parenting, even if conditions aren't ideal. It's a great resource for learning good communication skills.

Divorce and New Beginnings: An Authoritative Guide to Recovery and Growth, Solo Parenting, and Stepfamilies by Genevieve Clapp, Ph.D. (2000) John Wiley & Sons

There is an excellent section on divorce from the child's perspective. It is a good resource for information on single parenting and blended families.

Mom's House, Dad's House: Making Shared Custody Work by Isolina Ricci (1997) Collier Books/Macmillan

This set the standard for joint custody books for a generation.

The Co-Parenting Toolkit: the Essential Supplement for Mom's House Dad's House by Isolina Ricci Ph.D. (2012)

RESOURCES FOR CHILDREN

Divorced But Still My Parents by Shirley Thomas, Ph.D. and Dorothy Rankin (2011) Springboard Publications

Shirley Thomas, author of the classic ***Parents are Forever*** collaborated on this handbook aimed at children ages 6 to 12. It has interactive worksheets and helpful techniques tailored to the development stages of childhood. Children under 9 would benefit from this book being read to them by a parent. Get it at www.parentsareforever.com. Get a copy for each of your children so they don't have to share.

Dinosaurs Divorce, a Guide for Changing Families by L. & M. Brown (1988) Street Books/Little, Brown & Company

The classic divorce books for kids.

Two Homes to Live In, a Child's-Eye View of Divorce by B. Hazen (1983) Human Sciences Press/Plenum

This is one of the best for kids under 6.

Mom's House Dad's House for Kids: Feeling at Home in One Home or Two by Isolina Ricci, Ph.D. (2006)

Moving On after Divorce

Divorce Hangover by Anne M. Walther, M.S. (2000) Pocket Books (Simon & Schuster).

I found this a very practical guide to ending the "Endless Post-Judgment Minuet" which I refer to in Chapter 38.

A Healing Divorce: Transforming the End of Your Relationship with Ritual and Ceremony by Phil and Barbara Penningroth (2001) 1st Books Library.

This is based on an interesting premise. We begin a marriage with a ceremony, but there is no corresponding ritual to bring closure to the end. Phil and Barbara Penningroth developed a ritual to symbolize the end of their marriage. Ritual not only honors the transition into a new stage of life, but it also reinforces respect for the process. Interestingly, there are rituals for the couple to perform together, as well as rituals for partners to do individually. If the idea speaks to you, look this one up. Buy it at www.healingdivorce.com.

Life After Divorce by Sharon Wegsheider-Cruse (2012) Health Communications, Inc.

Full of practical tools for healing and moving on.

How to Avoid the Divorce from Hell

Men on Divorce: Conversations with Ex-Husbands by Ellie Wymard (1994) Hay House

Women tend to talk more about their divorces, and tend to rely more on support systems. Much less is written about men's experiences of divorce. By focusing on and interviewing husbands, Dr. Wymard adds an important perspective on how half of the population experiences separation and divorce. This one appears to be out of print. Look for a used copy. It is a gem.

PRENUPTIAL AGREEMENTS

Prenups for Lovers: a Romantic Guide to Prenuptial Agreements by Arlene G. Dubin (2001) Villard.

If you are considering remarriage you should at least think about whether a prenuptial agreement is right for you. This clever little book gives practical advice on how to broach the topic, and take it through to conclusion without destroying your new relationship.

POETRY

How to Survive the Loss of a Love by Melba Colgrove, Harold H. Bloomfield and Peter McWilliams (2006) Prelude Press.

This little gem of a book was originally published in 5,000 copies. It struck a nerve and has more than 2,500,000 in print. It is the best resource I know to help people surviving a loss through divorce (in fact, any kind of loss). I cannot recommend it highly enough. It is widely available.

Uncoupling in Three-Quarter Time: Life Affirming Divorce Poetry by M. Sue Talia

This is my divorce poetry, available for download at nexusbooks. com.

PART VII

Post Mortem

CHAPTER 46

Will You Be Able to Dance Together at Your Daughter's Wedding?

I REALIZE I have given you a great deal of terrible news. It is not done gratuitously, but with the intent to alert you to the existence of options you may not be aware of. I hope that by now you've not only made a firm resolution that if divorce is inevitable, you'll do it right, but have also found some suggestions to help you accomplish that.

There is good news. You *can* be friends with your ex-spouse. Divorce can be done honestly, openly and with dignity on both sides. I have seen clients do it, I have seen friends do it, and I have done it myself. If you do it right, you will be able to dance together at your daughter's wedding. You *might* even dance at your former spouse's wedding. I did. Not only did my life partner and I dance at my ex-husband's wedding, but I officiated at my step-daughter's wedding, with her father (my life partner) and mother (his ex-wife) and her mother's current husband together in the front row. It was a lovely wedding, without any hostile undercurrents. And yes, the bride's parents did dance together. We have a photo to prove it. Now, mind you, neither of the underlying breakups was without conflict and pain, and a certain amount of time was required to provide perspective, which it ultimately did.

Wouldn't it be wonderful if you could simply remember the good times, embark on a new relationship without feeling the specter of the old one constantly coming between you and your new lover, or watch your spouse get remarried and feel that you are attending the wedding of an old friend? That's how it felt to me. The last poem in my divorce poetry, *Uncoupling in Three Quarter Time,* referenced in the last chapter is called "My Good Friend Got Married Today," and was written after I returned from my ex-husband's wedding.

Not everyone can pull it off, but I am convinced that more people could than do. In many cases, the culprit is that you assume there is no alternative to war and enmity and that it "*has*" to be that way. It doesn't. Don't let your divorce turn ugly and messy simply because you assume divorce must be ugly and messy. It need not be. It is emotional, painful, and cathartic. I am fond of the Zen phrase "Pain is mandatory, but suffering is optional."

Do not start the process assuming that you and your spouse will be sitting across the courtroom from one another. Do not assume that you will have constant ongoing conflicts over your children. Do not assume that you must be adversaries for life. It is true that your interests and his are no longer the same. However, that does not mean you must have war.

I began this book somewhat sarcastically quoting a common client complaint of "But it's not *fair*." This is usually a client's response to being told something he doesn't want to hear. Typically, a person who complains about the lack of fairness is looking for the system, courts, judges or the attorneys to rescue him from the consequences of his own errors of judgment. There are thousands of situations which the legal system is simply not designed to redress, and frankly, I wonder whether abstract, absolute fairness even exists. We are all subjective human beings, experiencing our lives (and our divorces) through our own set of filters. Stop looking for abstract fairness and you will be much more likely to find equity and peace.

If you want your divorce to be fair, then you and your spouse must take responsibility for being fair with one another. The only fairness that you are going to find in the divorce process is the fairness you insist on *from yourself.* Don't look for it out there. Look for it in here.

I had lunch with a colleague recently who casually mentioned that the night before she had attended her son's soccer game and sat with her ex-husband and former father-in-law. The three of them watched the game and had a pleasant conversation with one another. These former spouses do not have an idyllic relationship. They both have complaints about the other, and there have been periods of serious disagreement since the divorce regarding child-rearing and money issues. Nevertheless, they resolve their differences by talking about them, and they can meet at a soccer game with perfect equanimity. I asked her how she did it and she credited the fact that neither she nor her former husband ever expected anything else from themselves and each other. That's quite revealing. If they expected war, they probably would have had it. They got the divorce they did because that is what they expected.

Your friends may be telling you that anger, bitterness and strife are inevitable. They lie. But the only way you will avoid those problems is to fully expect to do so.

Through the course of your divorce, you will have a hundred opportunities to turn it into war. Sometimes the temptation will be almost irresistible. The best thing you can do is be aware when it happens. These opportunities come and go and most people are not even conscious that they have a choice, that they can elect to fight or to disengage, to accuse or to detach. If you are not aware that you have a choice, you will not exercise it. Instead, you will simply react. So let your awareness of your options be your first line of defense.

Once you have done that, you will be less likely to opt for the knee-jerk hostile act which plunges you into full-fledged war. If you have done as I suggested and made a list of what is important to you in life, and if you have further reviewed that list periodically, you will have made significant progress. Take your list and devise one or two mental images which symbolize the goal, the ideal end result to you. Perhaps it is as simple as being able to attend the same swim meet or basketball practice as your ex-spouse and be civil to one another for the sake of your child. Perhaps it is a conflict-free interaction at graduation. Perhaps it *is* the image of being able to dance together at your daughter's wedding for your daughter's sake. Or meeting at the hospital for the birth of your first grandchild. Whatever it is that speaks to you should be imagined as vividly as possible. Then, when your awareness tells you that you have a choice of creating compromise or war, let this mental image help you make the correct decision and ask yourself whether firing off a salvo will make it easier or more difficult for you to realize that long term goal.

If you do it right, you can have healthy, well-adjusted children. You can get up in the morning and look at yourself in the mirror with the satisfaction of knowing that you did the best you could under the circumstances at the time. Frankly I don't think we can ask much more than that of ourselves. Your divorce can be a constructive, empowering life passage.

It's your choice.

Glossary

alimony Monetary payments which are made to a spouse or former spouse. This term is used in the federal tax code and in some states. In others, it is being supplanted by the less loaded terms "spousal support" And "maintenance."

arrearages Unpaid installments of either child or spousal support. In most jurisdictions, they accrue interest at the legal rate until paid. When the current interest rate is 3% and the legal rate is 10%, this can really add up.

buy out An agreement whereby one former spouse makes a lump-sum payment to the other in exchange for a waiver of alimony. When negotiated between the parties, these agreements are enforceable by the courts, but cannot be imposed by the court over objection.

consulting attorney An attorney with whom mediating or self-represented parties consult from time to time to ensure that they understand the legal issues and the consequences of the agreements being discussed.

child support Money payments from one parent to the other which are designated for the support of minor children.

custodial parent The parent with the primary day-to-day responsibility for the child and with whom the child primarily lives.

custody A term used to describe responsibility and control over minor children.

> **joint custody** An arrangement whereby each parent has responsibility and control over the children for significant periods. It may or may not represent equal time in each household.

legal custody Refers to decision making power over the children. It has little or nothing to do with where the kids actually live or how much time they spend with each parent, and refers to who makes the major decisions about the child's health, welfare and religious upbringing.

physical custody Refers to the actual place where the children reside. It is not uncommon to see an order for joint legal custody, but primary physical custody to one parent.

primary custody The terms "primary" and "secondary" custody refer to where the kids spend their time. They are generally preferred to sole custody and visitation, which can imply that one parent is in control and the other is marginalized.

shared custody Shared custody is frequently interchangeable with joint custody, and refers to an arrangement where the children spend significant time with each parent.

sole custody Refers to an arrangement where the children primarily reside with one parent, and visit with the other.

split custody In a split custody arrangement, there are two or more children who have different custody and visitation schedules with their parents.

discovery The formal legal process by which information and documentation are obtained to prepare a case for settlement or trial. It can include depositions, subpoenas, interrogatories (written questions answered under penalty of perjury) and numerous other methods.

guidelines Either mandatory or discretionary schedules created by a governmental entity and used to calculate child or spousal support, based on the income, and sometimes the expenses, of the parents. They vary

Glossary

widely from state to state, and sometimes even county to county within a state. Many are computer generated, and judges frequently have little discretion to depart from them in an individual case.

jurisdiction As used in this book, it refers to the fact that laws vary from state to state.

mediator A neutral professional who helps the parties work out their own agreement. Mediators who focus on custody and child related issues may be therapists or attorneys. Where money and property are the main issues, the mediator is almost always an attorney.

minor's counsel A lawyer who is appointed by the court in a custody case to represent and advocate for the child's best interests. Sometimes called a "guardian ad litem."

noncustodial parent The parent who has less time with the child. This term is falling out of use in many states, in favor of terms which emphasize the continuing importance of both parents in the life of the child.

parental alienation An unfortunate situation in which one parent, usually the custodial one, deliberately sets out to alienate a child from the other parent, usually with disastrous results for the mental health and psychological well-being of the child.

parenting coordinator A neutral professional who helps parents establish and modify co-parenting plans for the benefit of their children. They are usually experienced custody evaluators or therapists, but may be attorneys as well. Their role is usually a temporary one to establish co-parenting ground rules and help parents acquire the skills to interact with each other in a way that reduces the conflict and confusion the children experience.

private judge A judge who is hired jointly by the parties to resolve the case. It may be a judge who has retired from the public bench, or an experienced attorney who has built a reputation for specialized knowledge and ability.

pro se An individual who represents himself in a legal proceeding. The term pro per is used in some states. It means "for yourself," indicating that the litigant is representing himself without a lawyer.

pro tem A lawyer who is appointed "judge for a day" or for a particular case.

referee or special master. The terms are used virtually interchangeably, depending on the culture of the specific jurisdiction.

special master An individual who is either appointed by the court, or by agreement of the parties, to listen to the evidence and make the decision or recommendation to the court on a specific issue in the case. Special masters for custody and visitation issues are usually therapists or lawyers by training. Special masters for financial issues may be accountants, attorneys, or retired judges. Unlike mediators, who don't make a ruling, but help the parties reach their own decision, referees and special masters actually make a ruling or recommendation which becomes an order of court binding on both parties.

support Monetary payments, usually weekly or monthly, designated for the support of a spouse or former spouse, or the children. Sometimes called maintenance.

> **child support** Support which is specifically designated for the children.

Glossary

family support Support which is not allocated between child and spousal support. This is usually done for tax purposes, as it can frequently result in increased tax deductions and higher spendable income for both parties.

nonmodifiable support Support (usually spousal) where the parties have agreed to limit the jurisdiction of the court to modify the amount or the duration of the payments, usually in exchange for other concessions.

spousal support Support which is specifically designated for the spouse or former spouse.

tax intercept Federal and state laws which enable a recipient of support to collect unpaid installments by "intercepting" the income tax refund of the payor.

timeshare A less-loaded term than custody to describe the amount of time the children spend in each parent's household.

visitation Refers to the amount of time the children spend with the noncustodial parent.

wage assignment An order which requires the employer to withhold earnings from the payor of support and make the support payment directly to the recipient.

Index

About the Author

M. Sue Talia has been a practicing family lawyer in Danville, California, since 1977. She is a Family Law Specialist, certified by the Board of Legal Specialization of the State Bar of California. Her focus is on complex family law litigation. Since 1997, she has limited her practice to private judging in complex family law matters. She obtained her B.A. from Santa Clara University, her M.A. in American History from Stanford University, and J.D. from the University of California, Hastings College of the Law.

In addition to the practice of law, she teaches workshops for family lawyers, forensic accountants and individuals contemplating divorce.

Since the mid-1990s, she has been a leading national advocate of the practice of unbundling, or limited scope legal representation, and writes and speaks frequently on the subject. She has taught hundreds of workshops on the subject throughout the United States and Canada.

She has long been active in legal and community organizations, is a founding director of the Family Law Section of the Contra Costa Bar Association, and has long been an advocate of restructuring the California family law courts to make them more responsive to the needs of children and families.

She has written several other books, including a book on divorce poetry, a mentoring book for young family lawyers, and more are in the works. For current information about her other publications check out her website at www.privatefamilylawjudge.com.

She lives in Danville, California, with her life partner, Lee, and Rusty. their resident rescue Cairn terrier.

Made in the USA
Charleston, SC
26 January 2017